Auto/Ethnography

EXPLORATIONS IN ANTHROPOLOGY
A University College London Series

Series Editors: Barbara Bender, John Gledhill and Bruce Kapferer

Auto/Ethnography

Rewriting the Self and the Social

**Edited by
Deborah E. Reed-Danahay**

Oxford • New York

First published in 1997 by
Berg
Editorial offices:
150 Cowley Road, Oxford, OX4 1JJ, UK
70 Washington Square South, New York, NY 10012, USA

Berg is an imprint of Oxford International Publishers Ltd.

Library of Congress Cataloging-in-Publication Data

A catalogue record for this book is available from the Library of
Congress.

British Library Cataloguing-in-Publication Data

A catalogue record for this book is available from the British Library.

Front cover photograph: "Magritte" 'Bill Brandt © J-P Kernot'.

ISBN 1 85973 970 9 (Cloth)
      1 85973 975 X (Paper)

Typeset by JS Typesetting, Wellingborough, Northants.
Printed in the United Kingdom by WBC Book Manufacturers, Bridgend,
Mid Glamorgan.

Contents

Acknowledgements

I was warned by many colleagues that editing a book is a lot of work, but I must say that this project has truly been a gratifying one despite the fact that they were right! I want to thank the contributors to this volume, first of all, who not only provided excellent material for their chapters but were conscientious about deadlines and made my job as editor a lot easier in many ways than it might have been. When I first began to solicit work for this project, most of the contributors approached were working on interesting narrative materials but were not familiar with the term "autoethnography" that I proposed as a concept to "think with." The joint effort of thinking through, and with, this concept has been rewarding to all of us, and I am grateful to my co-contributors here for pushing my own thinking on this topic in new directions.

This book project had its debut as an Invited Session sponsored by the Society for the Anthropology of Europe and the American Ethnological Society at the 1995 American Anthropological Association Meetings. All of the contributors to this volume were involved in that panel, but the chapters by Michael Herzfeld and Henk Driessen appearing in this book were not part of the original session. I would like to thank the panel discussants, Ruth Behar and Henk Driessen, for their encouragement and, especially, for helpful comments that were incorporated into the resulting finished product you hold in your hands. I am also grateful to Nigel Rapport for a careful reading of the entire manuscript and for his useful suggestions. At Berg, the early and strong support of Kathryn Earle for this project guided its smooth development and helped make the entire process most positive.

To my husband, Martin Danahay, I must say "thank you for leaving so many interesting books lying around the house over the years." As a literary scholar who has worked on nineteenth-century autobiography, he has introduced me to some texts that, while not directly informing this project, helped me to frame some wider issues informed by a literary perspective as well as that of anthropology. I am also grateful for his help in finding the cover photo of Magritte. To my son, Ian, I apologize for tying up the computer at home when he wanted to play with his new "Star Wars" game. And to Emily, who, at 12, is just beginning to understand what it means to have a mother who is an anthropologist, I am grateful for a new sense of wonder at the business of writing books.

When the chapters in this book were first presented as papers in the 1995 AAA panel mentioned above, a young woman in the audience asked during the discussion period how she could convince her thesis committee that doing work on personal narrative was a worthwhile pursuit. All of us, knowingly, understood the issues she raised. Each contributor here has already done the usual, more standard "fieldwork" and published from that. Our newer projects reflected here, based on written materials, come out of new experimentations with genres of writing and their role in ethnography. This work is not intended to supplant participant-observation research and reports based upon it, but stands firmly on the grounding that such experiences have already provided each of us. The answer to the young woman's question is something that many anthropologists struggle with at this point in time, and I hope that this volume leads in some positive directions to help guide future responses to such a question.

Notes on Contributors

Caroline B. Brettell is Professor and Chair of the Department of Anthropology at Southern Methodist University. From 1989 to 1994 she served as Director of the Women's Studies Program. In addition to the book she discusses in her chapter, she is the author of *Men Who Migrate, Women Who Wait* (Princeton University Press, 1986), co-author of *Painters and Peasants in the 19th Century* (Skira, 1983), editor of *When They Read What We Write: The Politics of Ethnography* (Bergin and Garvey, 1993), and co-editor of *International Migration: The Female Experience* (Rowman and Allenheld, 1986), *Gender in Cross-Cultural Perspective* (Prentice-Hall, 1993; 2nd edition 1997), and *Gender and Health: An International Perspective* (Prentice-Hall, 1996).

Henk Driessen is Associate Professor of Cultural Anthropology at the University of Nijmegen, The Netherlands, and member of the Board of the Research School for Resource Studies at the University of Utrecht. His current research interests include shifting borders and boundaries in the Circum-Mediterranean Area. He is the author of *On the Spanish-Moroccan Frontier: A Study in Ritual, Power and Ethnicity* (Berg, 1992).

Michael Herzfeld is Professor of Anthropology at Harvard University. His publications include seven books: *Ours Once More: Folklore, Ideology, and the Making of Modern Greece* (University of Texas Press, 1982), *The Poetics of Manhood: Contest and Identity in a Cretan Mountain Village* (Princeton University Press, 1985), *Anthropology Through the Looking-Glass: Critical Ethnography in the Margins of Europe* (Cambridge University Press, 1987), *A Place in History: Social and Monumental Time in a Cretan Town* (Princeton University Press, 1991), *The Social Production of Bureaucracy: Exploring the Symbolic Roots of Western Bureaucracy* (Berg, 1992),

Cultural Intimacy: Social Poetics in the Nation-State (Routledge, 1996), and *Portrait of a Greek Imagination: An Ethnographic Biography of Andreas Nenedakis* (University of Chicago Press, 1997).

Alexandra Jaffe is Assistant Professor of Anthropology at the University of Southern Mississippi. She has published numerous articles on language ideology, literacy, and ethnic identity on Corsica, and is currently working on a project about the role of bilingual media in the articulation of hybrid linguistic and cultural identities.

David A. Kideckel is Professor and Chair of the Anthropology Department at Central Connecticut State University. He is author of *Solitude of Collectivism: Romanian Villagers to the Revolution and Beyond* (Cornell University Press, 1993) and editor of *East European Communities: The Struggle for Balance in Turbulent Times* (Westview, 1995). He is currently involved in a multi-year project analyzing the relationship of donors and recipients in privatization aid in East and Central Europe for which he continues research in Romania, Albania, and elsewhere in southeastern Europe.

Pnina Motzafi-Haller is Assistant Professor of Anthropology in the Department of Behavioral Studies at Ben Gurion University of the Negev and a Senior Researcher at the Social Studies Unit at the Blaustein Institute for desert research in Sede Boker. She has carried out research in rural Botswana and in Israel. Her research interests include historical anthropology, identity and power, and nationalism and transnationalism.

Deborah E. Reed-Danahay is Assistant Professor of Anthropology at the University of Texas at Arlington. She has written *Education and Identity in Rural France: The Politics of Schooling* (Cambridge University Press, 1996) and several articles on themes of cultural identity in France. A specialist on the work of Pierre Bourdieu and on rural French schooling, she is currently working on the analysis of published French regional autobiographies and childhood memoirs written since the turn of the century.

Birgitta Svensson is Assistant Professor in the Department of European Ethnology at the University of Lund. She has written books about the cultural complexity and power of landscape, environment, and identity formation. She has also written on schooling and the meaning of education in becoming a member of the middle-class elite. She is currently working on a criminology project concerning how the ideology of treatment in Sweden has been creating criminal identities during the last 100 years.

Kay B. Warren is Professor and Chair of the Department of Anthropology at Princeton University. She has authored *The Symbolism of Subordination: Indian Identity in a Guatemalan Town* (University of Texas Press, 1989), co-authored *Women of the Andes: Patriarchy and Social Change in Two Peruvian Towns* (University of Michigan Press, 1982), and edited *The Violence Within: Cultural and Political Opposition in Divided Nations* (Westview, 1993). She is currently finishing *Mayan Public Intellectuals and Indian Cultural Resurgence in Guatemala* and *Editing Latin America in Boston and London: Documentaries and the Quest for Fairness.*

List of Illustrations

List of Illustrations

Introduction

Deborah E. Reed-Danahay

The chapters in this book result from ethnographic work in contemporary literate societies, in which important cultural production occurs in the realm of written texts. This book responds to two major developments in cultural studies: debates about representation (by whom and about whom), and the increasing trend toward self-reflexivity in all realms of writing. The common thread linking the chapters together is that they are about life stories – sometimes our own, sometimes those of others, and sometimes both. The act of self-narrative and the tension between creativity and restraint associated with that act in various political contexts, is a central theme in this book.[1]

In 1984, while surveying approaches to life history in various national contexts and disciplines, Daniel Bertaux and Martin Kohli came to the conclusion that, in anthropology, "life stories are no longer fashionable" (1984: 231). They attributed this to an unfortunate trend toward "scientism." Their observation was made during a period lasting from the 1960s to the mid-1980s when, after earlier years of interest in "native autobiography" in anthropology, the study of individual lives was submerged and marginal to our discipline (see also Brandes 1982). It is difficult to see how anyone could make such a statement now, over a decade later. We are in the midst of a renewed interest in personal narrative, in life history, and in autobiography among anthropologists. The changing nature of fieldwork in a post-colonial and postmodern world, in tandem with new theoretical trends in anthropology since the 1980s, have, however, meant that studies of life stories and personal narratives are informed by different questions than were earlier approaches (Cole 1992; Watson and Watson-Franke 1985).

The concept of autoethnography, which guides this volume, reflects a changing conception of both the self and society in the late twentieth century (Cohen 1994; Giddens 1991). It synthesizes both a postmodern ethnography,[2] in which the realist conventions and objective observer position of standard ethnography have been called into question, and a postmodern autobiography,[3] in which the notion of the coherent, individual self has been similarly called into question. The term has a double sense – referring either to the ethnography of one's own group or to autobiographical writing that has ethnographic interest. Thus, either a self (auto) ethnography or an autobiographical (auto) ethnography can be signaled by "autoethnography." This book seeks to transcend this dichotomy, however, and to point to the ways in which the two senses of the term are related. The discussions in the chapters break down the distinction between autobiography and ethnography. When the dual nature of the meaning of autoethnography is apprehended, it is a useful term with which to question the binary conventions of a self/society split, as well as the boundary between the objective and the subjective. The postmodern/postcolonial conception of self and society is one of a multiplicity of identities, of cultural displacement, and of shifting axes of power. These are all reflected in the move toward new forms of theory and writing discussed in this book.

Autoethnography stands at the intersection of three genres of writing which are becoming increasingly visible: (1) "native anthropology," in which people who were formerly the subjects of ethnography become the authors of studies of their own group; (2) "ethnic autobiography," personal narratives written by members of ethnic minority groups; and (3) "autobiographical ethnography," in which anthropologists interject personal experience into ethnographic writing. Anthropologists are increasingly explicit in their exploration of links between their own autobiographies and their ethnographic practices (Okely and Callaway 1992). This trend is mirrored in other disciplines, such as literary criticism (Freedman et al. 1993). At the same time, "natives" are increasingly telling their own stories and have become ethnographers of their own cultures.[4] Practitioners of ethnography have become increasingly aware of the politics of representation and of the power relations inherent in traditional ethnographic accounts (i.e., Behar and Gordon 1995; Fischer 1994; Moore 1994; Strathern 1987b). Such issues are also reflected in recent work on "autohistory" (Sioui 1992); "ethnocriticism" (Krupat 1992); and personal testaments to political violence (Heyck 1990; see also Warren, this volume).

Anthropological Selves, Ethnographic Texts

This book does not represent a definitive statement of what autoethnography is or can be, nor does it have that task as its ambition. Rather, the aim here is to explore various intersections, various blendings of genres and voices (Brettell, this volume), in order to rethink several assumptions about the relationship between ethnography and autobiography. A variety of genres of self-representation is addressed in this volume, through which both the politics and poetics of representation are questioned. Several key concerns emerge. These are questions of identity and selfhood, of voice and authenticity, and of cultural displacement and exile. One of the main characteristics of an autoethnographic perspective is that the autoethnographer is a boundary-crosser, and the role can be characterized as that of a dual identity. While recently enjoying much currency in anthropology, literary criticism, and post-colonial studies more generally, this notion of double identity is not new. It is associated with late nineteenth-century ideas of "double consciousness" and has been central to African-American thought as articulated by W.E.B. Du Bois (Zamir 1995). The notion of autoethnography foregrounds the multiple nature of selfhood and opens up new ways of writing about social life. A dualistic view of the autoethnographer may be better substituted with one stressing multiple, shifting identities. The limitations of dichotomizing identities are usefully discussed by K. Anthony Appiah (1995) in a recent essay on his own European and African identities and the dilemmas of forging an "African Identity" within contemporary forms of discourse.

A second question raised by the concept of autoethnography is that of voice and its authenticity. Who speaks and on behalf of whom are vital questions to ask of all ethnographic and auto-biographical writing. Who represents whose life, and how, are also central topics of concern in our current age of bureaucratization. For the most part, autoethnography has been assumed to be more "authentic" than straight ethnography. The voice of the insider is assumed to be more true than that of the outsider in much current debate. However, as the essays in this volume show, this issue is more complicated, partly because of the multiple, shifting identities which characterize our lives. Double identity and insider/ outsider are constructs too simplistic for an adequate understanding of the processes of representation and power. The most cogent aspect to the study of autoethnography is that of the cultural displacement or situation of exile characteristic of the themes expressed by autoethnographers. This phenomenon of displacement – so linked to issues of rapid sociocultural change, of globalization and transculturation, as well as to the extremes of violence occurring in many parts of the world – breaks down dualisms of identity and insider/outsider status. Whether the autoethnographer is the anthropologist studying his or her own kind, the native telling his or her life story, or the native anthropologist, this figure is not completely "at home." The ability to transcend everyday conceptions of selfhood and social life is related to the ability to write or do autoethnography. This is a postmodern condition. It involves a rewriting of the self and the social.

What is Autoethnography? A Short History of the Term

The word "autoethnography" has been used for at least two decades by literary critics as well as by anthropologists and sociologists, and can have multiple meanings. A review of key attempts to characterize autoethnography (as method, text, and/ or concept) is given below. This history can be traced through two veins – that concerned primarily with ethnography and that with life history. One of the earliest references to the term is in a short article by Karl Heider published in the *Journal of Anthropological Research* in 1975. Heider reports on Dani concepts of "what Dani do," based upon his questioning of 60 schoolchildren, and labels this "Dani auto-ethnography." He explains his use of this term: "'auto' for autochthonous, since it is the Dani's own account of "what people do," and "auto" for automatic, since it is the simplest routine-eliciting technique imaginable (1975: 3). David Hayano published another early piece on autoethnography, which has a different meaning for him than it does for Heider, in *Human Organization* in 1979. Hayano defines "auto-ethnography" as a set of issues relating to studies by anthropologists of their "own people" (1979: 99). In his essay, he traces the term to a seminar with Raymond Firth which he attended in 1966 at which an anecdote was told about an argument between L.S.B. Leakey and Jomo Kenyatta concerning the Kikuyu. This raised, Hayano writes, issues of the validity of anthropological data depending upon the characteristics of the fieldworker. For Hayano, it is "insider" status which marks the autoethnography, so that any research conducted by an anthropologist "among a distinctly different group than their own" is excluded from the category. However, Hayano does not restrict the term to the "native." He allows that a researcher may acquire, through socialization or other intimate familiarity with a group, the perspective of the "insider." The important measure, according to Hayano, is that autoethnographers "possess the qualities of often permanent self-identification with a group and full internal membership, as recognized both by themselves and the people of whom they are a part" (1979: 100). With such a broad definition of autoethnography, Hayano concedes that the term refers to " a mixture of diverse researchers investigating different problems" (1979: 103). Hayano distinguishes between "auto-ethnography" as he defines it and autobiographical writing, and is dismissive of what he calls "self-ethnographic" texts, due to their limited applicability to other cultural members.

In a more recent review of new approaches to the writing of ethnography, John Van Maanen (1995: 8–9) suggests four types of what he calls "alternatives to ethnographic realism." These are 1) "confessional ethnographies", where the attention is on the ethnographer (the signifier) rather than on the "natives" (the signified); 2) "dramatic ethnography"; 3) critical ethnographies, like Willis' *Learning to Labor*; and 4) self- or auto-ethnographies, where the culture of one's own group is textualized, as in the work of Hayano (whom Van Maanen cites). Here, autoethnography becomes a form of writing wherein the ethnographer is the native.

Marilyn Strathern (1987: 17) defines "auto-anthropology" as "anthropology carried out in the social context which produced it." Here, as in the approaches of Hayano and Van Maanen, the emphasis is not on a life story but on an ethnography of one's own culture. By carefully distinguishing the autoanthropologist from the indigenous anthropologist, however, Strathern is skeptical of many claims about the "insider" view developed by a professional anthropologist. Because an anthropologist is part of an anthropological culture, the "home" culture or "inside" that constitutes the "insider" view in autoanthropology is not necessarily that of the "natives." Strathern usefully questions claims of authenticity and calls into question the entire insider/outsider dichotomy (see also Herzfeld, Motzafi-Haller, and Brettell, this volume).

Other approaches to autoethnographic writing stress the autobiographical meanings of the term. While not using the term autoethnography, Stanley Brandes' (1982) discussion of forms of life history used by anthropologists in the early 1980s, captured the burgeoning trend which has led to more recent theories of autoethnography. Brandes characterized "ethnographic auto-biography," on one hand, as a strictly first-person narrative told by "a commoner, an ordinary member of his or her society" (1982: 188–189). On the other hand, he identified an important new genre, which he labeled "anthropological autobiography," in which "the anthropologist himself or herself is the autobiographical subject" (1982: 202). Both of these forms of life history could be labeled "autoethnography" in the dual sense of the term mentioned above. As Brandes describes these genres of life writing, each has an ethnographic interest and tells about a culture at the same time that it tells about a life. He writes that "both types are, in their own ways, ethnographic, and from both we have much to learn." While Brandes sees may advantages for social science in the humanistic approach of life history, he remains committed to the project of describing social life through ethnographic methods. Life history, in his view, is of interest for what it tells about cultural phenomenon and does not have intrinsic interest.

Norman Denzin has more recently distinguished several different forms of writing in what he calls the "biographical method": autobiography, ethnography, autoethnography, biography, ethnography story, oral history, case history, case study, life history, life story, self story, and personal experience story (1989: 27). Denzin characterizes "auto-ethnography" as a text which blends ethnography and autobiography, and he cites Crapanzano's *Tuhami* as an example of this genre. The important characteristic of autoethnography for Denzin is that the writer does not adopt the "objective outsider" convention of writing common to traditional ethnography. For Denzin, autoethnography entails the incorporation of elements of one's own life experience when writing about others through biography or ethnography. Therefore, it differs from both straight ethnography and life history or autobiography.

In a different typology, literary critic Alice Deck posits a distinction between what she calls the "self-reflexive field account" (such as Shostak's *Nisa* or Crapanzano's *Tuhami*) and the "autoethnography" (such as Hurston's *Dust Tracks on a Road*). In the first genre, which is close to what Denzin would call autoethnography, the author/anthropologist employs a "hierarchy of voices" (1990: 246), relying upon reference to outside anthropological and historical sources to verify the indigenous voice. This is not necessary in the case of autoethnography as defined by Deck. The author of an autoethnography, according to Deck, is the indigenous ethnographer, the native expert, whose authentic firsthand knowledge of the culture is sufficient to lend authority to the text.

Philippe Lejeune, like Deck, is highly critical of outsider ethnography in his discussion of autoethnography. Lejeune (1989) uses the concepts of both "auto-ethnology" and "ethnobiographer" in his chapter on "Those Who Do Not Write" in *On Autobiography* (see also Reed-Danahay, this volume). Viewing the non-native ethnographer as highly suspect, Lejeune encourages the development of ethnobiography and autoethnology as a way to avoid what he sees as the gap, or screen, of ethnology. For Lejeune, authenticity is masked by ethnology and these other forms represent more directly the voices of peasants and the working classes. Lejeune's position is diametrically opposed to that of Strathern.

A third literary critic, Mary Louise Pratt (1992; 1994), links the concept of autoethnography to relations between colonized and colonizer, and to modes of resistance to dominant discourses offered by the native account. For her, however, autoethnography is a form of ethnography of one's own culture, rather than a piece of autobiography. In an analysis of a seventeenth-century Andean text and contemporary forms of Andean cultural production, Pratt defines autoethnography as:

> . . . a text in which people undertake to describe themselves in ways that engage with representations others have made of them . . . Autoethnographic texts are not, then, what are usually thought of as autochthonous or 'authentic' forms of self-representation . . . Rather they involve a selective collaboration with and appropriation of idioms of the metropolis or conqueror. These are merged or

infiltrated to varying degrees with indigenous idioms to create self-representations intended to intervene in metropolitan modes of understanding (1994: 28).

Pratt describes autoethnographies as forms of writing that address both the writer's own group and a wider, more dominant one. Texts or works of art that are autoethnographic assert alternative forms of meaning and power from those associated with the dominant, metropolitan culture, and, while Pratt is careful not to romanticize their use as forms of resistance, she does suggest that they serve as such. The bicultural nature of the autoethnographer is a theme in Pratt's work as in that of such scholars as Alice Deck.

A very different use of "autoethnography," although similar to that of Pratt and Lejeune in that it represents a critique of ethnography from a non-anthropologist, can be found in John Dorst's book *The Written Suburb* (1989). Dorst applies this term not to written texts but rather to materials and objects produced by suburbanites in regional arts and crafts fairs in semirural Chester County, Pennsylvania. He argues that these social and cultural artifacts constitute a form of autoethnography, in the sense of self-inscription and self-referentiality for the people of that region.[5] Dorst views autoethnography as a form of postethnography. He writes: "If the task of ethnography can be described as the inscription and interpretation of culture, then postmodernity seems to render the professional ethnographer superfluous" (1989: 2) and that ". . . the impulse for self-documentation and the reproduction of images of the self pervade our everyday practice" (1989: 3). These provocative statements call into question the relationship between ethnographic representations of others and self-representations. As anthropologists increasingly engage in their own "self-documentations" through autobiographical writing, the line between ethnography and autoethnography becomes increasingly faint.

One of the main distinctions in these uses of autoethnography is whether or not the accent is on autobiography or ethnography. For Pratt, Van Maanen, Hayano, Dorst, and Strathern, the concept relates to a form of "native ethnography," a study of one's own group. Here, issues of authenticity of voice and of counternarrative come into play when the autoethnographer is not a professional anthropologist. When the autoethnographer is an anthropologist, issues are raised about the methodological issues of doing an ethnography "at home," given the long-standing tradition in this discipline of studying "others."

When autoethnography is tied to autobiography, as in the case of Lejeune, Brandes, Denzin, and Deck, the concept relates more closely to ethnographic autobiography or to native autobiography, rather than to native ethnography. The life story has ethnographic interest. The multiple perspectives on autoethnography reviewed above articulate the difficulties encountered when trying to distinguish between an ethnographic or an autobiographic perspective. Increasingly, ethnography is autobiographical and autobiography reflects cultural and social frames of reference. Much recent work in the study of personal narrative done by anthropologists has already pointed in this direction. The concept of a "social poetics" as used by Michael Herzfeld (1985 and 1996) reflects this duality of self-reference and cultural reference that is integral to the notion of autoethnography (see also Herzfeld this volume).

In this volume, autoethnography is defined as a form of self-narrative that places the self within a social context. It is both a method and a text, as in the case of ethnography. Autoethnography can be done by either an anthropologist who is doing "home" or "native" ethnography or by a non-anthropologist/ethnographer. It can also be done by an autobiographer who places the story of his or her life within a story of the social context in which it occurs. This type of autobiography is quite different from the more standard approach criticized by Bourdieu (1986), in which the autobiographer divorces the life trajectory from any social constraints. In the chapters of this book, the authors combine several of these meanings of the term and develop its implications more fully than I can do in this brief introduction.

The Chapters

The chapters in Part One – Power, Documentation, and Resistance – deal with contexts of state repression and the possibilities for resistance inherent in life stories and autoethnography. The documentation of lives can become a source of resistance or a source of repression, depending upon the context. The connections between ethnography and other forms of documentation are contrasted in these chapters. This book begins with Kay Warren's consideration of witness narratives (*testimonios*) of state violence in Guatemala produced as part of the Pan-Mayan movement of the 1980s. Having rejected both traditional ethnography and autobiography, this movement has sought to transcend the binary split between the self and the social through genres of writing that provide "collective representations." The *testimonio* genre, Warren writes, mediates individual experience and wider structures of violence and repression. The main focus of the chapter is a set of *testimonios* collected and edited by Victor Monteja, a Mayan intellectual/anthropologist living in exile in the United States. Montejo has produced autobiographical and collective works in order to circulate more widely the insider voice of Mayans and raise consciousness about violence and repression among outsiders (particularly in the United States). Warren describes Montejo's *Brevísima Relacíon* as an "autoethnography of a contact zone." More open-ended than the expository works generally produced by anthropologists, this work is a "collage" of voices. Montejo links it to ancient Mayan texts in order to lend authenticity and authority to the messages it conveys. Warren compares Montejo's work to the interpretive ethnography she has, herself, produced based on fieldwork in rural Mayan Guatemala among those whose silences about violence (connected to continued fears) provide a rich contrast to the voices published by Montejo. The ways in which silence, voice, and violence inhabit the work of the outsider anthropologist (Warren) and the insider anthropologist (Montejo) are drawn by Warren as complementary forms of witness to the operation of a repressive state. Now, well in the 1990s, the silences are giving way to increasing modes of public discourse about the past violence, and Montejo's works can now be openly published in Guatemala.

In chapter two, we are transposed to socialist Romania, and to the autoethnographic writings of a village "folk ethnographer." Aurel Relu Bălan, a key informant and friend of David Kideckel's during his fieldwork, meticulously recorded both his own autobiography and ethnographic details of the households, social practices, and individuals in his community. This testimony to daily life under socialism was of necessity kept secret during Ceauşescu's repressive regime and was hidden in secret cavities built in Bălan's house. Kideckel argues for the importance of expanding "the ethnographic genre to incorporate work created to purpose-fully elude official authority." Bălan's work, which Kideckel labels "private folk ethnography," differs from professional ethnography in that it can more usefully challenge conditions of oppression due its secretive nature. An important paradox in Bălan's case is that the seeming silence of his activities ultimately provide a powerful voice of resistance to the official regime. Bălan's impressive corpus of poetry, essays, household censuses, ethnographic observations, and autobiography are now being released to public view since the downfall of socialism. Kideckel suggests that his work stands as a statement of resistance, of an underground voice that challenged the dominant regime, and as a powerful source of ethnographic information recorded at a time when state censorship of social science research prohibited much of the work carried out by Bălan. Kideckel's chapter points to the ways in which enforced silence can be resisted through alternative forms of representation. When official ethnographers were monitored and silenced within Romania, Bălan was able to do much recording that escaped the official gaze.

In chapter three, Birgitta Svensson considers themes of life narrative, representation, and power within the explicitly coercive context of Swedish prisons. She uses a variety of theoretical insights, including those of Foucault and Giddens, on the formation of modern subjectivities and on the construction of biographical selves, in order to argue that the necessity to narrate our own lives and those of others is a mark of the modern self. Svensson suggests that, in the modern world, we must construct ourselves as "good selves" or be constructed as "bad selves." For the mostly male prisoners in Swedish prisons, record-keepers construct narratives of their lives associated with a "bad individualism." The prisoner's life becomes distilled to a litany of past crimes, with other details of identity silenced. The welfare state's mania for recording and cataloguing individuals is taken to extremes in the institutionalized context of the prison. Recording lives becomes an instrument of repression. This is a striking contrast to cases discussed by Warren and Kideckel, where the recording of lives is used to resist repression and to stand as a testament to cultural and physical violence. When Svensson writes of her interviews with several prisoners and relates the ways in which they have come to tell their own life stories, we see the degree to which the power of the biographical project of the state and prison system has colored their own understandings of identity. In this case, one sees a form of symbolic violence that seems to almost erase the possibilities for autoethnography.

In Part Two – Exile, Memory, and Identity – the themes of
cultural and geographical dislocation, of multiple identities, and
of a search for origins come to the fore. Each of these three chapters
is connected to France, with Paris standing as the metropole/
diaspora for French peasants as well as for Algerians and Corsicans. Autobiography in each case becomes a vehicle for the
exploration of wider issues of cultural identity. In chapter four,
Henk Driessen takes us to both Algeria and France, in his analysis
of the "ethno-autobiographical" production of two figures in
Kabyle popular culture. The Kabyle are a Berber-speaking peoples
in Algeria who differ from the Arab-speaking majority culture.
Both figures discussed by Driessen are singers: Lounes Matoub,
a male based in Algeria who strongly identifies with, and
champions, traditional Kabyle values and the Berber Cultural
Movement; and Djura, a female who, while born in Kabylia, moved
to Paris as a girl and claims a more multicultural identity which
champions the cause of female immigrants in France. Both Matoub
and Djura published life stories at midlife prompted by violence.
Matoub wrote his life story, entitled *Rebel*, after being attacked by
Islamic activists. *The Veil of Silence*, Djura's book, was written after
an attack by family members connected to a feud in which she
became involved. Driessen shows how these two life stories are
selectively autobiographical, and deal mostly with issues of
cultural identity – issues that both singers struggle with and try
to express through their art and political activities. Given their
different positionings as Kabyles situated in Algeria and in France,
male and female, Matoub and Djura express different relations to
their homeland and to the French diaspora. As a male, Matoub
can unflinchingly identify with traditional codes of Kabyle values,
while for Djura, female liberation and life in the metropole entails
some rejection of aspects of this value system. Through Dreissen's
analysis and comparison, these two stories, written by figures who
"bridge the Mediterranean divide," provide insights into the
blurring of political and cultural boundaries and classifications in
contemporary times, and to the ways in which individuals respond
to such processes.

In chapter five, Deborah Reed-Danahay takes a different set of
two writers (male and female) who have origins in rural France,
in order to examine issues of cultural identity and displacement
that result not from a colonial and postcolonial system, as in the
case of Algeria, but from what might be viewed as a process of

internal colonization by the French state of its many distinct regions. The autoethnographers Pierre-Jakèz Hélias and Emilie Carles published, late in life, texts that combine aspects of autobiography, memoirs of peasant childhood, and ethnography. Each became educated through French schools. My primary focus in this chapter is the ways in which stories of education entail stories of leaving home, and I connect this to issues of home vs. away ethnography as well as the geographic dislocation associated with modern-day academic employment. Our fascination with self-reflective accounts and autobiography in current anthropology, I suggest, are connected to our own experiences of the type of multi-identity and cultural displacement expressed in such narratives as those written by Hélias and Carles. Their texts, which have enjoyed popular success in France and abroad, differ from each other in significant ways, based upon regional and gender differences of the writers. They have in common, however, their presentation of an either/or choice about staying or leaving home associated with becoming an educated person. Like the stories of Matoub and Djura, as Driessen suggests, quoting Geertz, these two books provide "a kind of commentary on one another's character." The life stories of Hélias and Carles also illustrate the perspective of selves who bridge or transcend different cultural systems – and, thus, point toward a questioning the native vs. outsider dichotomy often associated with such texts.

In chapter six, Alexandra Jaffe analyzes life histories and issues of identity and representation in yet another context of French cultural domination – Corsica. Here, the interesting dilemma is that pressures to produce "authentic" texts by Corsican writers, to truly represent Corsicanness, can come into conflict with other experiences of the self that are more complex and multivocal. As with the Pan-Mayan movement described by Warren, the desire in Corsica is to produce collective representations in order to reinforce cultural distinction and resistance to dominant culture, rather than individual accoun ; that stress creativity and difference among Corsicans. Through a series of vignettes of discussions regarding Corsican language use and an analysis of several Corsican texts, Jaffe shows the tension between the "I" and the "Isle" in forms of self-representation and forms of representation of Corsican identity. The experience of exile is key to issues of Corsican identity in the texts examined by Jaffe. As in the cases of Algerians and of French mainlanders who have strong regional attachments, cultural identity for the Corsican writers discussed by Jaffe is always expressed in relationship to a dominant French culture which stigmatizes and marginalizes Corsica. These contexts come together in Delaville's autobiographical novel, which chronicles a childhood spent in Algeria, and in which Corsican identity is composed in a complicated triangle of Algeria, France, and Corsica. The dilemma for the novel's main character, Jaffe writes, is that "he has a polyvocal life, but access only to a univocal text to tell and understand that life." As Jaffe's analysis usefully reminds us, autoethnography can be as subject to the politics of representation as can outsider ethnography.

Part Three – Voice, Self-Representation, and Genre – ends the volume with the three most self-reflective of the chapters. In these essays, the authors reflect upon their own previous ethnographic work and discuss their relationship to newer textual (auto-ethnographic) projects with which they have become involved. In chapter seven, Michael Herzfeld weaves a complicated analysis of his encounters with three versions of Greek culture and self-hood – that of sheep-thieves, of bureaucrats, and of the novelist Andreas Nenedakis. Herzfeld has been writing the biography of Nenedakis, who, he suggests, stands as a mediating figure between the Cretan shepherds (in whose villages he has his own origins) and the urban world of the bureaucrats. For Herzfeld, the seeming contradictions between the order and classification associated with the state and the disorderly citizens who confront and challenge its regime, lies at the heart of an understanding of the modern nation-state. Drawing upon Greenwood's *The Taming of Evolution*, Herzfeld suggests that "the taming of revolution," through which all nation-states are constructed, encapsulates this contradiction. The contradictions of the nation-state are linked to those experienced by the anthropologist himself, who is both attracted to and repelled by certain characteristics of his Greek "acquaintances." In a move toward self-reflection, which Herzfeld argues is necessary, following Okely (1992) and Callaway (1992), to a politically engaged consciousness of our own actions and forms of knowledge, Herzfeld considers these contradictions in terms of his own personal trajectory. In particular, he cites an experience that serves as an epiphany in his life: his first attendance, as a youth, at a performance of Verdi's *Nabucco* in 1961. Herzfeld's intense enjoyment of this opera, which celebrates nationalist ideologies of romanticism and patriotism, stands in conflict with his professional understanding, as a social anthropologist, of nationalism as a social construct. As a way of explaining these various inconsistencies, Herzfeld proposes that common cultural understandings shared by both himself and the diverse Greek characters he has encountered during fieldwork, which are based on concepts of accountability and self-regard (*eghoismos*), underlie the apparent discrepancies so prone to inspire classifications of distinction. It is the tension between selfhood and authority, understood by all subjects of modern nation-states, which informs the genesis of the nation-state. Herzfeld suggests that autoethnography is a form of "social realization of the self" which signifies these tensions. His analysis undermines such dichotomies as native or insider vs. outsider in the context of European ethnology, where a common cultural terrain produces mutually intelligible, if not completely shared, meanings.

In chapter eight, Pnina Motzafi-Haller confronts and questions the authenticity of the native anthropologist through an autobiographical journey of professional development and ambivalent identity. The impetus for this story is Motzafi-Haller's recent collaboration with another author in composing a manuscript about Misrahi ethnic identity in Israel, entitled *Birthright*. The question of whether or not she lends a "native voice" to *Birthright* prompts Motzafi-Haller to come to terms with her own personal trajectory. After describing details of her early schooling as a "marked" Misrahi child in an Israel dominated by Ashkenazim, and her increasing command over a scholarly discourse that erases the self, Motzafi-Haller writes of her graduate education in anthropology at Brandeis University. Trained, she asserts, to forget her own identity and search for the "other," Motzafi-Haller set off for fieldwork in Botswana. There, she faced an ambivalent status as both "white," due to her national identity and education, and, when trying to swim in a public pool in South Africa under apartheid, as "black," due to her dark skin and hair. Returning to the privileges of an affiliat on and office at Harvard, finishing her dissertation on Africa, Motzafi-Haller experienced a growing discomfort with her own position and professional/personal identity. When she was hired by an Israeli university and returned to live in Israel after several years in the United States, she had to again confront issues of the native vs. outsider position. In this chapter, Motzafi-Haller raises several important questions coming from her own ambivalent status and struggles as, following

Abu-Lughod, "halfie anthropologist." She rejects the claim that a native voice is necessarily more "authentic" or "true" in order to argue, instead, for a greater awareness of the ways in which the positioning of the anthropologist will influence his or her scholarship. It is the politically engaged scholarship of recent "native" anthropologists that is important, Motzafi-Haller argues, rather than their indigenous origins.

The final chapter of this volume continues the themes of the mixing of genres and of the blurring of insider vs. outsider. Caroline Brettell, like Michael Herzfeld and Pnina Motzafi-Haller, reflects upon the meanings of a new piece of writing that diverges from her previous ethnographic work. Here, the personal is taken to the farthest point in the volume, because Brettell has written a biography of her own mother. In this chapter, Brettell describes this endeavor and compares it to her previous work on the life histories of three Portuguese migrant women. She also considers other works produced by daughters about their mother's lives. The essay is doubly autoethnographic because Brettell is analyzing the corpus of writing produced by her mother, a former journalist for a Montreal newspaper whose columns combined ethnographic interest with personal narrative, and because Brettell is doing a form of autoethnography herself, looking inward toward her own family origins. This analysis is framed by an overall interest in women's lives and by the importance of allowing the voices of women to speak for themselves. As Brettell suggests, however, there are a variety of ways in which this can, and has been, accomplished in the growing literature on women's lives. Brettell traces changes in genre associated with life history that have made her more self-conscious of her own role as author since first writing the book *We Have Already Cried Many Tears*. She does not consider the stories told in that text by the Portuguese women to be autoethnographic, because she played such a strong authorial role in composing the text. But her book about her mother, and her mother's own writings, can be, she suggests, considered autoethnographic. Brettell is aware that in composing the biography of her mother, she is transgressing many ethnographic conventions and blurring the boundaries of a variety of genres. In giving details from her mother's life and including passages from the columns she wrote about the lives of Canadian women at mid-century, Brettell shows how her own life is intertwined with that of her mother. Does this, she asks, give her an authentic insider voice when composing her mother's life? In writing this biography of her mother, Brettell experiences some of the same dilemmas faced by other autoethnographers or native anthropologists. She is a boundary-crosser, both insider and outsider, as was her mother the journalist. At the close of Brettell's chapter, which is at the close of this volume, the reader is left with incertitude about the issues of genre and representation raised here. The open-ended nature of this volume, like the *testimonios* discussed by Kay Warren at the beginning of this text, is intended to provoke further dialogue, drawing from a multiplicity of voices, about ways to write the self and the social.

Notes

1. The growing literature on the ethnography of written texts cannot be sufficiently addressed here. Key examples include Eduardo P. Archetti's *Exploring the Written* (1994), Ivan Brady's *Anthropological Poetics* (1991), and Paul Benson's *Anthropology and Literature* (1993). Also of relevance to this volume is the recent collection *Creativity/Anthropology* (Lavie et al. 1993). The anthropological study of written life histories is also a growing field. Two recent volumes by Marianne Gullestad provide examples of this literature: *Imagined Childhoods: Self and Society in Autobiographical Accounts* (1996) and *Everyday Life Philosophers* (1996). On the recent, more general, growth of interest in personal narrative, see the *New York Times' Magazine* special issue (1996) *True Confessions: The Age of the Literary Memoir*.
2. There are so many references to "postmodern" anthropology in recent times that it is impossible to cite all sources. Key discussions of relevance here include that by Atkinson (1992), Fischer (1994), Strathern (1987a), and Van Maanen (1995).
3. See, in particular, the recent edited volumes by Smith and Watson (1996), Folkenflik (1993), and Ashley et al. (1995).
4. Since I grew up near to the region described by Dorst, his study constitutes the closest thing to an ethnographic description of my own culture that I have ever encountered, making it "autoethnographic" for me.
5. Examples of this include Bernard 1989, Hammel 1982, and Sioui 1992.

Part One

Power, Documentation, and Resistance

Chapter 1

Narrating Cultural Resurgence: Genre and Self-Representation for Pan-Mayan Writers

Kay B. Warren

> . . . we know that while intellectual debates wear themselves out with sterile rhetoric about how to understand "the other," indigenous people continue to live the most horrendous injustices which have been perpetuated across the centuries.
>
> Victor Montejo (1992: 3)

The public intellectuals involved in Guatemala's Pan-Mayan movement critique the ethics and politics of foreign anthropology and openly reject interview-based research and the ethnographic genre for their own writings.[1,2] They also distance themselves from autobiographical portrayals of cultural resurgence by arguing that the movement is at heart a collective effort. For these activists, this resistance represents a rejection of divisive individualism in favor of a transcendent Mayan identity for the 60 percent of the national population with indigenous backgrounds.

As the movement developed an institutional base throughout the highlands in the late 1980s and early 1990s,[3] Pan-Mayanists created a variety of genres of self-representation for different audiences: daybooks based on Mayan and Gregorian calendrics, school texts, point-of-view columns for editorial pages, collections of Mayan fables, conference proceedings, essays on Guatemalan racism, novels, testimonies, translations, poetry, linguistic research, reports to development organizations, social commentary, university theses, and statements asserting cultural rights.[4] As resurgence has gained momentum, these works have been published and distributed by Mayan presses, national newspapers and periodicals, international development funders, universities, the Ministry of Education, and other organizations inside and outside the country. Drawing inspiration from Mary Louise Pratt (1992), Marc Zimmerman (1995a, 1995b), Jonathan Boyarin (1993), Joanne Rappaport (1994), and anthropologists working on Mayan resurgence,[5] my wider project surveys the writings of Mayan intellectuals with an eye to the ways that marginalized groups represent themselves, interrogate the power structures in which they operate, and imagine alternative futures.[6] This research deals with the convergent and conflicting constructions of "the individual" and "the collective" in Pan-Mayan, traditionalist, and foreign portrayals. I am interested in the ways in which Mayan activists produce, circulate, read, and appropriate literature which now reaches hundreds of local communities through schools and nonformal education activities and by means of workshops, audio and video tapes, publications, radio programs, and the press. These materials find another axis of transcultural circulation through international meetings and courses in Latin American Studies in American and European universities and through organizations and journals supporting international human-rights struggles.

This essay discusses the prose of Victor Montejo, one of Pan-Mayanism's most prominent writers in exile. After fleeing Guatemala at the age of thirty in 1982, Montejo worked at Bucknell University, earned a master's degree at the State University of New York at Albany and a doctorate at the University of Connecticut at Storrs, and taught at Bucknell and the University of Montana before becoming assistant professor of anthropology at the University of California at Davis.

To use Mary Louise Pratt's insightful phrasing, Montejo has created "intercultural texts" – giving authority to subaltern voices through the *testimonio* genre – in order to describe the violence and existential dilemmas of Guatemala.[7] *Testimonios*, which have been widely used in Latin America to personalize the denunciation of state violence and to demonstrate subaltern resistance, gain their narrative power from the metaphor of witnessing. On the one hand, they represent eye-witness experiences, however mediated, of injustice and violence; on the other hand, they involve the act of witnesses presenting evidence for judgment in the court of public opinion. Drawing on Narvaez, Zimmerman (1995b: 12) notes that the literary *testimonio* involves

. . . generally linear first person narration of socially and collectively significant experiences, in which the narrative voice is that of a typical or extraordinary witness or protagonist who metonymically represents other individuals or groups that have lived through other, similar situations or the circumstances which induce them. By virtue of its collective representativeness, *testimonio* is overtly or not, an intertextual dialogue of voices, reproducing but also creatively reordering historical events in a way which impresses as representative and true and which projects a vision of life and society in need of transformation.

The Guatemala of Montejo's testimony is not the tourist paradise of colorful weavings and isolated peasant villages awaiting Western development, but rather a world of "contact zones," social spaces where disparate cultures meet, clash, grapple with each other, often in highly asymmetrical relations of domination and subordination" (Pratt 1992: 4).

Montejo's intercultural texts are both familiar and rebellious. They ignore the ethnographic conventions of anthropology which call on authors, sooner or later, to establish professional authority through abstraction, generalization, depersonalized narrative voices, and the theoretical justification of worthy research.[8] His books are also transgressive in light of Pan-Mayanist arguments against the autobiographical and ethnographic genres for the promotion of resurgence. Finally, while *testimonios* are most often autobiographical narratives edited by outsiders as acts of international solidarity, Montejo is an insider, a Jacaltec Maya who fled the extreme of rural violence in 1982 and met with other refugees, who in *Brevísima Relación* become peers working on a project of common concern:[9]

As an insider, my efforts are centered on the issue of how I (a native) can tell my collective story (of expropriation and exile) and, at the same time, elicit a strong commitment from anthropologists to promote issues such as social justice, self-determination, and human rights in the politics of native people. One of the most persistent struggles of modern Mayans is to get rid of their five century old denigrating images and colonial "representations." Thus, indigenous people have always complained that anthropologists do not listen to them, that instead they have represented native people with the anthropologist's preferred images: "primitives," "minorities," "backward," or just "informants." We Mayans find it difficult to deal with the academic world because if we tell the "experts" what is Mayan, they are reluctant to listen; instead they find it more scientific (comfortable) to tell us what it is to be Mayan, or to define Mayan culture. This is not to say that we possess the sole "truth," but as our culture is at stake, we regret that our views are not taken seriously. . . .. My aim has always been to make the sufferings of refugees more visible and to bring attention to their struggles to liberate themselves from continuous oppression and persecution. Mayans are again speaking for themselves and rupturing those barriers that have silenced us and positioned us in such unequal social relations (1993a: 16–17).

As a Mayan, a refugee, and an anthropologist, Montejo is aware of his own multiple accountability to readers with inherently conflicting politics and positionings. As an insider/outsider who studies displaced communities, Montejo must answer Abu-Lughod's question: "What happens when the 'other' that the anthropologist is studying is simultaneously constructed as, at least partially, a self?" (1991: 140).

Montejo has become an important interpreter of indigenous culture and Guatemalan politics during and after the counter-insurgency-guerrilla war of 1978–85, which killed an estimated 50,000 to 70,000 people, internally displaced 500,000 people out of a national population of 8 million, and forced 350,000 refugees to flee to Mexico and the United States, of whom 46,000 found shelter in refugee camps across the border in Chiapas, Mexico (Manz 1988: 30, 209). He argues that, just as the sixteenth-century Spaniards feared an indigenous uprising and used violence preemptively, so the Guatemalan army undertook a scorched earth policy in the early 1980s to undermine any incipient alliance between indigenous communities and the revolutionary move-ment which was then expanding into the western highlands (1993a). Montejo's writings, which have been published in Spanish, English, Jacaltec, and Italian, circulate in the United States, Latin America, and Europe. His works include *El Kanil; Man of Lightning* (1982), *Testimony: Death of a Guatemala Village* (1987), the collection with Q'anil Akab' titled *Brevísima Relación Testimonial de la Continua Destrucción del Mayab' (Guatemala)* (1992), *The Bird Who Cleans the World* (1992), and *Sculpted Stones* (1995). Some of these works are extraordinarily painful accounts of state terrorism in Guatemala. Others are bilingual compilations of Mayan fables from Montejo's home community, Jacaltenango, in the state of Huehuetenango, and poetry which recounts his journey from rural Guatemala to exile.

As it was for past generations, the issue for Pan-Mayan writers involved in projects of revitalization is to find a way to engage the terms of violence and racism and create space for something beyond extreme fragmentation. The challenge in the repressive environment of the late 1980s was to represent the formative experience of cultural difference in a multiethnic society without being labeled subversive. Perhaps it is fortunate that Mayan hermeneutics focuses on highly condensed symbolism, multiple levels of meaning, and veiled language. In the traditionalist past, community intellectuals, such as the *k'amöl b'ey* ritual guides, kept social criticism alive through religion and liminal ritual; today, national and regional leaders elaborate social criticism through the emerging field of Mayan Studies. The transnational field concentrates on Mayan languages, cultural distinctiveness, and prehispanic and colonial history – topics that, on the face of it, appear quite distant from contemporary politics. Yet, as I have argued elsewhere,[10] cultural and linguistic distinctiveness represent for Mayans an ethnogenesis that antedates and transcends the Spanish conquest. Colonial histories in service of the movement are presentist accounts which call on readers to see echoes of past violence in the cultural dynamics of the present.

Until very recently, writers in Guatemala were forced by death squads and state repression to veil their analyses and maintain extreme public caution when discussing politics. Mayan writers such as Demetrio Cojtí, Enrique Sam Colop, and Demetrio Rodriguez Guaján, and organizations such as the *Coordinadora Kaqchikel de Desarrollo Integral* and the Mayan press *Cholsamaj* showed great courage when they published on social issues in Guatemala. Those in exile were the first Pan-Mayanists explicitly to chronicle memories of violent displacement during the civil war.

Mayan Writers Outside the Country

Me Llamo Ribogerta Menchú y Así Me Nació la Conciencia (1985) is the most famous and controversial of the Guatemalan testimonial literature. As is clear from Elizabeth Burgos-Debray's preface, this is a highly mediated work, compiled by a Venezuelan anthropologist with European training who had a well-defined political agenda. Burgos-Debray did not know Guatemala well and spent only limited time with Menchú. Critics have argued that Menchú was an active participant in the literary process with her own political goals which shaped the product ethnographically and politically.[11] Used widely by solidarity organizers in the US and Europe "to embody and represent revolutionary possibility and hope in her country" (Zimmerman 1995b: 71), the work has unfortunately come to overshadow the writings of Pan-Mayanists living in exile[12] who have composed powerful personal testimonies, worked with Mayan refugees in Chiapas, and advocated cultural revitalization rather than revolution (Montejo 1987; Montejo and Akab' 1992). In the post-Cold War era, with the transition to civilian governments and the signing of the peace accords negotiated by representatives of the government, military, and the URNG guerrillas in 1996, it is particularly important to hear other voices and grammars of dissent.

Victor Montejo's writings take readers on a personal journey of violence, displacement, and cultural renewal. From the safety and free speech of exile, he was able to criticize state terrorism directly. In the United States, one of his goals was consciousness raising, to reach North American and international audiences so they would understand the human cost of authoritarian military regimes. To this end, he has lectured widely and participated in many forums on Mayan culture and on human rights.

While the rhetoric of anticommunism was used by Latin American governments to garner US financial support for counter-insurgency warfare in the 1970s and 1980s, human rights activists worked to convince Americans that the Guatemalan regime had an agenda which targeted armed guerrillas as well as unarmed civilian populations who were deprived of basic internationally recognized human rights.[13] The human-rights movement did achieve some success in pressuring the US government to cut foreign spending which directly financed state violence.[14] Another goal was to make Americans aware of continuing human-rights abuses and the unfinished business of the land crisis, refugee return, clandestine cemeteries, demilitarization, and peace negotiations after the war's de-escalation in the late 1980s.[15] To these ends, Montejo has participated in the Commission on Human Rights of the American Anthropological Association.

Over a period of several months at the end of 1982 and beginning of 1983, Montejo first drafted his own story of state violence and survival, *Testimony: Death of a Guatemalan Town* (1987), during his stay with relatives living in the Guadalupe Victoria refugee camp on the Mexico-Chiapas frontier. At that time, he visited neighboring camps to search for people he knew from his Kuchumatan homeland. He finished the book in the United States (Montejo 1992: 1–2).

Testimony tells of the September 9, 1982, massacre of San José Tzalalá, the village where Montejo had been in charge of the elementary school for ten years.[16] This deadly confrontation is initially presented as the consequence of a terrible mistake, which made the cost of joining the newly instituted "civil patrols" – locally organized to hunt guerrillas and monitor community members – the same as suicidal noncompliance with the policy of citizen involvement in the counterinsurgency war. When the army first came to Tzalalá to organize the patrols, wives and mothers protested the extra work and danger for the men, who dared not resist directly for fear of being jailed for not following orders. Later the men argued, to no avail, for the alternative of joint work on community improvement projects (1982: 29). Under President Ríos Montt's newly implemented policy, the men and youths of Tzalalá were forced in groups of eighty to 100 to hunt from six o'clock at night to six o'clock in the morning for guerrillas. They used clubs, stones, slingshots, machetes, and one ancient rifle as weapons against the insurgents. In Montejo's testimony, the contrast of their makeshift arms with the army's sophisticated Galil rifles and machine guns only underscores the hierarchy of human value implicit in the conflict. To demonstrate they could kill, the army commander – who like his subordinates remains nameless in this testimony – compelled the men to beat to death two of their neighbors on the pretext they had clandestine revolvers. Ten days after this brutal initiation, the villagers on patrol duty made the mistake of attacking a well-armed military patrol, dressed in unfamiliar fatigues.

Montejo recreates the tragedy from his vantage point at the schoolhouse: the eager shouts of patrollers who spotted the armed strangers they assumed to be guerrillas, the terrible sounds of machine-gun fire and grenade explosions, and the distant confusion which soon overtook the schoolhouse. Barring the doors and windows and yelling for the children to hide under their desks and pray, Montejo tried to protect and calm his terrified students.

Montejo uses an intimate first-person narrative to capture the immediacy of the unfolding massacre. His furtive glances under the slats of the schoolhouse window allowed him only partial experience and knowledge in the face of chaotic uncertainty. To portray the horror of families caught directly in the cross-fire, he introduces Doña Malcal, who saw the violent encounter first hand and tells of her only son's frantic search for his father, only to be shot. The occupying soldiers did not even let Doña Malcal comfort her son as he struggled to breathe: "[The soldier] pushed us out of the house, and I had to leave my son behind. That is why I am here now like a ghost, while my heart remains with my son, who by now is almost certainly dead" (1987: 34).

In this realist account, Montejo becomes a narrator-witness, a Mayan outsider who is not a member of this indigenous community, but rather a commuter on foot from a nearby town. After fantasizing an escape, he realized he would not. Given his authority and fluency in Spanish, he was needed to mediate between the villagers and the army, between the clash of interpretations. As the sergeant rounded up the surviving patrollers, some of whom were bleeding with shattered bones, anxious wives called out and begged him to explain the mistake. Montejo found the commanding officer and politely explained:

"I am the schoolmaster in this village and have come to let you know that the people you're holding captive are members of the civil patrol. By accident they mistook you for guerrillas."

"Don't come to me with those stories. These sons of bitches are guerrillas. That's why they attacked us, and I am going to execute every damn one of them."

I went on, unperturbed, "Up there by the chapel the rest of the men are waiting to clear up the situation for you."

"With me you have nothing to clear up. Everything is already clear. They've wounded one of my soldiers, and all of you will have to pay for it. What more do you want to know?" (1987: 25).

The narrative anxiously reveals the nature of brute power: the soldiers toyed with understanding the situation (or not) as they sacked the town, assaulted pregnant women, rounded up the townspeople, and burned their homes. After the roundup, the officer in charge reviewed the captives' identity cards against a list of alleged guerrilla collaborators someone had anonymously denounced, perhaps "for reasons of revenge or other personal reasons" (1987: 35–36). In a gesture, it becomes clear to the reader that the violent confrontation was no chance encounter.

Arbitrarily, some victims were sent to the school-turned-torture-chamber, where specialists unmercifully beat them to extract the names of accomplices. The identity papers of others were impatiently returned to them. Montejo's fate appeared to change dramatically when one of the accused, for no real reason, named him as a guerrilla collaborator. After defending himself by keeping calm in the face of physical threats and arguing his case of mistaken identity, Montejo was released only to discover the interrogators had slipped a noose around his neck. He was marked guilty as charged; even his friends shrank away from him in fear.

In a flashback, Montejo's account shows how quickly violence fractured the community *before* the massacre, turning neighbor against neighbor as the subsistence farmers were indoctrinated by their army commanders:

> ". . . we promised not to release anyone who fell into our hands," replied one of the heads of the civil patrol. "Not even if it's our own father or brother."

> This was the first time the civil defenders had begun speaking in these terms . . .. The defender was repeating to his own neighbor what the military had drummed into his head: Destroy, kill, even if it includes your own family. This military doctrine had gradually undermined the foundations of an indigenous culture, causing the Indian to act against his own will and best interests and destroying what is most sacred in his ancient Mayan legacy: love and respect for one's own neighbor, which translates into a policy of mutual support (1987: 63).

Moreover, the counterinsurgency war used indigenous troops – "alienated Mayans," "all of dark complexion and ill-educated" – to kill their own people on the distant command of the elite officers, who remain remote physically and culturally in this testimony. Since, in the army's minds "to be poor was to be a guerrilla" (1987: 56), there was nothing more to do in Tzalalá than to execute the six accused captives in front of their families. The commander of the foot soldiers would only be promoted for killing so many "guerrillas." Ironically, the troops trained in counterinsurgency techniques were called *kaibiles*, after the indigenous warriors who resisted the Spanish invasionary force in the sixteenth century.

Montejo narrates the tragedy of Mayan participation in the death of the village. He re-creates the process of indoctrination, never complete but compelling to some patrollers and soldiers, which exploits internal cleavages in communities, the poverty of foot soldiers, the reward structure for career officers, and the cynicism of the armed forces which from the president down was structured to compel Mayans to kill Mayans in the early 1980s.

At the end of the narrative, Montejo takes his readers along as he was dragged to the army base in his hometown, Jacaltenango, for further questioning, since "he seems to know so much." There is the hint of class antagonism here: How is it that a Mayan can be so articulate and direct in his explanations in the midst of more powerful soldiers who speak broken Spanish? Perhaps Montejo finds a noose around his neck not so much because he was falsely accused by a neighbor who is about to die, but rather because his interrogators wanted to negate the capacity the schoolmaster had earned (and been given by villagers) to mediate between the community and the armed forces.

For Montejo, the horror in Jacaltenango at the army installation is the coexistence of a space of mass torture and murder, institutionalized and normalized, within his hometown. This is a public secret, kept by signs that say "Forbidden Zone – No Trespassing" where the freshly incinerated bodies of torture victims were dumped.[17] Yet this move is also his salvation because his family was now to intercede on his behalf and pressure for his release. The Juan Bosh hell is run by drunken soldiers whose monstrous and capricious actions at night were only underscored by moments of the kindness in the morning. During his captivity, Montejo was grateful for gestures of humanity: a young officer who offered him a blanket and plastic poncho to sleep on as he huddled his first night wondering when his torture would resume, and as he awaited his fate in the morning others who brought a cup of corn *atole*, coffee from his wife, which meant there was hope for outside intervention, and a Bible which, as he read the Psalms of David, brought him equanimity. One soldier even coached him not to "betray any fear or let them catch you shaking" (1987: 92) at his interrogation. But it is clear to the reader that no one can really be trusted and no gesture is transparent. Nevertheless, Montejo insists throughout his accounts on seeing the soldiers as individuals and as victims at the same time as he exposes the collective cruelty of this torture center. Throughout his interrogation, Montejo was convinced that his own demeanor and actions could make a difference. If he only controlled his expression and stayed vigilant, his captors might not initiate the process which would inevitably consummate in the torture, screams, and death occurring all around him. Prayers to the Virgin and dreams of his brother, who had been killed the year before by soldiers and who reappeared to Montejo as a spiritual guardian, gave him hope. He was determined to show no fear or anxiety and maintain his straight-forward innocence when questioned.

In the end, he had to accept an unbearable bargain to win even conditional freedom. Montejo promised the base commander to report names of people he heard were involved with the guerrillas and to return to the base each day for continued questioning at the officers' whim. This, of course, was an unstable solution because someday he would have to accuse others and perpetuate this unending cycle of complicity. Hearing that a civil patrol had harassed his family and his name had appeared on a death list, Montejo and his family decided to flee to the United States where he had contacts from his earlier writings on Mayan culture (1987: 115).

Montejo began talking to other refugees about their experiences of violence during a visit to the Chiapas refugee camps at the end of 1982 and the beginning of 1983. In the summers of 1988, 1989, and 1992, in conjunction with his dissertation research, he returned to Chiapas and went on to Guerrero to tape stories of survival in the languages of their narrators. In 1993, he accompanied refugees in the first mass return from Chiapas to Guatemala. *Brevísima Relación Testimonial de la Continua Destrucción del Mayab' (Guatemala)* (1992) is the fruit of Montejo's collaboration with other Mayans to produce evidence of government repression against isolated highland communities near the frontier with Mexico. The name that Montejo gives his co-compiler of the collection – Q'anil Akab' evokes for him the collective collaboration inherent in the work and the inspiration he receives from Mayan culture in his writings. Q'anil Akab' is both many voices and the transcendant united diversity that Montejo advocates for Mayan culture in Guatemala.

Safety was an issue for the refugees who offered their personal stories of military abuse for publication: in the book, each is protected by the use of Mayan pseudonyms. There is, however, a complicated hopefulness in this naming: through assumed names, the witnesses to violence are identified with their culture, with the renewed practice of using indigenous names in Mayan revitalization, and with anonymity so they might return someday to Guatemala without fear of personal persecution for breaking the forced silence about violence.

Montejo structures his collection of testimonies of genocidal war to mirror Bartolomé de las Casas's famous description of the atrocities committed by the Spanish invaders against indigenous populations, as chronicled in the 1542 *Brevísima Relación de la Destrucción de las Indias* (Zimmerman 1995b: 114–115).[18] Readers are reminded of the continuities of violence from the conquest to the present by the intercutting of fragments from the las Casas account with each of the testimonies. The difference, Montejo reminds us, is that this *Brevísima Relación Testimonial*, unlike the original, contains the voices of Mayan observers.

The modern chroniclers celebrated the 1992 quincentenary of Spain's conquest of the New World with an open letter to the king of Spain, Juan Carlos I, whose sixteenth-century counterpart, Prince Felipe II, in his role as the chief negotiator with the Indies, was the audience for the original las Casas account. As in past centuries, the goal of the correspondence was to urge the Crown to direct its powers against colonial violence: "Here we present to your Highness a collection of testimonies, voices of the survivors of genocide, which the Guatemalan government has wanted to hide from the world's eyes" (1992: 9). Although Juan Carlos I did not, in fact, reply when the book was sent to him in 1992, the anti-quincentenary campaign brought together circles of indigenous leaders from throughout the Americas to share ideas for cultural demands in the face of continuing neocolonial violence.

Montejo signals other framings for the collection, both modern and ancient, by including the adjective *testimonial* in the title. This work is designed not as single-voiced synthesis of one narrator's survival, but rather as a multivoiced testimony to horror. *Brevísima Relación Testimonial* is a collective Mayan contribution to the *testimonio* genre which has long made a place for subaltern voices and politics in Latin American literature (Zimmerman 1995a,

1995b). Yet to mark this as an indigenous work, with its own cultural history that could not be assimilated into Cold War politics, the compiler offers an alternative subversive framing: the ancient prophesies by Mayan priest-diviners of a foreign invasion described in the Mayan *Chilam Balam* and in the Aztec chronicles of the conquest.[19] The editor imagines himself as *aj-tziib'*, as an ancient scribe and poet in the present. Thus, Akab' links the past and present when he ends the prologue with these prophesies:

> 1980: Signs and Dreams. In dreams we saw great golden signs that appeared in the skies. Others saw sharp-edged machetes that fell from the heavens. Many machetes, a rain of machetes fell from the sky to the earth. But the most common dreams were of fires that razed the crops, along with animals and villages. Weeping, much weeping among the women and sighs among the elders (1992: 12).

In Montejo's and Kaxh Pasil's testimony drawn from Kuchumatan communities, troubling signs of rare wild animals, grieving dogs, and the devil, quickly gave way to visions of naked tortured bodies which gestured from their perches in the trees at the banks of the river – long before the violence came to the region. Most disconcerting were the elders' dreams in which the ancestors and patron saints abandoned their towns. Then angry waves of violence came in 1980, 1981, and 1982. Montejo historicizes the omens and eyewitness accounts with a chronology of the militarization and massacres in the Kuchumatans. In these years, thousands of refugees poured out of the Kuchumantans toward the Mexican frontier. At first, the Mexican authorities forced the refugees back into Guatemala. Then, as the scope of the violence became clear, refugee camps were set up in Chiapas (see Americas Watch 1984a, Montejo 1993a).

The body of the work is composed of personal stories, called laments, which describe the physical intensity of military violence, the arbitrariness of torture and murder, and the double binds state violence created for civilians. Montejo's selection of these particular testimonies, among all the other possibilities, and his editing of the taped interviews would seem to reflect two interlocking and urgent issues: the public secret of "disappearances," which were in fact widespread brutal killings in isolated highland villages, and the involvement of Mayans in this violence.

These witnesses graphically describe the horror of watching individuals – young, old, men, and women – being hacked to death in front of unwilling witnesses because they were out of place or did not have the proper identity cards. They tell of others, who, after presenting their identity cards and found to be on ever-growing lists of accused subversives, were unspeakably tortured in secret at military bases, their bodies burned or thrown from bridges to be swept away by the currents.[20] The testimonies dwell on deaths for no meaningful reason, on people with no chance to defend themselves from the military's lawlessness. As Hulum B'aq, a civil patroller, observed: "Not one soldier or military official was prosecuted for these crimes against the lives of thousands of peasants. Well they were the authorities, but a criminal authority" (1992: 78).

To make sense of this senselessness, Montejo selects a very specific cross-section of voices for this collection: a former soldier and member of the intelligence section, civil patrollers, and civilians who escaped from torture centers at military bases. In what I would argue is an autoethnography of a contact zone, all the speakers can be seen as contributing their observational expertise to reveal the inner workings of the terrorist state: its tactics for civilian control and indoctrination, the treatment of prisoners and modes of torture at army bases, the structure of military-civilian authority, the relation of the armed forces to the death squads, ways of escaping from the bases, and the justification of violence as it escalated from surveillance to counterinsurgency sweeps to the extermination of civilian communities.[21]

Striking patterns emerge from disparate eyewitness observations. The bloody contact zone is portrayed as a chaotic cultural system which coerced complicity, transformed the subjectivities of its forced laborers, and generated a climate where torture and massacres were inevitable. Since, for Montejo, ruthlessness is neither an inherent predisposition nor a characteristic flowing from a person's social position, the line between "good" and "bad" can be continually blurred in this postorientalist collection of narratives. Individuals who become complicit in the violence find themselves learning to be murderous through their "own" experiences and are purposefully taught by others to think in certain ways as a result of punishing, fragmenting, and isolating indoctrination, built on a foundational hierarchy of "good people" versus "savages who deserve extermination."

By resisting the ethnographic tendency to sum up the moral of the story, Montejo offers *Brevísima Relación* as a polyphonic, interactive work, which calls on readers to see potential patterns for themselves.[22] In the testimonies, some indigenous individuals resist complicity in small ways, others are sympathetic to the army. Patrollers condemn the brutality of soldiers who gang-raped three young female Q'anjob'al guerrillas before killing them, and note how some soldiers in this detachment drifted slowly to join the patrollers who had physically distanced themselves from the unbearable spectacle of the public torture of an old man and woman. Yet both patrollers and soldiers rob "abandoned" homes and refugee camps of their meager possessions and farm animals. At the military base, some guards encourage prisoners out of real empathy, others only in a cruel joke of betrayal, to set them up for a terrifying end instead of their anticipated release.

Mayan complicity in atrocities is dealt with directly in the conflicted testimonies of Chilin Hultaxh, an ex-soldier and collaborator with the intelligence section, and Hulum B'aq, a former civil patroller – though, significantly, no one in this collection actually speaks of his own personal violence toward others. What is revealed is the widespread routinization of violence in the everyday practices of the counterinsurgency forces, the torture centers at army bases, and local civil patrols.

So, too, the testimonies illustrate small acts of resistance on the part of soldiers and civil patrollers, who would have lost their lives with more open opposition. Hulum B'aq and his companions angrily confront a fellow patroller who, out of his own worries, attempted to curry favor with the military by loaning soldiers his machete, even as fellow patrollers found successful excuses for why they could not:

> We knew that the unfortunate indigenous women who the soldiers had just killed were poor peasant women, not guerrillas, as the army is accustomed to accusing the thousands and thousands they have killed in the same way.

> "Why did you hand over your machete to them? Weren't you aware that they had their own arms with which to commit their crimes without our participation?" The man began crying with great sadness for having given them the machete, and in desperation threw the machete in the river. A machete that has been used to commit this kind of crime can't belong to us peasants (1992: 75).

Here the narrative shows Mayans insisting on the nonviolent domestic utility of their most basic tool, the machete, in feeding people rather than killing them.

In these testimonies, one impulse of these witnesses whose lives were swallowed by the violence is to identify *other* individuals who were harmed: Ignacia, a pregnant women; Gilbertino a 40-year-old with six children; Doña Tulis, an old woman who could not bear to shed her traditional clothing at the refugee camp; Akux Lenam, a civil patroller who fled his duties; Doña Cristabel, a woman who found the courage to go to the military to ask where her son was held (1992: 23, 27, 31, 35, 49). At the end of the collection, Montejo continues this naming "to demonstrate to the world not just the statistics and the drama of the injustice in which the Mayan people of Guatemala live, but also the names of these [302] victims" in San Francisco Netón who were massacred by the army on July 17, 1982 (1992: 121). The list is important "evidence" to a world that undervalues narrative genres for documenting violence.

Another impulse is to identify the authors of violence: the presidents Lucas García, Ríos Montt, and Mejía Víctores, whose regimes authorized violence and organized the command structure and death squads which carried it out (1992: 9, 28–31, 49, 63–68, 91–96). The naming of victims and protagonists by these witnesses is a powerful counterpoint to the victims of torture who were forced to name "accomplices."

Reading Autoethnography in Dialogue with Foreign Ethnography

How might one read the testimonial genre in dialogue with interpretive ethnography – in this case, with my descriptions of violence from those who stayed in San Andrés Semetabaj, a community north of Lake Atitlán and far to the west and south of the Kuchumatans? Thematically, the accounts have much in common, though the intensity of militarization contrasted in the two regions. Both deal with existential dilemmas, with the fragmentation of community life, loyalty, and trust, and with the agony of witnessing brutal physical violence when one cannot intercede. Yet in other ways there are important differences in experience and genre.

Montejo's testimonies come in the form of sustained first-person narratives of torture, survival, and escape. Their immediacy is maintained by the erasure of the interview process and the omission of any metanarrative, abstraction, or analysis that might have continued after their introductory remarks.[23] As I have already argued, that is not to say there is no overall argument, for clearly this work makes the strongest possible case for the transformation of the state to establish basic human rights, the dismantling of civil patrols, the demilitarization of the countryside, and the opportunity for refugees to return to their communities and fields.

Reflexively, however, the compiler is submerged in this variant of the testimonial genre as just another voice in a collage of different positions and experiences. As interviewer and editor, Montejo took great care to maintain the distinctive language practices of each speaker in the Spanish edition and to include enough information to clarify their backgrounds. By contrast, Montejo's personal narrative of exile in *Testimony; Death of a Guatemalan Village* includes an independent narrative voice which more actively intervenes to explain issues, such as indoctrination, to a readership which may lack direct knowledge of rural community life.

These testimonies address the issue of survivorship by the repeated twinning of the speaker's own surprising survival with companions who died terrible deaths in the same situation. Thus, readers see the arbitrariness of violence and survival. Hulum B'aq saw his connection with torture victims as he was on patrol duty:

> One day, when it was my turn to take care of the La Laguna bridge with my group, the soldiers came down to the bridge from Netón bringing three peasants who were all tied up. These three indigenous peasants looked so poor, just like us, the patrollers. We already knew the soldiers went down to the bridge at night to kill people they brought from different places and then they threw the bodies in the river to disappear them (1992: 73–74).

Kaxh Maal-Ya's testimony tells how he and his younger brother, Kaxhin, were taken prisoner by their civil patrol for being absent when a military patrol made a visit to their community. Feeling they were going to be killed at the regional base, the older brother convinced Kaxhin to join him in an escape attempt only to lose his younger brother at the base's perimeter fence while they were being pursued by the armed guards. Tumaxh K'em tells of a group of families, fleeing to Mexico, who were intercepted by their civil patrol and returned to the army base. Circumstances allowed the narrator to escape, while his neighbor, Jesús, was too weak from his beatings to follow. Shortly thereafter, another man was killed in Tumaxh's place. In both escapes, the survivors felt a moral compulsion, before fleeing across the border, to get in touch with the families of their counterparts to tell them the sorrowful news behind the disappearance of their loved ones.

Miraculously amidst all the violence, the survivors' immediate families are reconstituted on the other side of the border, creating the possibility for a constructive future in the midst of personal tragedy. The book's final section presents children's fragmentary accounts of almost identical transitions from terror to safety,[24] and begs the question of the impact of state terrorism on them. To fill some of the silences from their stories, Montejo includes children's drawings which give stark visual form to memories of soldiers shooting civilians and burning their homes.

Despite the shocking details, there are striking silences in these testimonies: memories of what it meant to torture others, not just to be a victim, children's enduring experiences after their escape, refugee families both reunited and broken by the experience, and the dilemmas experienced by Mayans in exile which render their stories more open-ended and unfinished.[25] These silences no doubt reflect editorial choices but, as Montejo explains (1993a), they also betray the great anxiety and fear of strangers, especially those who asked questions or probed memories of violence, that refugees felt in the camps.

On the one hand, the collage of first-person accounts (rather than an expository style) leaves more of the work of analysis to the reader. On the other hand, in remaining true to the genre testimonial genre, the book leaves the civil patroller's and ex-soldier's silences about their own violence as unfinished business which can pass without being directly interrogated. Nor do we hear from any ex-guerrillas who joined the flow of refugees.

In contrast to Montejo's testimonies, the San Andrés accounts I collected during five months of field work in 1989 were much more fragmented and veiled in the naming of protagonists and victims (see Warren 1993). Most likely this is because people were still directly subject to military terror and systematic political monitoring when I returned to Guatemala to talk to the families I had been close to in the 1970s. It is also possible that people had not yet learned how to tell their stories as testimonies, perhaps because they had less direct contact with human-rights groups than international refugees.

In San Andrés, I was warned by friends that the local military commissioner would routinely monitor my behavior and that I should make no attempts to talk to youths or former soldiers. Initially I decided not to pursue the topic of violence out of concern for everyone's safety; in the end, I was compelled to deal with memories of the civil war because public events and private conversations referred to *la violencia* obsessively but almost always obliquely in 1989. There were private stories of close escapes and of witnessing the disappearances of others (another version of twinning) and many cryptic stories of unidentified bodies on the highways. The denouement of exile was replaced in San Andrés narratives with a sense that "the violence, it always continues." There was no closure, no exit in sight at the end of the decade.

Like Montejo, I found that the civil war bred terrible uncertainty, all sorts of survival tactics in the face of military and guerrilla intervention in community affairs, and the fear that violence would be internalized as individuals were tempted to take advantage of community divisions and antagonisms for personal profit or to settle old scores. For a number of reasons, including its location away from major areas of guerrilla-military confrontation and the long history of collaboration of diverse groups in the community, San Andrés weathered four years of terror in the early 1980s with some killings, an overnight guerrilla occupation of the town, and the militarization of the region, but without major massacres. What weighed most heavily on townspeople, however, was the public secret of a nearby clandestine cemetery operated at the height of the violence by the military.

Another tragic consequence of the violence was the constant fear on everyone's mind that neighbors or perhaps even relatives would denounce them to either the military or guerrillas. In effect, one had to rely on people one could not trust in order to survive the violence. Silence, strategic evasiveness, and ambiguity were used as verbal tactics for almost a decade by townspeople who felt that one could not know for certain the allegiances of those with whom they routinely dealt.

My published account, "Interpreting *la Violencia* in Guatemala: Shapes of Mayan Silence and Resistance," began in conventional academic expository style with the insurgency/counterinsurgency war as the context for understanding the impact of violence on civilians in San Andrés. While the analysis masks the interactive interview process which accounts for my knowledge of the town, attempting to represent the violence forced me to erode and transform the unitary expository style into a more polyphonic text. From interviews, I quoted memories of daily life during the conflict to represent the immediacy and fragmenting experience of the violence for individuals and families. Given the political situation, however, the speakers remained unidentified in the publication.

My analysis argued that townspeople survived the silence imposed by the corrosion of trust in others in part by revitalizing traditionalist magical realist narratives of transforming selves to address the haunting issue of interpersonal betrayal. Departing from social scientific conventions to make my case, I quoted a long magical realist narrative – which on the face of it had nothing to do with war, but in practice had everything to do with the adversities it generated – and discussed Mayan hermeneutics to show that realist fragments were only one of a variety of ways Mayans used to represent the effect of violence on their lives (see Warren 1993 for the example). The social relations that mediated the process of revitalization were striking; among those who began to tell the old narratives were leaders of the very religious groups who had sought to displace traditionalism with new orthodoxies. Thus, like Montejo, I found that Mayan culture – both in what we would consider its realist and magical realist ways of representing the world – was used by particular individuals to address the existential dilemmas and human costs of a world spinning out of control. One sees here a convergence between the ways testimonial and anthropological accounts gain their authority and make their cases to readers.

In my ethnographic account, I had always wondered where to make space for my own presence and subjectivity as an outsider who had worked in Guatemala at various times for over twenty years and returned to continue research once it was finally "safe" to do so. Finally, with the urging of Begoña Aretxaga, I decided to add a self-reflexive epilogue through which I explored the role of anthropologists as witnesses to human-rights abuses, the issue of ethnography as a dialogical project, and the fact that the US political and military involvement in Guatemala was part of the problem. I considered the possibility that the silences I found were produced in part by my presence, not only induced by the trauma of the violence.[26] While that is doubtlessly true, I was struck with the curiosity community leaders expressed about unraveling the silence of other Mayans, in and out of town. The epilogue also gave me the opportunity to note that I too honored certain silences and ambiguities as someone who, as others in the community in the late 1980s, had been caught in a nighttime military sweep, and knew more than she could reveal at the time in public forums. My experience of state terror – though in no way comparable to those who lived through the worst of the crisis or those who have learned to survive longer periods of low-intensity warfare – had a fundamental impact on my own understandings and writings.

I suspect that the silences imposed on San Andrés by the civil war left community members hungry for precisely the kinds of accounts that Montejo and his collaborators produced to make sense of their own experiences.[27] But, certainly through the early 1990s, the question was whether it was safe to be in possession of such accounts in a country where military sweeps and political monitoring were still common. Thus, for some years, these testimonies had a wider readership outside the country and little distribution within.

In publishing first-person accounts of violent displacement, Montejo appropriated many of the conventions denounced by Pan-Mayan critics of anthropology: the use of ethnographic interviews and autobiographical accounts which underscore individualism and divisions within the Mayan community. Yet his multiple framings, denunciations of racism, focus on multiple-subject positions, and inclusion of Mayan narratives which transcend the conventions of realist testimony make the collection relevant for the current process of healing and revitalization.

The framing of the collection to stress a subjectivity shaped by Mayan hermeneutics fits in with Montejo's other works which were written throughout this time period and stress Mayan cultural struggles and their distinctive moral discourse. Across these works, Montejo argues for the resilience of Mayan culture in the face of fragmenting conflict and asserts that the experience of violent displacement is yet another source of Pan-Mayanism. For their part, Pan-Mayan activists in Guatemala see this work as an important aspect of their struggle for revindication.

Perhaps it is a hopeful sign of the times that the Spanish version of Montejo's *Testimony: Death of a Mayan Town* was published in Guatemala in 1993 with great acclaim and *Brevísima Relación Testimonial* will be published soon by the University of San Carlos Press in Guatemala. Personal testimonies of the violence during the civil war in other parts of the country can now be found at open-air regional book fairs in Guatemala, and Guatemalans are beginning to read Mayan publications at universities where the next generations of national leaders and professionals are being trained. Informal collections of testimonies are being produced by a variety of grass-roots groups for their own members.

In recent years, Montejo has been able to return to Guatemala to speak at public forums organized by Pan-Mayanists such as the 1994 *Primer Congreso de la Educación Maya* and the 1996 *Primer Congreso de Estudios Mayas*. Montejo's trips to his home town, Jacaltenango, to work with others to build a library and cultural center for adults and children represent still another encouraging sign. That he and others traveling through the highlands by bus and car have to fear for their lives because travelers are being routinely threatened, robbed, kidnapped, and killed by unidenti-fied gunmen, only shows that violence has taken new twists and turns on the eve of the signing of the peace accords at the end of 1996.

Notes

1. My thanks to Deborah Reed-Danahay for the opportunity to think more about the relation of Mayan writings to auto-ethnography and autobiography. This essay emerges out of recent discussions with a variety of writers in the Pan-Mayan movement, including Victor Montejo, Gaspar Pedro González, Enrique Sam Colop, and Demetrio Cojtí. As the analysis makes clear, I have tremendous respect for these public intellectuals and talented writers. However, I alone am responsible for the framing of this interactive analysis of Victor Montejo's works and my own ethnography.
2. See Sam Colop (1990) for the critiques and Montejo (1993b) for scathing reviews of foreign scholarship on the Mayans.

3. See Adams (1993) and Warren (n.d.d).
4. For a full listing of these sources, see Warren (n.d.d). Beyond the writers discussed in this essay, prominent voices would include the essayists Demetrio Cojtí Cuxil (1991, 1993, 1995), the novelist Gaspar Pedro González (1992, 1995), the lawyer-linguist Enrique Sam Colop (1991), the poet Humberto Ak'abal (1993, 1995a, 1995b), the historian Víctor Racancoj (1994), legal writers Miguel Angel Curruchiche Gómez (1994) and Edgar Esquit Choy and Carlos Ochoa García (1995), and the linguists of Oxlajuuj Keej Maya' Ajtz'iib' (1993), among many others. Institutional sponsors would include the Mayan press *Cholsamaj* which publishes widely in service of the movement, the University of Rafael Landívar's *Instituto de Lingüística* and the Ministry of Education which publish teacher training books and texts, the *Academia de Lenguas Mayas de Guatemala* and *Centro de Estudios de la Cultural Maya* which publish conference proceedings, and the *Coordinadora Kaqchikel de Desarrollo Integral (COCADI)*, *Maya Wuj*, and the *Consejo de Organizaciones Mayas de Guatemala*, which publish the widely used daybooks and educational materials on cultural rights.
5. See, for example, Wilson (1995), Fischer and Brown (1996), Adams (1994), England (1992), Hale (1994), Smith (1990, 1991), and Watanabe (n.d.).
6. See, for example, Warren (1996, n.d.a, and n.d.c).
7. See Zimmerman (1995b) for a useful overview of *testimonio* literature in Latin America and the genre as practiced in Guatemala.
8. That Montejo is fluent in these norms is clear from his dissertation (1993).
9. In other ways, he has had a very different experience in exile in the US. See Hagan (1994) on Guatemala refugees in Houston and Burns (1993) on refugees in Indiantown, Florida.
10. See Warren (1966 and n.d.a.).
11. See Zimmerman for a very important survey of the critical literature on Menchú and for an insightful reading of Menchú against Sexton's testimonies of Ignacio (1995, vol. 2).
12. See, for example, Zimmerman (1995b: 96) and the Stoll and D'Souza controversies described in Zimmerman (1995b).
13. For examples of human rights discourse for the Kuchumatans in the early 1980s, see the Americas Watch and Amnesty International citations in the bibliography.

14. In part this goal was achieved in that the US, after Congressional hearings, cut direct support of the military. Yet indirect support continued through US programs and military advisors which trained Guatemalan officers in counterinsurgency techniques, using development funds redirected to paramilitary police forces and C.I.A. involvement with the military, which has come to light recently.
15. See the Americas Watch Committee publications cited in the bibliography. For a view critical of the human rights community, see Stoll (1993).
16. This is a pseudonym.
17. See Taussig (1991) on terrorism.
18. See also Sam Colop (1991) for another critical approach to colonial history.
19. See, for example, León Portilla (1974, 1984). For more on the history of the Kuchumatans, see Lovell (1992).
20. I have made the editorial decision *not* to reproduce excerpts which detail acts of torture or killing. They are too graphic for a short essay where, unlike a contextualized longer work, their shock value displaces other issues and orientalizes the other.
21. As Montejo discusses in an expository mode in his dissertation, military rhetoric "shifted from Indians as savages to Indians as communists who threatened to seize private property and introduce a totalitarian system . . .. Indians were equated with guerrillas, subversives, and instruments of communism" (1993a: 59–60).
22. See Clifford (1988), Clifford and Marcus (1986), and Fox (1991) for discussions of ethnographic authority, the diversification of anthropological narrative strategies, the politics of authorship and representation, the recent concern with representing the plural voices that contribute to ethnographic knowledge, and the realization of the culturally diverse audiences for ethnography. Nichols (1994), who deals with another domain of realist representation – documentary films and fictions – demonstrates the earlier self-awareness of these issues for filmmakers.
23. Montejo made a self-conscious decision here, given that he is fluent in North American academic conventions through his graduate work (see Montejo 1993a).
24. These were written at the camp's school under the supervision

of the school master, which no doubt accounts for their similarity.

25. That violence and the state take new coercive forms after exile is clear through Montejo's dissertation research (1993a) as well as the studies of refugees in the US by Burns (1993) and Hagen (1994).

26. Montejo (1993a: 9–11) deals with the issue of refugee reticence, explores its social and political sources in the camps, and deals with the Mexican government's political structuring of the camps. His interviews were conducted in camps outside formal government control.

27. Another issue for many is the difference for social activists between those who stayed and those who fled to exile.

Chapter 2

Autoethnography as Political Resistance: A Case from Socialist Romania

David A. Kideckel

If you do not write, you forget . . .

    Aurel Bălan, 'Hîrseni Commune: Families from Past to Present'

Ethnography: Public and Private, Native and Folk

Ethnography, both process and product, is a public phenomenon. This essay considers the implications when it isn't. As a public act, ethnographic production entails external observation, interviews, and measurement – activities which mostly occur in an observed and seeing community. Imparting ethnographic knowledge is as public as the process. Its vehicle is the written monograph, essay, or video or audio recording. All give ethnography a corporeal reality on which it depends for enabling intercultural subjectivity. Consequently it is oxymoronic to speak of private ethnography. Without overt research populations or audiences, ethnographic realities ought to disappear like the sound of trees falling out of human earshot.

Despite this public quality, there are myriad examples of private ethnography. A review of cases shows that in most, politics drives the process. For example, significant ethnographic work has been commissioned by powerful interests intent on knowing subject peoples to better administer or control them. Such was the case with some practices of the Rhodes-Livingstone Institute in colonial Africa (Kuper 1973: 123–149), the US Bureau of Indian Affairs research earlier in this century, and work in 1960s and 1970s Latin America and Southeast Asia.[1] Here, though some observation and writing was accessible to the public, much was reserved for its sponsors.

Conversely, other examples of private ethnography include attempts by the disenfranchised to understand those who control them or how their lives are affected by such control. As a threat to established power, such ethnography is particularly dangerous to both observer and community. Private ethnography serving subordinated peoples is thus frequently carried out by native peoples themselves, due to issues of trust and subversion inherent in it. A recent example concerns the revolutionary situation in Chiapas, Mexico. While professional anthropologists have produced an abundance of work describing indigenous Mayan conditions, as Kay Warren discusses (this volume), much recent ethnography has been created by Mayans themselves in an attempt to control their own history.[2]

Private ethnography, especially of the latter variety, frequently falls into that category described as "native anthropology" (Bernard and Salinas P. 1989; Hofer 1969; Jones 1970), where members of cultural groups undertake to describe their group. However, I further distinguish trained native ethnographers like Jomo Kenyatta, Malinowski's student and author of *Facing Mount Kenya* (1965), from a "folk ethnographer" like Badea Cîrțan, the nineteenth-century Romanian shepherd who traveled on foot to Rome to understand Romanian origins and who wrote about his people and travels in poems and monographs. Native ethnographers derive from the culture they describe, are trained in ethnography, and return to engage their origins. Folk ethnographers, on the other hand, are both untrained and immersed within the milieu they describe even as they describe it.

What, then, are the implications of private folk ethnography? This essay considers how it develops, its similarities and differences from "professional" ethnography, and the extent to which it is a legitimate ethnographic enterprise, an accurate depiction of cultural conditions, and above all, politically effective in challenging the conditions of oppression under which it is often carried out.

The lack of discussion about native/folk/hidden ethnography in some recent highly regarded texts on ethnography (Clifford and Marcus, eds. 1980; Geertz 1988; Marcus and Fischer 1977) implies a range of analytical difficulties in the genre besides that of subjectivism. How does ethnography undertaken sub rosa, with knowledge that its product must be kept from public view, shape the manner by which data are collected or presented? Are data collected in this manner too selective and thus invalid for general use? Most important, does ethnographic secrecy deprive ethnographers of their voice and their work of its political power, its initial impetus?

These are not idle questions. World political change demands that subject peoples regain their voice and that anthropology integrate such indigenous accounts into its own canon. Many of the essays in this volume in fact suggest that ethnography, biography, and autobiography have become critical battlegrounds in the war between constituted authority and local populations (e.g. Motzafi-Haller, Svensson). Consequently, if we are serious in our support of a critical anthropology and a participatory politics, as Rosaldo says (1989: 147–149), we must take the narrative analyses of others as seriously as we take our own. We must expand the ethnographic genre to incorporate work created to purposefully elude official authority. It potentially has greater insight than its overt counterparts as it need pay scant attention to publishing conventions or hedge its voice in proper phraseology. It is raw and to the point.

This essay considers some of the foregoing intellectual and political issues in folk/hidden ethnography by examining the life and work of a remarkable individual. In ten year's time, during the worst days of Romanian dictator Nicolae Ceauşescu, Aurel Bălan, a pensioned and nearly blind former chief accountant of a village collective farm and consumers' cooperative, produced over fifty volumes of family histories, autobiography, poetry, and daily logs and financial records. Known at first only to a select group of friends and relatives, this work was hidden in a water-proof, fake window well to prevent its discovery by authorities. Since Ceauşescu's fall in 1989, Aurel's work (he died in May 1989) has now been made public. Its significance occupies me here.

Reviewing Aurel's work, it first appears overly romantic, polemical, and subjective. Furthermore, the semisecret way by which he gathered data and produced and safeguarded his work also implies its ultimate political irrelevance. However, the following discussion suggests otherwise. Not only was his work an accurate commentary on daily reality in a Romanian village, but through his process of data collection and production Aurel sharpened his critique of the socialist state, provided his family with lessons about it, and thus fostered their survival, even prosperity, within it. Furthermore, as he "gathered his data" and subsequently as his work was revealed, it validated the rejection of socialist practice for many villagers, testified to the worth of their small-scale struggles, and served as a model for political behavior in a modern state system. Paradoxically the hidden ethnography of Aurel Bălan was eminently useful for the community where it was carried out and for the articulation of its interests and culture in the past, present, and future.

Romanian Ethnography, Subterfuge, and the Socialist State

To better understand Aurel Bălan's work and, by extension, other hidden/folk ethnography, it must be seen in the context of Romanian ethnography in general. Romania has long social scientific, native, and folk ethnographic traditions to which Bălan's work clearly relates. Professional Romanian ethnography dates to the work of Dimitrie Gusti and his students between the two world wars (Barbat 1941; Cotaru 1938; Stahl 1936) though there were even older native and folk ethnographic traditions (Cernea 1981). The earliest examples of these are a detailed description of Moldavian life by Dimitrie Cantemir (1715) and a number of economically oriented descriptions of Romanian regions by agronomist Ion Ionescu de la Brad. The Romanian village monograph tradition especially developed through the nineteenth century when priests, school teachers, and local autodidacts generated great numbers of written descriptions. Many were spurred by growing Romanian ethnic consciousness or, as in Ionescu's work, to point out critical social and economic needs.

Whatever their nature or source, the circumstances of Romanian ethnography changed radically with the socialist advent at the end of World War Two. Immediately after the socialist capture of power, ethnography and the social sciences in general were anathemized and threatened with extinction. They were deemed too positivist in a dialectical world and too oriented to cooperative and corporate communities where class struggle and state corporatism now reigned. Ethnography, in particular, was assumed to celebrate popular tradition and custom and thus was conceptually opposed to international proletarian revolution and the mobilization of the productive forces.

As socialist power consolidated, however, the social sciences again became appropriate tools to facilitate societal management and integration. Sociologists and others were contracted to state agencies to observe and measure local behavior on social problems and issues like labor migration, the organization of agricultural or industrial production, or the proper distribution of settlements over geographic space. Among others, ethnographers were put to work in factories and on collective farms to document the socialist realities aborning.

The life of sociologist Traian Herseni[3] provides an example of ethnography in the socialist period. A student of Gusti who participated on his team study of Drăguş village (Herseni 1944) in Transylvania, Herseni went on to serve as one of the last ministers of education prior to the socialist advent. Arrested, beaten, and jailed in the late 1940s for his science and his politics, Herseni was released in the late 1950s and joined an approved sociological research institute. In this part of his career he headed the team that produced an ethnography of a major Romanian chemical plant commissioned in honor of its fiftieth anniversary (Herseni et al. 1972), wrote an ethnography and analysis of the *ceata feciorilor*, the "traditional" village young men's associations (Herseni 1977), and a general text on sociology (Herseni 1982).

Other ethnographers worked at the Ethnographic Section of the Romanian Academy of Sciences, renamed the Institute of Ethnography and Dialectology in the mid-1970s. Some, like Romulus Vulcănescu, retained their political independence, but were marginalized from positions of real authority and influence, though their work retained a sizable audience (Vulcănescu 1966, 1970). Most others didn't have the cachet to keep their scientific independence. They were charged by the party-state to invent folklore and ritual to serve its purposes, especially those of national integration. The Institute's greatest elaboration (some would say its greatest shame) was the national folklore contest, *Cîntarea României* (Song of Romania), a forced, homogenized national competition of folk song, skit, and dance based on socialist themes (Kideckel 1993; Kligman 1988).

Politicizing ethnography in socialist Romania severely limited its role for Romanian self-knowledge. Much formal ethnographic practice was diverted into state-defined spheres and folk ethnographers, an important source of social knowledge in all societies, were forced underground. In other times and places such people, motivated by love of community and senses of history, recorded observations and feelings about their communities. However, practicing ethnography was folly in the insecure socialism of the Romanian state which evaluated all written observations for their political content. Many people recorded observations during the early years of socialism, but few works saw daylight. For example, one Babu Ursu was arrested, tortured, and killed after his work, which included commentaries about Ceauşescu, was discovered (Michael Cernea, personal communication).

Some folk ethnography reemerged after the party consolidated power and began to emphasize nationalism in its ideology (Verdery 1991). This especially took place between 1974 and 1979 as a range of party programs to expand citizen cultural production and participation were introduced. Under control by "Committees for Socialist Education and Culture," also responsible for organizing "Song of Romania" folklore events, the substance of such activities were rigidly channeled and prescribed. One typical event in which both Aurel and I participated was the "Scientific Session on Hîrseni Commune: Past Present and Future." This Sunday program drew a crowd of about 100 locals and a few politicians from Braşov, the regional capital. There were seven presentations: a discussion of local geography, an essay on local life under feudalism, a summary of the community's goals in the 1976–1980 five-year plan, a paper relating local toponymy to Romanian terms for the natural world,[4] two papers about local folklore, and Aurel's history of the Hîrseni consumers' cooperative (Bălan 1979, see below). When I arrived in the commune days before the event, the organizers also asked me to contribute. I wrote a brief presentation on the relationship of households to collective farm but was only allowed to read it after it was vetted by the organizers for impolitical phraseology. Such were the possibilities for local ethnography in the socialist years.

The Making of a Folk Ethnographer in Socialist Romania

Aurel (Relu) Bălan didn't begin adult life with ethnographic purposes in mind. However, his life's circumstances combined

Figure 2.1: Aurel and Victoria Bălan outside their home in Hîrseni, Romania.
© D. Kideckel.

with his voracious intellect drew him to the ethnographer's craft. Once inspired, he used it for both personal and critical ends and, in my estimation, expanded the genre under the most trying of conditions. Not only did he preserve the history of his family, community, and region, but he also used ethnography for instruction in household and community. He thus assured himself a voice beyond the grave.

Aurel Bălan was born in 1932. Except for a stint in the army in the early 1950s and a few months of travel by motorcycle throughout Romania, Relu lived his entire life in Hîrseni village in the Olt Land region of southern Transylvania (Kideckel 1993). A staunch defender of village interests and partisan of its citizens, he nonetheless was psychologically distanced from them. This relationship manifested itself his entire life. For example, though his parents owned an estate of eight hectares before World War Two, Relu never yearned for property like his siblings or fellow villagers. Prescient about collectivization, he formally renounced his landed inheritance for support for his education after returning from the army. Once educated, despite his passion for history and travel, he stayed in his native village and ventured forth mainly in books. During this time Relu discovered his joy in writing. In the army and immediately after, he wrote long letters to his future wife, Victoria, and romantic poetry about community, family, and the love of his life, such as "My Native Village" translated below.

Relu became a bookkeeper. With his head for details and the growth of state-controlled organizations and record-keeping requirements, it was a perfect career. As a community activist he helped found and operate the local consumers' cooperative. During his tenure the Hîrseni cooperative added a bakery, bootmaker, hair stylist, and soda bottling workshop, among other services. Because of his success at the consumer's cooperative, he was named head bookkeeper of the village collective farm when it began in 1962.

In the late 1960s, Relu's life changed dramatically. Suffering from a rheumatic heart and diabetes, he was forced to retire from the consumers' cooperative and collective farm. Limited by his health and diet, Relu spent the next decade observing village comings and goings from the door of his household (cf. Rosaldo 1986). Unlike Rosaldo's discussion of Evans-Pritchard among the Nuer, Relu's vantage point neither resulted from, nor contributed to, his political isolation. He sat on the bench in front of his home and stopped passersby to question them about their household, family, and community events, past and present. Paradoxically, though physically and psychologically distanced from his surrounding milieu, Relu became the conscience and memory of the community to some (and remarkably presumptuous to others). People visited him with economic and organizational questions and the corpus of his knowledge and poetry grew.

My Native Village

You are always in my mind
Village which I've left,
Your beauty shows the pride
With which I grew up.

It was in you that I learned
To write and read
And to know many things
In which I take pride.

Your hardworking people
Are easily admired
Working their land with care
With love of their possession.

Your new and plastered houses
Done up in brilliant colors
Evokes pleasant thoughts
And are works of great fertility.

The view of one who passes
Through my native village
At once senses a desire
To settle there as well.

With love one considers
The world which you comprise
And you are loved by myself
With much soulfulness.

In you I see my past
My years of growing up,
The joys which I lived
In a short time of my life.

This short time until leaving
Passed unconsciously
I go with will now to the army
Leaving in you my desire.

A gift which you still have
That is known to all
Is your heavenly location
That much pleases people.

There, flowing water
Trickles from the mountains
And by the streams with joy
Young men and women revel.

At any holiday time
In the green meadows
A new and visible world
So beautiful is found.

In games and dance they pass
the time,
Your native youth
They have great love for
The traditions they keep.

Along with your chosen beauty
Which you have, my village
Add my great love
Which I take with me always

My love for you is known
By the one of whom I think
A beautiful dear girl
Whom I truly love.

This is my village
From which I have left,
Which I will remember always
Wherever I may travel.

Relu's knowledge of his community and its key institutions, insatiable curiosity, and his restricted activities, all contributed to our relationship. I can't remember how we first met in 1974. It might have been because he lived near places I frequented while in the field – two courtyards from the school and across the street from a retired agronomist, the son-in-law of the wealthiest precollective village landowner. Perhaps I was encouraged to visit by our mutual friend, eighty-year-old Toader Dîmboiu, the collective farm's cashier and also an amateur poet. Maybe it was because he had a used bicycle for sale. Whatever its origin, our relationship blossomed instantaneously.

Throughout my fieldwork, Relu was consistently one of my best friends and informants. His natural ethnographic sensibility and affinity for Geertzian "thick description" served us both well. Like key informants everywhere, he clearly understood the knowledge I sought and the implications of the social facts and relationships we discussed. For example, while teaching me backgammon (*tablă*) one rainy afternoon in 1974, he spoke of who plays the game in Romania, different styles of play, some historical reasons for the game's presence, dice manufacture, the general unavailability of *tablă* games in Romanian commerce, and no doubt some other topics I failed to note.

Two running discussions we had especially illustrate our mutual process of ethnographic discovery. One was about a wager he made over which a six-month argument ensued and which, to me, seemed suggestive of local social and political coalitions. The other was about household nicknames, their origins, and significance.[5] At first he was amused by my interest in two such mundane topics, but quickly warmed to their significance. Instead of simply describing who supported the People's Council vice-president (the reluctant bettor) or teasing out the etymology of nicknames like "Georgie, the Sun" or "She-Fox," Relu recognized what each theme said about village coalitions in the first instance and inheritance issues in the second.

My presence figured in his work as much as his did in mine. He questioned me closely about what I wanted to understand about village life, how and why I asked the questions I did of the people I did, who benefitted from my research, and other pertinent issues. He was also keenly interested in the books I read and about any aspect of life in other countries, especially mine. Though we became close friends, he only ever requested one material thing from me, a home diabetic test kit to analyze his blood and urine. My most sentimental possession of Relu's is a poem he wrote dedicated to myself and my wife whose title, "Strangers But Friends," echoes a basic ethnographic theme. The ultimate test of our relationship came in the 1980s. As Romanian life soured under Ceauşescuite economic privation and political repression, alone of all my friends, Relu continued to write lengthy letters to me describing village life in detail. One letter about his eldest daughter's marriage is a classic piece of ethnographic description. Furthermore, only he was willing to host me in a month's stay in 1984.

Relu's Oeuvre: A Decade of Production

Relu went from observer to recorder of village life due to a horrible accident. One day in 1979 as he broke up clumps of caustic soda for household need in his courtyard, a large amount flew into his eyes resulting in his total blindness in his right eye and partial blindness in his left. He could no longer read, his favorite activity, without great strain, and his resulting depression was immense. However, after a lengthy hospital stay and thorough introspection about his future, Relu seemed to sense a new measure of political freedom and sharpen the insight needed for his ensuing life as folk ethnographer.

No longer content to write the occasional poem, letter, or smattering of household budgetary data, he began to systematize his knowledge and extend his textual reach. His romantic poetry quickly turned to sharp political examinations of village and family events, often combined with a wicked humor. Viewed in hindsight, his poems offer general comments on life chances in socialist communities caught in the grip of "Ceauşism."

For example, four poems about his youngest daughter, Gabriela, take her from receiving a university rejection notice (*O Zi de Neuitate*, or *An Unforgettable Day*) to finding work on the local collective farm (*Gabi la Servici la CAP*, or *Gabi Goes to Work at the CAP*)[6] to two others about meeting and marrying her husband, Sorin. The first two are especially forceful discussions of critical issues in socialist villages. Written with a wry, angry, politically insightful, humorous and hopeful voice, they evoke love and understanding for his daughter and for other youth with similar fates. *O Zi de Neuitate* counterposes the beauty of the day and nearby Carpathians with the "storm" that ensues after the family learned of Gabi's rejection for admission to the University of Bucharest's cybernetics program. One of the brightest of her high-school class, she was probably rejected for university admission since, like so many others in Romania then, she hadn't the connections to bribe her way in.

Relu's poem not only addressed the injustice done his daughter but also named other deserving Hîrseni students who suffered Gabi's fate. Next to each name Relu placed asterisks referring to a list of households from which each derived. Now, this could merely be a "Who's Who of Hîrseni Rejections." However, he seemed to have a larger purpose. When cross-referenced with Relu's note-books on Hîrseni family histories (see below), the list celebrates the propriety of these young people and their forebears, implicitly contrasting them with the miscreant influence-peddling of Ceauşism. In *Gabi la Servici la CAP,* Gabriela, now without a seat in university, leaves home for her first day as a bookkeeper at the collective farm. Though the poem describes Gabi's extraordinary disappointment, it also expounds in a bittersweet way on the sanctity of labor and the essential worth of all honest work.

Relu also wrote on other cultural and political economic themes. What I call his PCR[7] Trilogy, written in summer 1980, explicates the main stages of Romanian political life: Pioneers, Communist Youth, and Party member. *The Communist: The Ideal and The Real* (below) is especially hard-hitting and illustrates Relu's growing disenchantment with political life. An early member of the Party, he was originally attracted to its egalitarian and developmental ideology. Later, when he encouraged his daughters to join, he did so only due to the Party's role in career advancement. This bothered him tremendously, and this poem reflects that in discussing the forced quality of party membership, members' careerist orientations, their unfair advantage over others, and the violence and hypocrisy of Party life.

The Communist: The Ideal and the Real

The Communist should be a man	But the party takes good care
Who is first in front of all	Of the biggest communists
His spirit a model	Who get the best of everything
Of honesty and righteousness.	And this way keep their power.

His character should be
Beyond reproach of any,
A man of great humanity
Who acts correct with each.

To become a communist, though,
Is not a difficult task.
Whether or not you were UTC[8]
Is really irrelevant.

If they want you, you're in.
No big deal, nor even planned.
They do not even ask you,
But oblige you very calmly.

One part of the communists
Are forced to join the Party.
They are talked to endlessly
Until they can't resist.

Other party members join
Only for their own interests
Even if not so thrilled
With the way communism
works.

After they join the Party
Nothing matters . . . good or bad.
They're as distant as tourists
When you ask them for aid.

Most pay their dues
Go to meetings
And even on occasion speak
So the leaders may hear them.

It's necessary to speak
If you want good things.
But never criticize
Or they'll mess you but good.

They'll do to you like
Pîrvulescu[9]
Even if you were important
And seen as such by Ceauşescu
They can bring down anyone.

Goods of highest quality
Food of all kinds is theirs
Fine meats and fresh produce
Only by attaining this goal.

The party is the mother that
Makes them rich and heroes,
Who gives them a good life
Without worries or needs.

For them doors are always open
Both from front or from back
They only need to push a bit
To enter where they want.

There are stores for them
That are listed as closed;
Stores and restaurants
Labeled "no public access."

But the Party rank and file
And all others
Hear only of "norme"[10]
And "good practices."

These guys forget their past
And from where they began.
Today they are like boyars[11]
Living in villas like palaces.

For the biggest communists
The meeting is everything;
Written transcripts, speeches,
Total engagement.

They yell so furiously
As the meeting ends.
You think they've taken sick
With criticism and advising.

They shout their work is hard
But they do it for the party
But you needn't wait too long
Until they foist it on the
innocent pauper.

Figure 2.2: Bălan's son-in-law, Sorin, shows the location of the secret cache. © D. Kideckel.

Other poems on endless topics inspired by chance occurrences, provide detailed descriptions of quotidian reality. *S-îmi Daţi Un Pic de Pîine* (*Give Me a Bit of Bread*) discusses the widespread hunger of the mid-1980s, a discourse prompted by the appearance at his doorstep of a poor village widow. *Leicuţa S-a Pilit* (*Leicuţa Is Soused*) tells of a drunken old woman unsteadily weaving down the street, though it is mainly a metaphor and moral commentary on the poor state of familial responsibility in late socialism. *Aragazi şi Butelii* (*Gas Stoves and Propane Tanks*) is a discourse on shortages and dependency. *Brutării* (*Bakers*) speaks of socialist work conditions. *Să Vină 23 August* (*August 23rd is Coming*) discusses people's apathy on the eve of the Romanian National Day. And the haunting *Soarta Mamei Mele* (*My Mother's Fate*) tells of his mother's suicide in response to a family crisis.

Though poetry was Relu's love, his ethnographic skill was better expressed in other work like his twenty-two volume auto-biography titled simply *The Story of My Life* (*Romanul Vieţii Mele*). Also important was the vast and diverse kinds of household evidence which Aurel recorded daily, if not hourly, after the loss of his sight. The autobiography is too vast to consider here. The household evidence, however, is not only accessible but remarkably telling.

As an accountant, Relu was enthralled with numbers and kept particularly close track of his household budget. He recorded virtually every *Leu* that entered or left his home over a decade's time including the cost of wedding gifts, bribes, income from wagers and prizes, and the value of gifts like the blue jeans my wife and I gave his daughters. Relu also kept lists of anything that lent itself to listing. This included village library hold-ings, telephone calls made and received, prices of items at the consumers' cooperative, and even phone numbers of world personalities and institutions including Pope Paul VI, Helmut Kohl, François Mitterand, the White House, and Buckingham Palace.

There is an explicit politics in many of these records. Thus, Relu kept an annotated record of the formal correspondence between his family and the local militia, who threatened to fine his wife for not weeding collective farm potatoes on time. He kept lists of Romanian folk singers and musicians, noting those who came under political suspicion. He listed people who died in the Romanian earthquake of 1977, informally checking state announcements with known realities. Politics was even evident in the organization of the volumes. Each spanned the same time period as state Five Year Plans (1980–1985 and 1985–1990) and thus provided a local set of data against which to measure official "progress." He purchased a new notebook and entered the title page for 1990–1995 two weeks before he died in 1989.

The History of Hîrseni Households

Of all Relu's work, his most anthropological effort was entitled "Hîrseni Commune, postal code 2322, Braşov County, Families from the Past to the Present: A Small Encyclopedic Monograph." So important was this project to him, he hand-wrote two separate copies in 1979, each running about 400 pages.[12] To an extent, the project grew from our many discussions about community families and histories. However, the inspiration for the volumes was Relu's and, as this essay's epigraph suggests, it allowed Relu to systematize and retain his vast local knowledge.[13]

In a three-page forward, Relu first pleads for continued recording of genealogical information and then discusses the organization of the notebook. The first twenty pages group village households into ten neighborhoods. On the left page, a color-coded map of each neighborhood indicates the location of each household. The facing page provides a running list of neighborhood buildings with households listed in green and institutions in red. Both the neighborhood/household map on the left page and the list on the right are designated numerically based on current street number. Each household entry further lists the household head, household number, and a running count of households. It also includes the household's street number before World War II.

Relu's definition of neighborhoods is a key to much that is significant in local life. Hîrseni neighborhoods were not formally defined as in other nearby villages heavily influenced by Saxon German practices (McArthur 1976, 1981; Stahl 1936). Instead they were defined loosely by village streets and by emic distinctions based on history and prevailing social relations.[14] To him, as to all his co-villagers, such informal household groupings provided the most frequently mobilized set of social ties and obligations. Thus to focus on the neighborhood as the context for locating houses and institutions was an important ethnographic datum.

After the list of households and institutions, Relu provides a detailed and color-coded schematic of his own courtyard, gardens, and buildings. The drawing shows the orientation of every household feature from bedrooms and kitchen to pig sty, outhouse, chicken coop, and garbage pile. It also includes an exacting drawing of the elaborate flower garden pattern that took up most of the courtyard's interior. In some ways, the drawing is out of place. It should appear later in the book where Relu lists his own household's genealogical history. Thinking about the drawing, then, I see it as an elaborate, ethnographically nuanced "I statement." That is, it simultaneously illustrates the author's world, gives a detailed portrait of his unique household, and sets it somewhat apart from the households listed later. Orienting the reader to both author and subject, this is an essential introduction to village life and the notebooks which describe it.

A Table of Contents and village map comprise the last part of the introduction. The Contents show that the notebook includes: 1) village map; 2) each household's recent genealogical history with Relu's personal observations (pp. 15–176); 3) brief histories of the land used for the village airstrip and sports field (including a list of the members of the local football team); 4) a table listing and discussing each village family name with information on the number of families who left the village, the number remaining, number of total persons of a given name, the community of origin of each name, and whether the name would soon disappear; 5) a table of villagers living and deceased, who had a professional education, including a list of their "important functions" and places of work; 6) a table of Gypsy households; and 7) a list of village social institutions, whether state-controlled like the militia or communal ones like the cemeteries or churches.

The main part of the notebook describes each household's genealogical and personal history, the data for which derived mainly from Relu's extraordinary memory. If he didn't know something he asked those who walked past his house. A typical household entry first includes a heading indicating the old and new household numbers, color-coded to indicate the neighborhood on the initial map. After the heading is a list of household members, both living and dead, organized by genealogical relationship. The earliest generation remembered was listed with Roman numeral I and its offspring from eldest to youngest with Arabic numerals 1,2,3, and so on. The household heir from the current generation, who generally derived from those Arabic-numbered offspring, was then listed along with spouse and children. The latter were listed from eldest to youngest with letter designators (a, b, c). The heir (a, b, or c) was then listed, and so on. Next to each individual entry, Aurel briefly described their particular fate (e.g. married in household x, married out of village in community y, and so on). Further, each new family name listed for the household (as when a female heir brought in her husband) was underlined. Relu's accuracy is fairly impressive. In fact, household members are not only listed in number, name, and birth order but are also cross-listed with other Hîrseni households.[15]

After listing household members, their relationships, and fates, Aurel provides a narrative discussing *inter alia* a household's nickname, its origins, and critical facts about household history and member biographies. There are fewer observations about lower-numbered households, even for some prominent village residents, than households with larger numbers. This suggests that either or both: 1) Aurel knew more about people in his own, southern half of the village where numbers were larger; or 2) his interest in recording information increased as the project wore on. A typical page from one of the briefest entries, looks as follows (with my notes in Italics):

16A (*pp.#*) Nr. 2(*hsehld #*)/ 4 (*neighborhood*) 2 (*old Hsehld #*)

I. *Tăulea* Vasile wife Elisabeta Taulea (Hîrseni 77) (*her home of origin*)

1. Victoria married in Hîrseni 15
2. Maria " Mediaş
3. Ioan, wife Elena Popa from Mărgineni

3. Ioan *Tăulea* wife Elena Popa from Mărgineni

a. Vasile-Viorel
b. Elena

Observations: the nickname "Vasile from Toader" comes from the father of Vasile whose name was Toader. Vasile Tăulea was a well-read man, as people said. I knew myself that he had many novels that he read, and I heard he read voraciously as a youth. His daughter Maria is an excellent high school teacher and her husband is also a teacher. Vasile Tăulea had a sister, Maria, who was married to Ioan Bălan from Nr. 183. (*Ioan Bălan was Aurel's first cousin*).

The household on the next page tells another story.

Nr. 3/4 *(no old household number)* 16 *(page)*

I. Ioan *Rînea* wife Raveca (Iaşi *her village of origin*)

   1. Ioan married in Bucharest

obs: Ioan Rînea is the son of Iacob Rînea of Nr. 19. He was the only son with whom Iacob couldn't get along. Ioan left his father's and settled here and built a house on land purchased from Toader Tăulea. He died a young man of 35 as he had become a drunk. After his death Raveca moved to Făgăraş. The house was demolished by Tăulea Vasile from Nr. 2

As these entries indicate, Relu's "History of Hîrseni Households" was more than a listing of village families. There was an essential morality and political orientation indicated which was far more than the sum of the parts of the individual household entries. In fact, the volume offered a running commentary on the requirements for a "proper" *(cumsecade)* life as defined by Hîrsenites through the twentieth century. Elements of propriety emphasized in the notebook included commitments to family, household, and village expressed in the preservation of property, the perpetuation of family, the rejection of divorce, and the proper upbringing of children. Intergenerational respect and continuity figure especially large in Relu's analysis of household transformations, though this was as much a collective community sentiment as it was a personal one.

Paralleling Relu's concern for appropriate social relations is his running, though veiled, critique of the socialist system. This is especially seen in his narratives about village people or properties related to the institutional life of the community. The pages of historical description concerning the wealthy family who were exiled from the village and whose property was ultimately taken over by the collective farm for its headquarters is a good example. Thus, Relu implicitly contrasts the success and hard work of this "poor boy made good" who built a small inheritance into a diversified economic power with the decrepitude that the property had fallen into by the end of the 1970s. Similarly, the families that contributed directly to the onset of socialism are viewed with a degree of sometimes mild, sometimes extreme opprobrium. Such

Figure 2.3: The camouflaged window-well used as a document cache.
© D. Kideckel.

was the case with I.T., one of the founders of the Hîrseni collective farm. Relu describes him thusly:

> ... I.T. finished four years of schooling in Făgăraş in order to become a primary teacher. He quit this. He had many other functions, none of which he ever concluded favorably. He likes to drink a lot which is a real shame since the man is not stupid. His household is exactly the way it was when his father left it to him, with the single addition of electric lights.

Uses and Significance: Some Conclusions

Aurel's ethnographic work, both processes of information collection and finished product, operated at many levels of significance for himself, his family, and community. First, of course, it was a personal testimony written for his own consumption and as witness to his life having "made a difference." The last twenty years of Relu's life, after all, were spent in treatment for one or another illness, on special diets difficult to obtain in a Romania of permanent shortage, with constant hospitalization and imminent threat of death. Clearly he sought to negate these adversities by his autobiographic and ethnographic work.

For his family, Relu's work was a guide to negotiating and surviving in a corrupt social system, though one open to manipulation and achievement. Relu's family was thoroughly familiar with his activities as he shared his production with wife and daughters at the end of every day. "Daddy's poetry reading" was ritualized and knowledge of his work intimate. His lessons were fairly direct. Though his writing celebrated hard work, honesty, family, and community, it did so with a certain hard edge. It indelibly traced the outlines of the socialist system, the practices necessary to survive within it, and the relationships critical to success. Thus, Relu's work provided a blueprint for survival even as it explained the personal struggles that made life so difficult. Today Relu's daughters and sons-in-laws are successful and upwardly mobile in their own right. These qualities were shaped in part by the mirror Relu held up (and still holds) to their surrounding milieu.

Less clear is the extent and manner by which Relu and his labors contributed to his community and society at large. In this regard it is remembered that Relu's work was essentially secret and intended only for a limited audience (he told his wife and daughters that the autobiographies were for their eyes only). Though he had little personal fear if they were discovered, he was quite concerned at their implications for his family should they come to light.

Still, even this knowledge did not prevent him from sharing much of his writing with people able to disseminate it. The people who came to know of his projects were mainly of this ilk. Besides his immediate family and myself, his activities were definitely known to a local history teacher and to a few friends and his physician in the near-by town of Făgăraş. Additionally most of his immediate neighbors[16] and some consumer cooperative employees were cognizant of Relu's work. After the fall of the Ceauşescuite state in 1989, the strategic position of some of those "in the know" enabled an even wider dissemination of knowledge of his work to regional political and cultural figures. Last year there were even initial discussions about making some of the work available at a Făgăraş museum/cultural center.

As far as his fellow villagers were concerned, that Relu shared his fact-gathering widely gave some an inkling of what was transpiring inside his courtyard's walls. Other villagers, queried by Relu as they passed his courtyard, were mostly in the dark about his projects but provided community news or verified a nickname or long-deceased family member. Some surmised that Relu recorded the information they provided, but others saw his requests as the product of boredom and inactivity. Whatever their degree of knowledge or insight, however, Relu's public questioning stood in stark contrast to the enforced silence and jealously guarded privacy in the pervasive socialist state. No matter the destination of the information he gathered, his actions provided credible witness that the vaunted power and ubiquity of the corporate state was really a hollow and ineffectual shell.

This returns us full circle to my initial discussion about the potential political importance that native and folk ethnography can and must play in authoritarian and culturally oppressive environments, but its difficulty in doing so. As the case of my friend, Aurel Bălan, clearly shows, it is especially under the most extreme circumstances of political restriction that ethnographic practice can realize its inherently critical and liberating mission. Even when carried out in the closest of secrecy, ethnographic practice potentially stands in strong opposition to regimentation, restricted knowledge, and the suffocation of public discourse. Above all, then, Aurel Bălan's ethnographic accounts of self, family, and community were political. They were written at a time of enforced public silence, without foreknowledge of the coming demise of Ceaușism. It was a time when all but the most protected voices went unheard and all but the most foolhardy kept their heads down and their relationships as predictable as possible. Relu's work and life thumbed its nose at these conventions. He "told it like it is/was" and provides an extraordinary archive of daily life in late socialist society. His struggles were not in vain. His voice is louder today than ever.

Notes

1. Such activities prompted original promulgation of the Code of Ethics of the American Anthropological Association.
2. A recent example of joint work of folk ethnographers and trained anthropologists concerns production of a Mayan play, "From All for All," on the sociopolitical conditions behind the Chiapas uprising. It is written by Mayans but "with the anthropologist as dramaturg and impresario" (American Anthropological Association 1995: 41).
3. Herseni's work was ethnographic and cultural anthropological. However, as Romanian anthropology was largely restricted to its biological aspects, Herseni practiced as a rural sociologist.
4. Focusing on the Latinate roots of regional place names, the paper was a thinly veiled support for Romanian autochthony in Transylvania.
5. See also Salzmann (1981) on the origins and significance of nicknames in Romanian villages.
6. CAP is the acronym for Cooperativă Agricole de Producția, the Agricultural Production Cooperative or collective farm.
7. Partidul Comunist Român, i.e. the Romanian Communist Party.
8. UTC, or Uninunea Tineretilor Comunist, was the Union of Communist Youth, the RCP's equivalent of the Soviet Komsomol. It was originally said in the Party's early days that you

had to first prove yourself worthy as a communist by invitation to join UTC.

9. Constantin Pîrvulescu was an RCP elder. At the Party's 12th Congress in 1979, he defiantly accused Ceauşescu of placing his and his family's interests above the country. Later, Pîrvulescu's delegate credentials were invalidated, his speech stricken from the record, and he later disappeared from view. He was rumored to have been killed or sent to an insane asylum (cf. Shafir 1985: 82–83).

10. The standard way to measure work and pay in socialist Romania.

11. Frequently absent large landowners.

12. Relu numbered his pages 1a, 1, 2a, 2, etc. Thus, though the last completed page in the volume is 187, there are a total of 374 pages.

13. He gave one of two copies to me as a gift in June 1979.

14. Unlike in Hîrseni, these village neighborhoods more clearly had corporate functions like mutual assistance (Stahl 1936). In Hîrseni, Party cadres responsible for collective farm formation used local streets to define farm work teams. They inadvertently combined households that saw themselves as belonging to different neighborhoods (Kideckel 1983, 1993).

15. I checked Relu's listings with local census documents. His knowledge was most vague about recently born children.

16. Almost directly across the street from Relu was the former home of the largest presocialist village land owner. One wing of the home was occupied by the state postal and communication agency (PTTR) and one by his widow and son-in-law, a former collective farm agronomist. Relu and he were particularly good friends.

Chapter 3

The Power of Biography: Criminal Policy, Prison Life, and the Formation of Criminal Identities in the Swedish Welfare State

Birgitta Svensson

> The image of biography is everywhere. A human life becomes conceived of as a story. . .. A soul is a pilgrimage through life.
>
> Ian Hacking (1995)

> Next to killing, imprisonment is the strongest measure of power at the disposal of the State . . . nothing is so total, in constraints, in degradation, and in its display of power, as is the prison.
>
> Nils Christie (1993)

As the welfare state weakens, demands are heard for tougher action against criminals and a clearer distinction of what is good and what is evil. These demands are part of the criticism of the welfare state. Sweden has changed from being a country with an international reputation for the humanity of its correctional treatment to one based on repression and rendering prisoners harmless. What was a system of justice has been converted into a system of crime control, as Nils Christie puts it. The causes of criminality have been redefined from a societal problem into an individual problem.[1] The criminal is turned into an evil person who differs from good people. Biological theories become fashionable once again, and the criminal is described in general as something different, something resulting not from defects in society but from pathological defects in the individual himself.

Responsibility and guilt are modern feelings. The subject is encumbered by the burden of the past. In modernity, people must assume responsibility for their own lives on the basis of their own subjectivity. The sense of guilt and "bad selfhood" is reinforced when the explanation is to be sought inside oneself. A country's way of handling its prisoners says a great deal about its cultural value patterns, norms, and habits. Criminal policy ultimately shows how everyday life, identities, and biographies are constituted. Criminal policy is thus really about cultural policy.

Prison has never diminished either the crime rate or the number of criminals, but rather increased them. The number of prisoners in prison does not reflect the crime rate in society. Instead it should be looked upon as a figure that says something about the distance between people, the type of legal system, and so on. Criminal policy is naturally also a matter of the self-understanding of society. The reason for retaining a system like this is its effects on morals in society (cf. Foucault 1977: 265).[2] Even most governments know that crime is not diminished by putting people into prison. The political strength, however, in punishing those who do "wrong" is enormous (cf. Hobsbawn 1994: 342). "They" are locked up and taken away from "our" world, or, as a conservative politician expressed it, "they should be inside so that we can be outside."

In ethnographic research, there has been a tendency to shape self-identities solely on the basis of individuals' experiences, regardless of discursive formations and historical contexts. But, as Hannah Arendt has said, right from birth we are a part of narratives which make us both subject and object. History is inside us, it is a part of our own self-understanding.

The aim of this chapter is to reflect about the power that is exercised in autobiographical accounts. Since the life course has been growing in importance in late modernity, it has also become the mantra of ethnographic research. My identity as an ethnologist is as much that of a biographical worker as are the social experts within the prison context. In analyzing the biographical discourse, however, my aim is the opposite, not to construct but to deconstruct the descriptive organization of lives in biographical terms. I see it as a way of dis-embedding the disciplining power of individuals. With a Foucauldian perspective, I regard individuality as a form of social control that the individuals exercise in telling their lives. The individual is constituted by the biography but is, at the same time, its vehicle (cf. Foucault 1980: 98). Biography is a way of constructing coherent pasts that make sense to the present. Viewing the life from such a constructionist perspective makes it possible to examine how representations of the life course are used as means of social control (cf. Gubrium et al. 1994).

To understand the critique of the welfare state, one must analyze the cultural processes that created its subjects (cf. Svensson 1994). The criminal policy of the Swedish welfare state was founded on the ideology of treatment and social engineering. This in turn developed from the emergence of new forms of the exercise of power and concomitant new forms of knowledge during the nineteenth century and gave rise to the shift of focus from the body to the soul or what Foucault calls the "knowable man," conceptualized in the terms of subjectivity, personality, and individuality (1977). The new knowledge of the individual also produced a new reality, where one had to subjectivize oneself as an individual, good or bad.

In Swedish criminal policy today, the concepts of care and therapy have been replaced by punishment, and the focus is once again on the crime rather than on returning the criminal to society. "There is no reason at all to feel sorry for a person who is sentenced to prison," according to a typical statement from a politician. "He's in prison because he was willing to break the law in order to gain an advantage at the expense of other people." In postmodern society, people are questioning how efficient the efforts at treatment have actually been. As early as the 1970s, the optimism about correctional care was replaced by a rejection of prison, with the argument that it was obsolete as a form of care.[3] What was advocated instead was the development of noninstitutional care, with more concrete efforts to change the attitudes, thoughts, and actions of the convicts.

A penal outlook that had been characterized for almost 200 years by a desire to prevent people from committing crime, has been replaced today by retribution. The preventive ideology, formulated by Jeremy Bentham at the end of the eighteenth century, was based on the idea that punishment can only be justified if it has the effect of preventing crime.[4] The idea was later developed in the direction of what is called individual prevention, which seeks to readjust the criminal to a normal life in society.

The role of imprisonment in controlling and readjusting a small, deviant criminal minority is insignificant. The more often punishment is used, the less effective it becomes. It erases all forms of moral responsibility in the person to whom it is applied. As one prisoner said to me, "I grew up in this prison, so it's no punishment for me any more." Prison today is therefore used primarily to segregate evil. It creates order in social life by defining what is dangerous and what keeps society together. The good acquires its shape in relation to the evil. The state thus defines the legal order. Prison life is a training camp which tests how norms can be imprinted and identity formed. One of the most significant instruments in this formation has been the biography.

In my study of prison life, I will try to show how criminal policy constitutes specific forms of criminal identities and biographies. Looking at the prison as a training camp helps me to see how the norms are impressed on people, the criminal identity is formed, and the frameworks for the biography are outlined. As Zygmunt Bauman says, criminalization, incarceration, and the penal practice of modern society serve as a laboratory where the tendencies attenuated and adulterated elsewhere can be observed in their pure form (1993: 122). Ironically enough, this was also how anthropologists traditionally used to describe and justify their studying of "primitive" society.

There are relatively few persons in prison in Sweden, but they play a normative and standardizing part in the public debate about problems of late modern society. The Swedish prisoner is a man. Less than five percent of the prison population are women. Most prisoners have no job, no home, and have been convicted before.[5]

I have carried out a cultural analysis of prison as an arena where ethical patterns are trained and demonstrated. In the exercise of power as well as in the criminals' resistance strategies, I believe it is possible to see how the ideological changes in our society have been displayed in everyday standards and ways of thinking. My intention is to describe how the Swedish criminal policy, by the use of imprisonment and the philosophy of treatment, has contributed to a way of biographical thinking among the convicted. I start with a short description of the general setting of the prison and the life inside from the point of view of both the staff and the inmates. This also includes some life stories told by what I think are typical inmates in a "real prison" like the one where my study was done. I have given them the names Ben, Jimmy, Jack, and Tony. We will also meet them later on in the text. "Real prison" is what they themselves call the prisons with the highest degree of security, the most long-term prisoners, and the strictest rules. Some of these institutions, like the one I visited, are very old cell-houses from the mid-nineteenth century, and they are equipped with high walls, wire fencing, alarm systems, supervision cameras, and the like.[6]

Prison life and criminal careers

When I arrived at the prison for the first time, doing fieldwork in the spring of 1995, what struck me most was that it was so noisy – gates and doors being locked and opened, locked again, and so on, and people moving between different places all the time. But there was also a friendly atmosphere that surprised me, among the inmates, among the staff, and even between inmates and staff. This is when it is "normal." In a prison, for a person coming from outside, unusual things happen all the time. "The funny thing about prison life," says a prisoner, "is that it is so routine, monotonous, and boring but at the same time not like that at all. There are always things happening that people can get involved in" (RR 1995: 113). One day there is a strike in the workshop because a racist activist has managed to get people to support him in a demand that whites should not work together with blacks. On another occasion a person with AIDS has to be moved to the infirmary because the others do not want to have him around. In this case, however, as in so many others, the problem was not really about AIDS but about conflicts over card-playing. Since they cannot play with money they play with phone cards or charge cards, and the credits become difficult to settle. Cash is not allowed since card-playing with money results in high debts and quarrels. The inmates, however, find ways of ignoring this and consider their charge cards as money.

This is a man's world, with coarse jokes, constant petty quarrels, and many men doing bodybuilding.[7] Nearly all of them are tattooed, with typical motifs being snakes, knives, dragons, syringes, skulls, Vikings, pictures of women, and women's names. They have tattooed themselves and each other during different terms in prison. They think that the tattoos express strength and manliness.

The prison routine can briefly be described as follows: The inmates are wakened at 6:45 a.m., when they go to the bathroom and wash. After breakfast they work until lunchtime, and after lunch they are allowed to spend an hour walking in the exercise yard. Then comes the afternoon work, followed by dinner at 4:30 p.m., after which they are free to do what they want for two hours before they are locked in their cells at 7:45. Their free time is mostly spent chatting, drinking coffee, and playing cards or billiards.

There is a library and a kiosk open twice a week. You pay for what you buy with a charge card. A radio is standard equipment in the cell, but television sets have to be rented or bought by the inmates themselves. You are allowed to make telephone calls in your spare time but you have to tell the staff in advance and you are not allowed to call more than three different numbers. You pay with a phone card. Inmates are searched every day, as are their cells. The inmates are obliged to submit a specimen of urine, to check whether they are using drugs.

Meetings are regularly held to discuss the inmates. Once a week there is a board meeting where the staff discusses the various biographical data on the inmates, plans for their release, or transfers to another prison. Discussions are also held about where it is suitable to place different types of inmates. Great effort is expended on sorting the prisoners and putting suitable constellations together according to principles such as the type of crime for which they are sentenced, ethnicity, age, unruliness, and so on. The last part of the discussion is devoted to general problems. The nurse once brought up the problem of not having condoms in the visiting room. In the morning the guards meet to discuss what to do during the day. They get together when all the inmates have been brought down to their workplaces. The discussion topics concern the everyday life in the departments, such as a fight in the workshop: who is to blame, should they be called in for questioning, and is a written report necessary? Often the fights are about trivial matters, such as the taste of the coffee, the price of the cigarettes, or somebody having borrowed a few stamps. Sometimes the fights are so serious that an inmate is transferred to another prison. The prisoners have to write an application for everything they want or have views about. There is quite a complicated pattern of grievance procedures in prison, concerning everything from being disturbed by the ventilation system to issues concerning their personal treatment.

Being a guard in prison is not esteemed very highly outside prison, so they are reluctant to talk about their job. When they do so, many of them claim that the reaction is often prejudices and statements that prisoners are pampered. Most of the staff spend a large part of their lives in the same environment as the inmates. Their life is shaped in interaction with the prisoners. This takes place at different levels, however, depending on their different professional roles. The majority of the staff are guards, whose duty is to handle day-to-day contacts and to see that all runs smoothly. The guards are in an intermediate position. Their task is to implement decisions from above and simultaneously to resist pressure from below. One of them told me that they are often sent on courses to learn fine, new progressive ideas that can be used in their work, but all to no purpose "because when you get back to the prison it's still the same old order that rules." Today, however, it is rather the case that the prison governors have a more liberal attitude and try to introduce new ideas, which the guards find difficult to implement. The newly appointed warden of the prison that I studied, for example, is a psychologist.

There is a high turnover among the guards. Not many have been in the job more than ten years. Many started because they were unemployed. They had never intended to take a job like this, and they are not very happy with it. Others would have liked to become policemen but, lacking the qualifications to get into the police academy, they thought that being a prison guard was a near enough alternative. The uniform has proved to be very important for the guards. Staffing policy has changed: nowadays people who are interested in taking care of people are employed, whereas military training used to be the right qualification.

The social workers in prison are usually more devoted to their jobs. When a woman from a clergyman's family was asked why she chose to work as counselor in a prison, she replied that her mother had been horrified by her choice of career and had tried to dissuade her. The daughter was not afraid, however, since she thought that although the inmates had done wrong, they could no doubt be improved and reformed. "It was partly a desire to bring salvation," she said. "I always sided with the ones that I felt sorry for, the ones who had failed." When she had started her job in the prison, she was warned by the warden not to become the kind of case that they had just had in the prison system: a counselor who fell in love with a client. Female staff often hear the same warning example.[8]

People working in the prison administration do not have very much to do with life inside, which makes them a bit more alienated from it. A woman who has worked for forty years in the prison office describes how it felt to come there in the 1950s. "It was terribly exciting. It was a completely different world." Some of the inmates helped in the office. The woman had recollections of dreadful, menacing killers and of "nice lawyers, businessmen, and real-estate agents."

The guards agree that the relationship prevailing in prison is one of "us and them." Honesty and direct encounters can be the most dangerous thing. Both sides have to be flexible and adopt a clever negotiation strategy if all is to work well. It is often a question of making the prisoners govern each other. The guards are assisted by the existing hierarchies among the inmates and usually reinforce them. The position of an inmate in the hierarchy is clearly seen in the way he walks along the corridor. A seasoned prisoner walks easily and with self-respect, while younger ones and newcomers seem to keep a low profile. It has been said that prison employees have no interest in the individuality of the prisoners (cf. e.g. Irwin 1985: 70f.) but I think that it is rather a question of the setting of the prison creating a very special individuality.

The crucial part of the negotiation process is the ability to develop consensus and construct the right groups of inmates. There are few places where banal everyday issues become as significant as in prison. A person must have special cultural competence to be able to handle life in prison. His situation depends on how successful he is in his negotiations. It is a question of divide and rule. It would not otherwise be possible for a small number of guards to govern several hundred inmates. They are particularly difficult to supervise since they really have nothing to lose. The formal power is exercised by the guards, but the inmates can manage to take over and get the real power. There is a formal rule system inside – the institutional routine – and there is an informal set observed by the prisoners.

The voice from inside: Ben

Ben is a lifetimer who has spent most of his 58 years in prison. In terms of the norms of society he is classified as a dangerous murderer, which is hard to fathom when you know him. After many years in prison he has become a well-adapted, exemplary prisoner; he is quiet, he doesn't smoke or take drugs, he is fit and active, he reads a lot, and has developed a kind of intellectual lifestyle, listening to classical music and spending much of his small earnings on daily newspapers to keep himself informed about life in the society outside. He also gives money to the Red Cross and other charitable institutions; I learned this not from him but from the staff, who think that he does this to make amends for the crimes he has committed. He is highly institutionalized, talks like a book, and conforms to the prescribed norms of the prison, which is why the staff like him. After many stays in mental care, talking to psychologists and psychiatrists about his life, he has learned to analyze himself and tell his life story as a life history of a criminal. It starts, as for so many others, with a childhood with a drinking father and a big family: eight persons living in a flat with one room and a kitchen. His mother died when he was ten, but by then he had already left home and been taken in charge by the social welfare office – since he was only seven.

Ben played hooky and pilfered already in his first year at school. He stayed in a reform school until he was 14, but never learned anything there, he says. He just wanted to get away. "I have never managed to adapt to those institutions," he explains. He escaped several times and rebelled in different ways. What he found most upsetting was that they were not allowed to read newspapers or listen to the radio. He read quite a lot already as a child and he dreamed of becoming a doctor or a private detective.

His first prison sentence came when he was seventeen. When he was young he committed no violent crime; it was petty theft, car theft, and drug abuse that brought him to prison. "It was all for the thrill and excitement of committing crime," he says (cf. Katz 1988). "The violence came in later years . . . the fact that you do certain things." He doesn't want to talk about it. His abuse started when he came into prison. It was both liquor and junk, which in turn led to new crimes when he was out again. By then it was also easy to get different kinds of medicine inside and he abused it. "I was generally di ficult, I must admit," he says.

The only time in his life when Ben has lived something that looks like a normal life was in the mid-1970s, when he was in his late thirties. This was also the only time he had a relationship with a woman. He met a 29-year-old librarian inside. "She came along with her book trolley," he says dreamily. "But it didn't work out so well," he observes quickly and soberly. He goes on to tell how he sent a card to her a year ago: "I thought it might be nice to find

out how she is. We had a lot of fun together." His longest continuous period of freedom was when they were together. The
relationship lasted from August 1975 until June 1977. Otherwise,
his longest spell outside prison was five months. He calculated
that he had been out of prison for a total of two and a half years
since 1945. "I have never made such an effort as I did in '76 and
'77," he continues. "But I was deep into drugs on and off at the
same time." He also worked for a few months, and for a short
time he had his own apartment, for the first time in his life. "But it
didn't work out, partly because of my drug-taking, partly because
I had no interest in work," he observes as a matter of fact.

Today Ben thinks that he idealized his situation, imagining that
the woman would solve all his problems, but actually not much
worked out. It was entirely his fault that the relationship did not
hold, he admits. "It could have worked if I hadn't messed around
so much. She really tried. But, you know, I never felt any joy. There
was no excitement in being with her friends, everything felt dead
and lifeless, I thought. What I was really interested in was living
it up and taking it easy. When you're out of prison, life has to be
the exact opposite of life in the can. I noticed that things weren't
going well. And I felt so indebted to her, I had a guilty conscience
for all the trouble I caused in different ways. I couldn't talk about
it. So I did a spell in '77 and '78, and when I came out it was over.
I was put away for violent crime for the second time. I had
quarreled with a watch salesman, we got into a fight, and he got a
few slugs and a couple of kicks. I left my bag behind there, so
they were able to identify me. Then I broke into a pizza parlor.
Then I got the sentence for all of that together . . . even though he
said that it was just an ordinary fight . . . then it was over, all I got
was a card where she said that I would have to look after myself
from now on. We spoke on the phone once or twice, but then her
tone got sharper. In 1979 she told me not to call her anymore. I
threw a foot-scraper through the window of her apartment, but
the police came right away. She was evicted after that. 'You got
me evicted, too, you bastard,' she said. I don't know where she
lives now, but she's in the book. She'll be fifty next birthday, on
my name-day."

A very reflective and thoughtful person today, Ben seems to
have been growing in harmony with life inside. But when I ask
him if he can cope with this life, he rapidly answers, "There are
no good prisons. You never get used to life in prison, you just get

used to some of the routines." Because the prison regards him as an escape-prone security risk, Ben is not allowed any leave of absence. For six years and three months he therefore refused to go at all. Then he had three hours' leave of absence under the supervision of the warden and a guard. They visited a nature area and then had Christmas dinner in a restaurant. He often discusses different methods of committing suicide, but says that there are no good ways of doing it in prison. "I cut my Achilles' tendons once when I felt down," he says.

Virtually all of his life has been lived in exile, in prison, but Ben still uses expressions such as "I was last home in 1988" about his most recent experience of freedom. This is probably part of a wider notion of "home" as a nostalgic term in contemporary life, as Deborah Reed-Danahay points out (in this volume). He has not had a home to go to for many years and has no contact with the world outside. No one comes to visit him, and he gets no letters. He has tried to get in touch with relatives and other people, but they just hang up when he calls. Many criminals say that being sent to prison saved their life. In Ben's case that is true. Now he is probably never going to leave prison, while others come and go.

Prison as a microcosm of society: Tony

Tony is an easy-going, jovial chatterbox who used to be in prison repeatedly during the 1960s and 1970s but after that he managed to stay outside until a few years ago when he robbed a bank. He has a palpable criminal identity although he has been outside for many years. It should not be forgotten that most crimes are never detected. He is big, tough, and rather good-looking, though many years with needles and dope have taken their toll. His body is covered with tattoos; for instance, he has a big eye on the back of his head.

Tony has a long criminal career behind him. When a prisoners' council was started in 1969 (cf. Rutherford 1986: 73ff.), he was elected as one of the leaders, and now, on returning to prison, he was one of the leaders of a big prison revolt in the summer of 1994. He used to be a drug addict in his younger years, having started in the late 1950s. He was violent then, too, and often imprisoned for assault. Now he is doing a term for a failed bank robbery he attempted after he lost his job and was unable to keep up the payments on his house. He also ran a kennel. His ex-wife cheated him out of both of these, he claims, but he can do nothing about it when he is in prison. This is his first sentence for bank robbery. Another part of his sentence this time is for illicit distilling.

Tony finds it easy to talk and he has an approachable, engaging manner. He has roughly the same background as most other criminals: divorced parents, sent to a children's home at an early age, starting a criminal career in his teens. What is different about him is that he is of the old school: he misses the sense of community and honor that he claims used to exist. But he says as an afterthought, "Maybe prison is just a microcosm of society. It's not just the penal system that's got tougher, it's life in general." Just as morality and honesty are discussed a great deal in society when the boundaries for right and wrong are diffuse, he says that it is difficult to know whom one can trust in prison when the old honor among thieves has disappeared. "Everyone snitches on each other, boasting and running to talk to the guards far too much," says Tony. "That old moral code could be found throughout society, but it was stricter in prison. If you didn't follow the moral code, you could be killed." As a "native" he is able to anthropologize the terms in society, since he experiences them in their pure form inside prison.

Tony remained outside prison for many years because he had found salvation in the Pentecostal Movement during the 1970s. That made him live an orderly life with wife and children and work as a bus driver for many years. He stirred up some trouble in the congregation, however, and left it all. That brought him back to his old friends living on the fringes of society.

Depersonalization makes faceless inmates: Jack

When they are near the age of 40, many criminals try to make a turning point in their life, which is very commonly associated with meeting a woman or finding religious salvation. Psychologists such as Walters claim that there is a criminal burnout at that time in many criminal careers (1990: 123). The same is the case with Jack, who spent a few good years living outside in the mid-1970s together with a woman. He was then earning his living as a musician, since he managed to release a record of prison songs in 1972. During his first term inside, he started to play guitar and to write songs about prison life. In the 1970s, he had a big audience in the left-wing movement that dominated the public spirit of the time.

Jack's earlier life history was a darker one, and since he has told it so many times there are several versions of it. To the public he had a version of where he was born that was sad and tragic, his life having started inside a jail where his mother was an inmate. In fact, he tells me today, he grew up in an ordinary, well-behaved working-class family. That kind of background was no basis for a good story, he thought, so he actually borrowed the first part of his life story from a fellow inmate who was born inside. He spent his childhood together with both his parents and a sister until he was eight years old. His father was an attendant at a mental hospital and his mother was a cook at the same hospital. He liked his mother very much, but he detested his father, who was very hard on him and hit him a great deal. He tells, for instance, about the severe beating he received from his father when he got busted for drunkenness and burglary at the age of eleven.

Jack describes his school days as one long fight. He often played hooky. He came to a reform school at the age of 8 and at 12 was sent to another reform school. "Reform school, you know, it sounds nice," he says, "I was supposed to get treatment there. But they locked me up. And the first day, one of the other snotty kids came and told me to come with him: 'You should come down to the basement because the other guys want to talk to you.' When we came down into the basement he pushed me into a dark room where they were all sitting. I got a hell of a going-over in that room. But the next time I was supposed to get a new beating . . . you know there was really a lot of bullying there . . . then I stabbed a son-of-a-bitch with a knife. Yes, that's what I did. They left me alone after that. I stayed there for five years."

With the exception of those few years during the 1970s, Jack has spent most of his life in prison, though always for rather short periods and for minor crimes connected with drugs and alcohol. His life has been one of petty crime; at the same time, he has become a notorious jailbird. Coming to prison for the first time is a rite of passage where one has to make a good impression on one's fellow inmates. Jack proudly tells about when he came to a "real prison" for the first time, since he had been on the front page of the local newspaper. He said, "I was like a rooster when I got to prison the first time. I had a knitted cap and things on . . . I had been in the paper . . . the whole god-damn front page . . . and there I came, you know, there were these old dynamiters . . . but it was good, I got on well there, and they didn't want to have me back in the reform school!"

Most prisoners arrive at prison with a previous criminal background and knowledge of life inside. This experience is very useful in the entry into prison life. Hesitant negotiations take place at every new arrival, to make the newcomers find their position (cf. Little 1990: 108). The first days are devoted to finding one's place. It is mostly other inmates who take care of the introductions. The old identity is peeled off and replaced by the prison identity, which gradually merges with one's own. Among prisoners it is called "not getting away" (cf. Gadd 1991). This way of taking normal life away from you becomes what Goffman calls a "mortification of the self" (1991: 43). I rather think it makes these people develop a self in opposition to normal life.

To many of us on the outside, prisons evoke bars, escapes, uniforms, tough rules, and a life of military control. I would say that it sometimes looks more like a nursery. Many of the inmates curl up in their beds in their soft, comfortable tracksuits, looking like very big children in rompers. This is also the way they are treated. The inmate does not have to have any daily routine of his own, everything is decided for him in a strict order and with fixed times signaling when to get up, to eat, to work, and so on. Modern prison depersonalizes the inmates and makes them faceless (cf. Christie 1993). Jack's way of putting it is that "you're brought down to the childhood stage . . . where you have no say, they just talk about you, above your head, as if I had nothing to do with the things that are being decided. Other people make the decisions. You're not allowed to influence whatever the hell it is you want. If you want something, then somebody else does it for you. After a while you get so damned lethargic that you ask them to do it for you. And they do it. So you let go. And then you get out. Then there sure as hell ain't nobody who's going to pick things up after you."

To tell a criminal's life story: Jimmy

Thirty-year-old Jimmy, this time sentenced to five years in prison for gross drug crimes, describes his life: "I grew up without any fixed relationships, I don't know who my father is . . . I lived with my grandparents till I was six. Then my mother came and took me back to a stepfather and it all went wrong there because they had my half-brother. But nothing really happened until I was in the sixth grade. I started to get unruly. . . so I went away to my first foster home." The story continues with trouble in school and Jimmy being restless, so finally he was expelled from school. Then he tells about how at the age of fifteen he became more disorderly and how "they decided that I should go to a reform school, but I hadn't done any crime, I had never done any real crime." When he came there, he found it very hard, there were many threats and quarrels. "You got beat up . . . you had to. That's where I learned to be a criminal, you were forced out to steal by the older guys there. And then you had to escape for the sake of escaping. I didn't want to run away, but I did want to get home . . .. So then you had to steal a car. That didn't work. We always got nailed." When he was 18, he came to a new foster home and he got a job, but soon he started taking amphetamine. "So you began to slide, and finally you were totally hooked on amphetamines." But he managed to do his military service, which is unusual in his situation. After that he started to take dope again and got his first prison sentences, mainly for minor crimes. And so it has been going on since then, with the exception of one year when he met a girl, had a daughter with her, and found a job at a day nursery which he really enjoyed. The job was just temporary work he was given to help him into "the right kind of life;" when it ended, both he and his girlfriend were unemployed. "She was out of work too, so there we were, getting on each other's nerves, and then an old abuser like me . . . then . . . I left. That's the situation. So I started to turn on. So we fell out with each other." After this his story is filled with narratives from the different crimes, his drug use, and how he got caught. Jimmy is a nice guy, he says himself, and even the staff thinks he is nice; he bakes and fixes things. But he is considered an escape risk so he is not allowed to have any leave of absence from prison, which irritates him a great deal.

At the beginning of this last five-year sentence, his girlfriend visited him once a week with their daughter, but one time she didn't come as agreed and he went mad and screamed at her on the phone. "Yeah, you get a bit like that when you're inside . . . if a visit doesn't work out . . . you get really jealous and suspicious . . . you say a lot of stupid things on the phone. So now we've stopped, you know, we've broken up, but she'll be coming with my daughter." It is the usual story; most women leave their men when they go to prison.

Jimmy tells about his daughter, that he loves her very much and that he was the one who mostly took care of her, since "I'm domesticated, it was me that looked after the food and all that, and it was mostly me that tucked the baby into bed. And then suddenly the cops come and take you away, you know . . . they've ruined so much." He thinks that there is a great difference between him and the sort of criminals doing time for violent crimes or sexual crimes. He claims that he did what he did because he had problems. He has sold and taken drugs, nothing else, he maintains. While the criminal himself appears to create circumstances around him as an eternal loser, he simultaneously accuses the people around him for causing his problems (cf. Walters 1990: 81).

When asked what is the best thing in life that has happened to him, Jimmy answers that it was when one of the Swedish ice hockey teams went to the final. He keeps telling how happy he was then and that he even committed crimes to be able to go to their matches. On his arm he has a tattoo with the name of the team.

His plans for the future are to study for an examination during this sentence and then go to a residential college for adult education and become a youth worker. If only he got the chance, he claims, things would work out well for him. Even the teaching has been individualized so that if you are allowed to have an education, it is on your own. Older prisoners say, "In the old days they had folk high schools in the jails, and the group work gave rise to a sense of community, but they don't exist any more. Now there's just private study." The problems entailed by what was called "prisoner communities" or subcultures have been met by individualizing life inside, which also means that the only way to get an identity today is to be highly self-centered. Many inmates find it difficult to see other people and their problems. This is reinforced by an isolated existence, where masturbation, for instance, plays a major role. During the term in prison the inmates become increasingly alienated from life outside. Fantasy has to take the place of reality. Equality and solidarity become a threat, according to an old jailbird. Instead one becomes "ruthlessly self-centered – I've only got myself to think about . . . you're not allowed to care" (Gadd 1991: 11). Drugs have also contributed to this. In the past it was mostly stimulants, but now there is more and more heroin, which makes people just lie passively. In addition, it has meant that people inform on each other. As Jack says, "The day room is empty during the day because they're all lying in their cells with that god-damn horse. It's terrible . . . and they cheat each other. There was one hell of an atmosphere in the can last time I was there."

Jimmy maintains that it is crazy that he has been sentenced to five years for having smoked hashish. "OK," he admits, "I have been selling it too and I lived a rather good life on the money, but I wasn't exactly rich." Regarding his life expectations as a child, he says that he wanted to be an engine driver. He liked school but he didn't like his home. He has no contact with his mother; she doesn't even send him a postcard, he says. He says his brother told him that she mostly feels sorry for herself, having a son like him. As for prison, he thinks that it is needed for the worst and most dangerous criminals like serial killers,[9] "but there is no treatment," he says. What he wants is to be locked up and forced to get some "real treatment." His plan now is to get a nice house, a good job, and a family. "But on the other hand," he says "this is not America, where you can be what you want, here it is difficult to get a new chance when you have spoiled so many before." The British sociologist Michael Little (1990), who has interviewed young men in prison, considers these as universities of crime which simultaneously produce bitter, angry, and lonely men living in a fantasy world.

To my final question, that of whether he thinks that this interview differs from those conducted by the probation staff, Jimmy answers, "Yes, it's play-acting, it's not the same thing . . . you want to get off as lightly as possible. There are some things you can't say." He finishes off by saying that sometimes it is the parents who should be locked up. His parents are the ones who destroyed him, he thinks.

Prisoners in exile

Many inmates can tell of people who are unable to cope in the outside world, having been completely destroyed by prison life. "As soon as you make a person adjust to an institution, it's really difficult, you know, for them to manage outside. There's no one out there to put the god-damn food into their mouths," says Tony. They commit new crimes to get back into the prison where they feel safe, since they know the rules here. Jimmy tells how good it felt every time he got caught: "It was a relief, like, you know, Christ, isn't this nice . . . but three years . . .." And he talks about another time when he said to the policeman who caught him, "Christ, what a relief, I can make a new try, I thought . . . that was the first thing I thought."

Jack tells about how good it felt to come back and: "the guys were standing in the window saying, 'Hi, Jack.' It felt like coming home. Then you went down to the store and fetched the things that you had placed there before you were released." One can develop a sense of belonging even in exile, but the full belonging, the warm sensation that people understand not merely what you say but what you mean, can only come when you are among your own people in your own native land, according to Michael Ignatieff (1994: 7). The same can be said of prisoners, except that for them, as they grow into the criminal identity, their homeland changes from being a home outside to being a home inside. Prison is no longer an exile but becomes the place where they belong, where they understand the tacit code and do not have to explain themselves. Here they are recognized and understood.

The Politics of Difference

The American feminist philosopher Jana Sawicki has developed Foucault's power analysis, calling it "the politics of difference," since it assumes that not all differences can be bridged. The starting point can be sought in the people who are subordinated and segregated. The exercise of power can be studied in their lives. She also says that Foucault has shown how power relations can only arise where there is resistance; that is to say, where there is a conflict and someone wants to influence another person's behavior. Power enlists resistance strategies into its own service, partly by labeling them, by establishing norms and by defining differences (Sawicki 1991: 25ff.).

The segregation process by which evil identities are separated from good ones in criminal careers can be compared to what Elaine Scarry calls the structure of torture. What the process of torture does, she says, is to split the human being into two, to make emphatic the ever-present distinction between a self and a body, between a "me" and "my body." The "self" . . . is embodied in the voice, in language. The goal of the torturer is to make the one, the body, emphatically and crushingly *present* by destroying it, and to make the other, the voice, *absent* by destroying it (Scarry 1985: 48f.).

The usual way of piling up a criminal's life in the court records, as well as in the newspapers, is to refer to his life as if it simply consisted of his crimes. Headlines concerning "Sweden's most dangerous criminal" could look like this: "33 years of crime." Under this comes a box containing ten criminal acts: in 1959 at the age of 14 he is sent to reform school; in 1962 he gets his first prison sentence, escaping after three weeks; in 1969 he commits armed robbery; in 1972 he escapes from the most high-security prison in Sweden; in 1979 he robs a post office, shooting and injuring three policemen; in 1981 he stabs a prison officer with a sharpened toothbrush during an escape attempt; in 1983 he is sent to a mental hospital for psychiatric care; in 1986 he robs a post office; in 1990 he robs a gas station; in 1992 he does a bank robbery. This person is described as a symbol of evil. Stories are created in the papers, provoking the kind of "moral panic" described by Stanley Cohen (1985). Dreadful crimes hit the well-behaved middle-class, who feel threatened in their everyday lives. They are the ones defined as victims, while the criminals are regarded as ruthlessly calculating individuals deliberately committing their crimes. There is no regard for the fact that most crimes are committed by people under the influence of drugs or alcohol, often frightened and under stress, or that the acts are often badly planned or unpremeditated, leading to minor injuries which mostly afflict people in the criminal's own circle; in other words, people who are also socially vulnerable.

Since their voice has been taken away from them, they cannot really be heard. "You can't show your anger, for you know that it will recoil on you even harder. . . you adopt a 'never mind' attitude, but under that the hate and revenge is growing. You develop a basic hatred of society" (Gadd 1991: 147). A common tattoo among prisoners is HATE spelled on the four fingers of the right hand. The body becomes the place where a person shapes the self, with the aid of an outsider's physical language. By portraying oneself as terrible and dangerous, with a well-built, tattooed body, big earrings, special haircuts, and the like, one shows one's resistance to enforced silence and marginalization. Prison tattoos differ from others in that they often have special motifs such as a heart pierced with a knife or a snake coiling around a knife. In addition, they are often unprofessionally executed, messy, and with little aesthetic appeal. Some of them have motifs more directly connected to prison, such as barbed wire around the neck; one man has tattooed on his arm "Criminal boys don't pay, they steal." Prisoners also have large numbers of tattoos and in places where other people do not normally have them, such as the head, the hands, and other visible places. They say of their tattoos, "Well, it's a sign that you've done time." Yet they also express their pride and claim that it strengthens their identity: "I know that I've got more tattoos than nearly anyone in here . . . and I think I am one of the top men, too."

Socialization is the vehicle of classification and differentiation, as Zygmunt Bauman remarks: "The management of social order consists first and foremost in the activity of classification and differentiation of socially assigned rights and duties which combine into identities carried individually or shared within categories of individuals." In modern society it was not the differentiation into selected identities that took place, but rather the freedom of moving and choosing between different identities. Freedom was on the other hand unevenly distributed and paved the way for inequality and differentiation. Few people managed to be the choosers, the rule-setters, the self-makers, and the proper individuals. The rest were denied moral capacity and the ability to live in freedom (Bauman 1993: 120).

Almost all criminals relapse. Prison strips you of your former life, and when you come out again there is usually no option but to become a criminal once again. Prison professionalizes people, as Foucault has pointed out (1980: 42). "And the treatment you were supposed to get," Jack declares bluntly, "rather ought to be called mistreatment. But you have to have prisons in a society with such a bloody social structure as this. It is always good to look down on somebody whose life is more screwed up than yours. The jail is at the bottom . . . they can say, 'at least I'm not like them.' And imagine what an apparatus it is that feeds on drug addicts and prisoners."[10] Living in prison gives Jack the same kind of appreciation of society as a Foucauldian anthropologist gets from studying it.

Life Politics and Identity Politics

People have always organized their lives in different ways, but traditionally this was done through rites and life phases which were collective. In modern society, every individual must create his self with the aid of his individual ability to link his past to the future. One's personal cultural competence is then decisive for who one becomes, the identity one acquires. A sure self-identity is important if one is to be able to identify what one wants, which in turns expresses who one is. The choice directly reflects the self. Recognizing the choice is a fundamental precondition for reflexivity (Giddens 1992: 91f.). Life stories require reflecting people.

The central question of life in prison is how to accommodate and still maintain some kind of identity and self-respect (cf. Cohen & Taylor 1993). One must reflect on every aspect of everyday life in prison, since it can be used by the prison staff to manipulate one as a prisoner. Most inmates, however, adopt a cultural identity that they are used to from previous terms in prison. The criminal identity is strengthened when it proves to be successful. "You turn everything over. And everyone wants to be identified with something, in some way" (Gadd 1991: 9).

As Walters has pointed out in his book *The Criminal Lifestyle* (1990), the criminal is an individual who sets himself up to lose in ways that are both dramatic and destructive. He finds refuge in the criminal world, since he fears so many things; above all perhaps things like responsibility, commitment, and intimacy. This fear of failure grows with every crime and is what makes the criminal continue to fail and lose. At the same time, the criminal finds the immediate gratification of crime more reinforcing than the stable conformist life (cf. Åkerström 1993). This is diametrically opposed to the life perspective that is preached in official records and by social workers, where a person is instead expected to learn to wait for the returns.

The reflexive project of the self is both emancipatory and coercive. One fulfills oneself as subject and is constituted as object. Writing about oneself can therefore reveal compulsions and ascribed identities, and help the narrator toward a "rewriting of the narrative of the self," as Giddens has put it. In traditional society, when people followed learned habits and patterns, self-characterization was not so crucial for the way one was identified as a person. When there were not many possible choices, the self-presenting narrative was not so significant. People were not forced to negotiate their identities on the basis of individual choices (Giddens 1992: 74f.).

Today, concepts such as individualism and freedom have become cardinal values that organize all other meanings (cf. Dumont 1986: 16f.). It is therefore important to have a clear individual identity and to make the right choices in life. Your biography can be said to confirm how well you have succeeded; in other words, it is a kind of documentation of your stewardship of your freedom and whether you have been able to make the right choices so as to become a good modern individual. In the same way, biographies are written to tell us what bad individuals are like.

Much research has found that criminal identity has been shaped by society, reinforcing a deviant identity through stigma, labeling, and institutionalization. The researchers, however, have not considered what the life process and the life circumstances of the person involved have meant for his identity forming. Prison does not just create a biographical knowledge that the prisoner enters; it then goes beyond and reinforces this identity. The criminalization does not just become a self-fulfilling prophecy; the criminal also creates a more distinct criminal identity. The internal punishments that occur in prisons, for example, not infrequently lead to promotion in the criminal identity formation. One man describes the experience of solitary confinement as follows: "suddenly you got a star on your shoulder, you were at least a captain in the criminal army. You had been chosen, in a way" (Gadd 1991: 17).

Jean Genet, the French writer who also was a thief and wrote his first books in prison, said that he could not experience his freedom as anything but that of a thief, since the good citizens early in his life labeled him as a thief and an evil person. But he made the choice not to accept prison life as a punishment, and then the punishment became senseless. Instead of letting himself be humiliated as criminal and ending up powerless, he chose to make the humiliation into an election, a coronation. He writes: "The only way to avoid the terror of the terrible is to throw oneself into the arms of the terrible" (1967). This way of handling his situation, which is also very common among ordinary criminals, is reinforced when society today is not just bearing the impress of neomoralist movements but also shows a serious lack of interest in those who are separated as different. The American president Bill Clinton expressed this recently in words aimed at youth criminals: "You get three strikes, then you're out!" After three relapses into criminality, no respect is shown to their person. They are just rendered harmless and incapacitated. We see the same development in Sweden.

Identities are formed from the biographical constructions of which the life stories are a part. These narratives differ from pure fiction in that they retell certain memories. Memory has been described by George Marcus as the fundamental medium of ethnography. Memory is decisive for recognition and acknowledgment in identity formation. It relates history to identity and vice versa. This means that questions of how and what we remember are important. In modernity, however, it is difficult to grasp how different kinds of memories are structured. The boundaries between the private and the public in everyday life have become obscure. Memory is not a collective construction as it was in traditional society, when it was communicated and handed down in oral traditions and storytelling; now it is expressed in individual memories and autobiographies. Even the collective memory is passed on in modern society through the individual memory (Marcus 1992: 316f.).

Identity is not a given which a person learns just by living, but presupposes a self-aware reflexive process. One must create one's own identity (cf. Giddens 1992: 52), which is not necessarily the same as having the freedom to determine one's own life. It can also be a coercion. A person must act as an individual regardless of the conditions and opportunities on offer.

Prison punishes by depriving a person of his freedom. If you cannot handle your freedom properly, it is taken away from you. If you do not follow the prescribed lines in life, if you try to make choices but these choices happens to be the wrong ones, then you are put into prison and acquire an identity as a criminal, needing treatment to be brought back to orderly behavior and a well-accepted identity within society. Being sentenced to prison, however, is not synonymous with being criminal. On the contrary, it is sometimes said about a client of correctional treatment that "He's not criminal," although the person in question may have been sentenced to several years' imprisonment. It takes more than committing a crime to acquire a criminal identity. To bear the designation "criminal" one must have assumed an identity synonymous with that of the delinquent, by acquiring a distinctive way of living, with its own ideas, habits, traditions, and so on. One can therefore be called criminal even if one has not committed any crime for the moment.

The construction of the subject is interwoven with the construction of society and of history, and identity is defined in modern society in a multitude of subjectivization processes (cf. Foucault 1982: 209ff.). Identities are formed in interaction between the objectivizations that society makes of persons and groups, and the subjectivizations that people themselves are able to create. I use a perspective which understands the constitution of cultural identity as an interaction between the subjective life story and the objectivizing life history. Another way of expressing this is that every cultural formation occurs in the encounter between the strategies of power and resistance.

We have to distinguish between the concepts of life history and life story or life narrative. There is a *life history* outside the individual. Sometimes your biography is written regardless of whether you participate actively or not. The state compiles biographies of the citizens' lives, and institutions like the prison can construct a more detailed biography of the inmates than they themselves are able to do. *Life stories*, on the other hand, are part of the way people constitute themselves socially and culturally. Life history and life story relate to each other in the same way that the formal prison rules relate to the rules among the inmates.

A discursive practice is developed where inmates tell their life-stories in accordance with the experts way of creating life-histories. The life stories of Tony, Ben, Jack, and Jimmy are not just personal testimonies of a life, like the biographical story of Kideckel's folk hero, Bălan, and they are not sensible and elaborated stories like those written by anthropologists themselves, but rather stereo-typed stories written in concert with their life histories. Life stories can be said to be narratives in which one presents oneself on the basis of a structured perception of the self. They mainly refer to internal cognitive processes, however, not to the identity one acquires from identities assigned from outside. We must thus distinguish between self-presentation or personal identity and social and cultural identity, which is a result both of the interplay between different people and of a historically complex context. Life and the way it was lived was constituted as a political problem when the Swedish welfare state was being built up. People's lives become a subject for bookkeeping, registration, stocktaking, investigation, and cataloguing. An individual's way of life became the most important ground for assessing his identity formation. From a world of condemnation, we moved into a world of evaluation.

Evaluating the Biographies of Prisoners

"Biographies" of prisoners were compiled as early as the 1870s. The prison chaplain had the duty of filling in preprinted forms with headings such as family situation and development; parents' position in life and moral conditions; the models emulated by the inmate and the company he kept; whether he was prone to drinking, loose living, or other disorderly behavior; previous crimes; moral sense; and so on. Later these data were referred to as "individual communications" and "biographical notes," but the headings were still roughly the same. From the 1940s until now, this work has been done by social workers, who have used forms with items such as "attitude to society" and "moral development." Today the guards are expected to draw up a "treatment plan" for each prisoner. It is very simple, containing only a formal history of the subject's life. This is a further way to stereotype a life history.

The social life of the offender is completely forgotten. As Nils Christie puts it, "there is no point in exposing childhood dreams, defeats – perhaps mixed with some glimmer from happy days – social life, all those small things which are essential to a perception of the other as a full human being" (Christie 1993: 138). For every sentence there is a record of the points in the criminal register showing the life history of the person. It is also told in expressions like: "He is to be found under 30 items in the criminal register."

Before every sentence in criminal cases, the person is studied to determine the most appropriate form of punishment. The idea is to give the court a picture of the person who is to be sentenced, in order to assess how he should be treated. A forecast is made on the basis of the life that a person has lived hitherto. The presentence investigation consists of a statement from the suspect himself, along with data from criminal records and any other previous documents from correctional treatment and other records. Many normal Swedish rules of confidentiality are waived in connection with this investigation, which is made public when the case is heard in court. The accused are exposed and sorted as persons by being made the object of different kinds of treatment and assessment. The court judges on the basis not only of the crime but also of the presentence investigation; that is, the assessment of a person's life by a social worker or probation officer. A number of pages about the person's childhood and adolescence and any previous crimes are followed by comments on his life situation such as "X's life has been rather a mess . . . he has been slightly irritated and broody. . . problems with girlfriends" and concluding assessments such as "fixed rules of conduct can steer and guide him and strengthen his self-esteem and hence reduce the risk of recidivism." Here the assessment is based not on such considerations as that people with a good education should know better than to commit a crime; on the contrary, if there have been criminal tendencies in the family, if the person is poorly educated, unemployed, and so on, then the assessment is harsher (cf. Christie 1993).

The assessment of the court is also preceded by a different assessment. The investigating policeman transforms the event that is defined as criminal into writing, based on the oral statements of the people involved. In this process the investigator's language is substituted, so that, for example, a fight becomes a case of assault. The course of events is also structured into a coherent picture on the basis of police norms (cf. Jönsson 1988). Both the event and the life of the accused are thus filtered through many agencies before the verdict comes. If the sentence is imprisonment, then, as we have seen, there is further assessment and sorting. Apart from the above-mentioned biographies and treatment plans, the authorities continue to build up data on the inmates with the aid of personal files and other records such as police descriptions from the "rogues' gallery," with photographs and descriptions of tattoos and other distinguishing marks. Their life has been objectified into specific human destinies.

Outsiderhood and Selfhood

Prison helps criminals to build up a life as losers which some of them convert to a more active outsiderhood as rebels who resist every attempt to normalize them. Expressions like Jack's "No one is gonna be able to suppress me, they'll never crack my pride and my integrity" are typical. Inmates talk about themselves as losers, but they are proud of this since they do not want any part of the society around them. Prison treatment has always been predicated on remorse and guilt, but many inmates are imbued with a powerful hatred of the society that excludes them. This is expressed in statements such as: "Crime is a way to hit back, to show that you're good enough and that you don't bow to authority." Prison de-individualizes a person, and the only way to become someone who is treated with respect is to strengthen one's identity as an outsider.

Power is represented here by the Swedish state and its criminal policy, which has made outsiders of the individuals who are supposed to be treated in Swedish prisons, while resistance is represented by the criminal individuals who have developed an opposition and a selfhood in relation to, and in interaction with, the objectivizations that the state has made of them (cf. Svensson 1992). The main instrument of power in the construction of outsiderhood was the biographies compiled of the inmates. They were also to play a decisive role in the criminals' formulation of their subjective selfhoods. Since a large share of their lives is spent in institutions, their own narratives are also formed in interplay with authority and its language. They have no tools of their own for structuring their life stories.

The biographical text of a life history becomes a process which creates the construction that is the criminal. The construction then becomes something on the basis of which the criminal acts in his narrative. Power has an ability to define differences, to give them names, to create concepts, and to establish norms. The aim was to get the criminals to reflect about their lives, to internalize the biographical perspective and rewrite themselves and their "moral careers" (cf. Fraser 1989: 178). The result has instead been the development of a criminal culture; that is, prison produces and reproduces criminals. The resocialization that was supposed to give these individuals a place as "normal people" in society has entailed a criminalization, a negative socialization into a criminal identity. Prison is counterproductive. Hate and separation from society become a seedbed for organized resistance on the part of criminals. As Foucault puts it, penal techniques and the criminal interact as a technological whole. Criminality is prison's revenge on justice (1977: 255).

Criminals have different values and norms from those current in society, and they uphold these against the prevailing social system. One cannot assume that they will adopt the same value patterns as normal people and accept a life as passive deviants on the margins. They should instead be regarded as active practitioners of resistance (cf. Mathiesen 1965) as a precondition without which power could not be exercised. They have no reason, after all, to take any active part in the punishment process. As Jack says, "This is like a tiny mirror of the society outside, for Christ's sake. You find every god-damn level of society, and you see in miniature what's outside. And when you know that, there's nothing you can support outside . . . . I don't think so . . . . I don't want to be incorporated in this society because it's sick . . . its totally sick this society. I just need to look around and see how sick a prison is to know that it's even sicker on the outside." The resistance is, however, temporary, individual, and adapted to the governing system. We see what James C. Scott has called Brechtian forms of resistance, which cloak their resistance in the language of conformity – a kind of cultural weapon used in the everyday struggle for moral dignity (1990).

What distinguishes criminals from "normal" members of society is not differences in the form of characteristics but something that is created in relations between people. This can be described as a game in which people ascribe characteristics to each other so that they can distinguish themselves from others. By judging certain actions to be criminal and separating those who commit them by putting them in prison, we segregate them as criminal individuals. Those who have the main power to make distinctions and segregations are the social experts whose duty is to produce investigations, evaluations, and personal biographies of certain people and who have the power to determine what kind of measures can be taken against them. The experts shape their own professional identity and society's value system, while the criminal simultaneously shapes his criminal identity or contributes to the cultural construction of outsiderhood. Power defines and delimits the criminal as an object, while the criminal himself uses various external signs such as special tattoos when creating himself as a subject. They become his strategies of resistance to create differences.

Cultural identity becomes a question of us and them, or how one creates oneself as a subject while simultaneously constructing others as objects. It is in negotiations between these resistance strategies and this exercise of power that different identities are formed. One's success in shaping both one's own and other people's identity is crucially dependent on whether one has preferential right of interpretation in society – access to the proper channels of discourse and the power to define what is right and what is wrong.

But this also requires a certain distance between people. Without differences, *the others* would not be otherwise. Criminal identity presupposes outsiderhood, and this identity is strengthened the greater the distance from society grows. Prisoners are aware of the interaction between what is ascribed to them and how they turn out: "They lock me in here for six years. Isolate me, don't give me a single leave of absence, and treat me like some dangerous monster. Does anyone really believe that the day I stand outside these walls I've become a well-behaved person?" Prison is a storage place which makes the inmates incorrigible, giving them daily training in "bad" individualism; that is, they are proud of having a defiant reputation as "bad" (cf. Katz 1988: 261f, 312). They adopt the criminal identity and reinforce it. This gives them a sense of community and relations in their state as outsiders. They become visible, identified, and proud of having a reputation of being bad.

The Power of Biography

Biography means simply writing life. This has acquired a normative power in modern society, a way to order life and time just as a map orders the world and space. Lifetimes have become an experimental field where one writes biographies of oneself and others. The constructions, however, are not just subjectivizations but also objectivizations. We must consider what constructions are socially, historically, and politically possible and how they are part of a larger metanarrative.

We live in a biographical era, where there are different life scripts to relate to. Both life and time are biographically ordered in modernity. Apart from the fact that we construct reality biographically, we also live our lives biographically. Modern existence is ordered as an autobiographical presentation. On the basis of different life perspectives, we shape the present against the background of our earlier life history and with our sights set on the future.

Autobiography requires great self-knowledge and a well-developed reflexive self, and some people are more skilled than others at writing their lives in harmony with the spirit of the age. Experts on treatment are a part of the good identity, the one that serves as an example. Throughout the modern project, they have led the social and cultural fields in Sweden and shaped the knowledge of what is right and wrong, good and bad. The "bad" people have had their biographies written by these experts, who have made forecasts, assessments, and studies of them in different phases of life. Writing a biography of the bad people has become a goal for the entire social field since the latter half of the nineteenth century and increasingly so in the twentieth century. With the aid of biography, the experts have adjusted the treatment of these people to bring their lifetime into harmony with the modern project. They have taken those subjects who are outside society and turned them into objects of knowledge within society (cf. Beronius 1994: 135). They have exercised this authority in the name of welfare and justice.

The prisoners that I have talked to seem to find it impossible to tell me about anything but their own lives. I have tried several times to talk about everyday life in the prison, but the answers I get are always related to themselves and the part things play in their lives. They have been trained to tell their life stories for so many different social experts inside and outside so they simply can't see what I mean by asking questions about relations and community. When they leave prison, many of them have not had any other contacts than those with persons in authority and with other prisoners.

The biographical power could be said to be a therapeutic power, not a repressive one. It creates forms of subjectivity in accordance with a particular discourse. There are many different projects inside prison to bring the prisoners in line with a proper self. One way to treat personality disorders – defects in identity formation – in prison is to teach the inmates how to handle normal everyday life, with the aid of courses for fathers and an improvement program called "cognitive skills." It can be described as an attempt to instill in prisoners the middle-class values that prevail in society. Many of the inmates are highly critical of this influence, which they say gives them a different identity from the one they want.

They are well aware of their subordinate position in dialogues of this kind, where the other party has been professionally trained to influence them. The basic idea on which prisons still rest is that the imprisoned individual should think over his crime, feel remorse, and acquire an inner relationship to himself so that spontaneous individualizing and self-disciplining occurs (cf. Foucault 1977: 237f.). Foucault says that biographical knowledge and corrective techniques go hand in hand; the punitive technique bears upon a life. The causes of his crime are to be sought in the story of his life, "the 'biographical' . . . establishes the 'criminal' as existing before the crime and even outside it." A notion is formed "of a 'dangerous' individual, which makes it possible to draw up a network of causality in terms of an entire biography" (1977: 252). Differences and power relations in society give people different opportunities and conditions for making their biography. Those who have lived a life as a project also have the ability to document their life in tidy narratives (cf. Svensson 1995). A few people, however, have their lives described by other people in biographies which have the character of normative recommendations about what their lives should have been like. Inside the walls there is a mutual identity-formation process in which the treatment experts develop their professional identity and the criminals define the criminal identity. They are both part of the power that is exercised in the form of biography. The actions of the subject – the self and the body – become the object of new technologies which are, in turn, the result of the new expertise in managing people's lives.

The power of memory is to be found in a person's biography. Little was known about memory before the nineteenth century, when the "sciences of memory" emerged (Hacking 1995). Then there was also created a new genre of biography, the recording of criminals' lives. This recording meant that criminals could be identified by their biographies, they became objectified as criminals and accessible for the exercise of power. This identification then also became a part of their own self-understanding. The treatment that was supposed to give criminals a good biography has instead given them a bad one. The voice they got from inside was on the one hand telling a stereotyped story about their lives along the lines of the formal institutional narrative technique, on the other hand it was filled with hate, disgust, and bitterness. Together these two parts of a biography, the life history and the life story, help the inmate to develop a behavior as bad, dangerous, and terrible, which brings him into harmony with the modern order. This is identity formation on the basis of what I call "bad individualism."

In using autobiographical accounts, the power structures which prison reflects gives the inmates a collective voice. At the same time, state surveillance has made them culturally different in the same way as other groups that interrogate the power structures in which they operate. This can be compared to the cultural standardization that Kay Warren (this volume) analyzes among the Mayan intellectuals.

Terms in prison strengthen the criminal identity. Inmates adopt it, and when they get out they further reinforce it. The stronger the identity as an outsider and a criminal, the more visible your identity is. All inmates speak about how this "gives a feeling of self-respect." Prison life organizes criminal careers in the same way that the normal educational system organizes professional careers. Jack says, "It's like a vocational school, but the wrong way around. The occupation you learn is crime." Continuous and compulsory education takes place. The resistance of criminals brings out political and cultural meanings in society. The rhetoric of criminal policy states the norms on which society is based. Modern society relies on responsible individuals making conscious choices. Authority is exercised on the basis of good order, that is, the classification of right and wrong, good and bad. The measures of criminal policy thereby become a means for the self-understanding of individuals as well.

Notes

1. Zygmunt Bauman (1993: 244) argues that the dismantling of the welfare state is a process of putting moral responsibility among the private concerns of the individuals. This in turn means that the moral selves have to calculate gains and costs and that society is a marketplace where individuals satisfy their moral wants. In this situation, moral discussions tend to deal

with chiseling out good people and bad people, to reduce the number of citizens who need to be paid for.

2. The effect of the prison is not therefore that of a "failure," writes Barry Smart, but should rather be considered a "success" in so far as the form of illegality it produces has proved useful (1992: 75, cf. Cohen 1992: 106). It serves as an extension of methods to supervise the social body (cf. Foucault 1980: 40).

3. There is a widespread disbelief in prisons as correctional institutions among criminologists in Europe (see for example Bondeson 1989 or Mathiesen 1990). Foucault states that for the last 150 years the proclamation of the failure of the prison has always been accompanied by its maintenance (1977: 272).

4. The same Bentham was also encouraging the use of statistics concerning criminals (Beirne 1993: 49).

5. The prison population in Sweden today is a good 5,000, which is a 20-percent increase over the last five years (KOS). Around 15,000 people receive a prison sentence every year; half of them very short – less than two months. In the prison I visited, most of the prisoners are doing a term of more than four years.

6. In Sweden most of the prison population spend their time in small, local, newly built prisons with medium or low security (KOS; cf. Rutherford 1986: 66). The normative effect, however, comes from the big ones.

7. Women's prisons also develop a tough atmosphere similar to that in men's prisons, but the shame is twice as great for a woman in prison. She has overstepped the limits in two senses: she has committed a crime by breaking the law and she has transgressed the boundary for accepted feminine behavior.

8. The first women employed in correctional treatment were counselors and other social welfare officers, as well as office staff. Female guards are also found in women's prisons. In the last few years, however, an increasing number of female guards have also been taken on by men's prisons, as well.

9. We actually do not have any serial killer in Sweden, but Swedes in general are highly influenced by what they see on the television from the USA.

10. Instead of having this negative welfare, the main means of effectively approaching problems of poverty and social exclusion could be what Giddens calls generative politics. "It

works through providing material conditions, and organizational frameworks, for the life-political decisions taken by individuals and groups in the wider social order" (Giddens 1994: 32). He also calls this a positive welfare. Since life today is much more of a construct than a destiny, the life-political measures have to connect autonomy with personal and collective responsibilities.

Part Two

Exile, Memory, and Identity

Chapter 4

Lives Writ Large: Kabyle Self-Portraits and the Question of Identity

Henk Driessen

Introduction

September 25, 1994: Lounes Matoub, a popular singer from the Berber-speaking Kabyle minority in Algeria, is driving home after a visit to his hospitalized father in the capital. Darkness and pouring rain make the driving hard. Matoub stops at a roadside bar. Chance would have it that precisely this bar has been targeted out this evening for a cleaning-up operation by the Armed Islamic Group (GIA). This Islamist guerrilla movement has been responsible for the most atrocious killings since January 1992 when the Algerian Army cancelled the elections about to be won by the Islamic Salvation Front (FIS). Matoub is recognized and abducted by a gang of fifteen armed men. Shortly after this raid Cheb Hasni, another well-known singer, is murdered in Oran. Matoub's disappearance brings demonstrations, strikes, and searches in many parts of Kabylia. On October 2 more than 10,000 people demonstrate in the Kabyle capital of Tizi Ouzou to demand the release of their singer and recognition of their Berber language by the government. To everybody's surprise Matoub turns up alive on October 10. He is the first who is set free after having been kidnapped by the GIA. Kabylia celebrates the singer's release on a large scale. After the initial euphoria of those first days, however, Matoub is tormented by nervousness, fear and nightmares. He retreats for a while to France where he feels lost, cut off from his cultural roots. Assisted by a journalist, he commits his life story to print.[1]

Paris, June 1987: Djura, "wearing a floral Kabyle gown, which hangs loosely on my seven-months pregnancy," founder and leader of the successful Djurdjura band and her French partner are assaulted and wounded on their houseboat by a younger brother and niece of Djura. The attack is a climax in a feud involving her entire family. In order to overcome the violent split with her family, she sets herself to writing the story of her life.[2]

The aim of this chapter is to consider Matoub's book as an example of ethno-autobiographical writing that speaks to issues larger than the events of his personal life. The leitmotiv is Kabyle identity, and I will argue that the traumatic experience of being abducted has not only triggered the story of his life but has also turned the singer's life into a metaphor of the predicament of a besieged ethnic minority. This point is further illustrated by briefly comparing Matoub's book with life history material provided by Djura, a female singer of Kabyle origin in France. Although there is not enough space to fully develop Djura's case, her written experience is more than just an afterthought. It highlights the complexity of Kabyle identity.

Rebel with a Cause

Lounes Matoub was born in 1956 in a village in the heartland of Kabylia. He was raised by his grandmother and mother in the absence of his father. Matoub attended a school of the White Fathers, an educational congregation that was very active in colonial Africa. His illiterate mother initiated him into the oral culture of Kabylia. He was a difficult boy with a proclivity for fighting and petty theft, spent some time in jail, and worked as a mechanic in Algiers until he was drafted into the army. He began singing and playing the guitar at celebrations in his village. Some old men taught him how to play the mandolin. Seduced by freedom and adventure, Matoub left for France where he performed in Kabyle cafés. Here he met the famous Berber singer Idir who served as his role model. He produced two cassettes and spent a month in la Santé (a large prison in France) for wounding his producer in a fight. In the course of the 1980s, he got involved in the Berber Cultural Movement (MCB). During a demonstration in 1988, a year of serious bread riots in Algeria, Matoub was gravely wounded by police bullets while distributing pamphlets. His recovery took several months in various hospitals in Algeria and France. In 1990 he participated in a march of half a million Berbers in Algiers to demand "Tamazight being declared an official and national language." Later that year he was again seriously wounded in an escalated fight with a neighbor in his village and had to make another tour of hospitals in Algeria and France. After recovery he visited Canada and the United States as a guest of the US-based Association of Berber Culture. In the deteriorating political climate of Algeria during the early 1990s, militant Islamists placed Matoub on a deathlist as "an enemy of Allah." He received threatening letters and calls, yet continued his public life and performances until his abduction in the fall of 1994.

Matoub's book purports to be a factual account of his life from his birth through the end of 1994. It is a passionate tale with a strong conversational imprint. The account of events is arranged more or less chronologically and is interspersed with comments and ethnographic notes on Kabyle culture and Algerian politics. The tone is at times detached, at times indignant and emotional. Some events are described in great detail, in particular his endless medical odyssey in Algeria and France, his abduction and the two weeks he is being held in GIA camps which is the *pièce de résistance* of the book. Matoub presents himself as an ambassador of the Berber cause. His struggle for Berber identity in fact constitutes the leitmotiv and mission of his songs and autobiography.

To the east of Algiers lies the Djurdjura, the great mountainous enclave that has been called "the small African Switzerland." Until recently, its Berber-speaking inhabitants were a fragmented sedentary peasant population distributed over complex mountain ranges. Villages were usually split into hamlets with a marked defensive look.[3] Matoub was born in this region two years after the Algerian war of liberation broke out. Kabylia and the Aurès provided the first base areas for the leaders of the Algerian revolution which meant that the Berbers became deeply involved in the struggle.[4] Matoub relates that he was fascinated by the *maquisards*. At five he almost set fire to his village while playing guerrilla. In his own words: "As little boys, my friends and I, we played war. There was one going on before our very eyes that served as our model . . . .. I always wanted to be a *maquisard* because for me it was the freedom fighter who always won . . .. I was a *moudjahid*, in spite of my age of five" (pp. 13, 27–28). This model of the freedom fighter seems to have been a formative influence in his life.

A second factor of importance was his strong bond with his grandmother and mother and through them with Kabyle language and oral culture, in particular traditional songs and stories of Kabylia. In the early part of his book, Matoub evokes images of women picking olives and singing Kabyle songs. Several of his statements on Kabyle identity are in fact fueled by recollections of childhood experiences.

A third major impact on his life is the basic education he received from the White Fathers who made him conscious of Berber history and identity. From them he first learned about Jugurtha, the Berber king who defied the power of Rome. Matoub praises the White Fathers for their respect of Kabyle culture and their teaching of the principles of republicanism, democracy, and secularism. In fact, the educational policy of the missions and the French government played a decisive role in the development of Kabylia. Although there has been no Berber policy in Algeria similar to the *divide et impera* ethnic politics in Morocco, stereotypes of the Kabyle did influence colonial policy. Berbers were considered to be the only natives capable of being assimilated to modern values (*évoluable*). It was assumed that Islam had only a superficial impact upon their way of life. The colonial media depicted Kabyles as a reasonable, hard-working, thrifty, enterprising, courageous, and basically democratic race.[5] Before public education was set up in the rest of Algeria, Kabylia already enjoyed primary and secondary schools run by the missionaries. From 1891 to 1950, practically all the Algerians recruited by the school for teachers in Algiers came from Kabylia.[6] One of the consequences of Matoub's school education was that he received instruction neither in Islam nor in Arabic. Later he simply refused to learn Arabic.

A fourth important condition of his growing-up was the almost permanent absence of his father who had to work in France to make a living. Out-migration is in fact a structural phenomenon in the history of Kabylia. The pressure of the growing population on the scarce resources forced many inhabitants to seek a living outside their region. Even before French colonization, Kabylia furnished gardeners and construction workers for the towns of the littoral. Large-scale migration to metropolitan France started during the World War I. More than 50 percent of the Algerian immigrants in France are of Kabyle origin, whereas Kabyles constitute only one fifth of the Algerian population.[7] The wide-ranging networks of Kabyles in France and their families in the homeland were an important power resource for the *Armée de Libération Nationale* which counted among its members a disproportionate number of French-educated Berbers. Thus Matoub's homeland had an intellectual and administrative elite, as well as widespread experience of emigration, several decades before the other rural areas in Algeria. This made Kabyles well-suited for the role of economic and cultural brokers between France and Algeria.

The experience of becoming aware of a separate Berber identity through French education and migration is a recurring theme of *Rebelle* and many of Matoub's songs. For instance, his Berber background is brought home to him during the two years in the army in the west of Algeria. He is being mocked and humiliated by Arab soldiers because of his inability to speak Arabic and confronted with the Arab stereotype of the "primitive Kabyle mountain dweller."[8] Such experiences probably accelerated his Berber activism: "When I left the army I was more rebellious than when I entered it" (p. 64). Revolt, resistance, and struggling are the motto of his life story: "I was turbulent as a boy, I still am and I'll remain a rebel for the rest of my life" (p. 12). During the dictatorship of Boumediene, a policy of forced Arabization was implemented: "I refused to learn Arabic" and "Each time I speak my mother tongue, I commit an act of resistance" (pp. 41, 43). His songs, all with Kabyle lyrics, were banned for being subversive yet circulated widely in Algeria on pirated cassettes.

Matoub repeatedly tries to anchor his character traits in Berber history and culture. He views the Berber language as the repository of what he calls the trinity of Berber values: honor, dignity, and vigor (p. 44). Each time he ends up in a fight he evokes the honor code as the bedrock of Berber culture. Matoub presents himself as what North Africans call a *nifsi*, a man with a strong sense of honor.[9] On the other hand, he did not defend himself when he was kidnapped even though ʌ e carried a pistol. He also admits to having been terribly afraid during his captivity and of praying with his captors, renouncing his ideals in order to save his life: "Better to be a living coward than a dead hero" (p. 176).

In spite of these traumatic experiences "struggle remains my priority" (p. 143). The statement, "I am not an Arab, nor am I obliged to be a Muslim" (p. 244), links up his life to the Berber cause: "I owe my name, my life, my popularity, to the people of

Kabylia . . .. My songs, my music, my struggle will be stronger
than ever. They deserve it. They are my reason for existence . . ..
My wealth" (p. 253). His "miraculous" release made him an even
greater hero. Before his abduction his struggle had been restricted
to the Kabyle cause. After his release he fights for the greater cause
of democracy as well: "I have a few qualities and a lot of faults.
But above all I am a poet, a buffoon, someone who loves life, a
vagabond, running from one corner to another, fighting for truth,
justice, peace, and recognition of fundamental rights" (p. 266). This
larger claim is recognized outside Kabylia and Algeria when
Matoub is awarded the *Prix de la Mémoire*, presented to him on
December 6, 1994, by Madame Danielle Mitterand.

A striking characteristic of his life story is that much of his
domestic life remains outside the scope of his memoirs: here and
there he praises his beloved mother and briefly mentions his father
and sister. The first time he mentions his wife is on page 137 when
he relates their divorce. He adds that she is the daughter of a great
Berberist, persecuted by the military secret service and who died
in a traffic accident, suggesting that this was staged by the secret
police. If he discusses domestic matters at all, they are mostly
bound up with the Berber cause. This lack of attention to domest-
icity is linked to the virtual absence of women in his book. Matoub
mentions women only to stress the colorfulness of their Kabyle
attire and the absence of veiling; in other words, as markers of
Kabyle identity. In his code of honor the domestic domain is the
female sphere *par excellence*. There seems to be a change of mind
after his release. Towards the end of his book he admits that it is
very important that women join his struggle for democracy: "If
our women surrender, our country will slip further and further
into barbarism and obscurantism" (p. 279). The fact that the more
intimate aspects of his life are played down may be in line with
the attitude of Berbers and Arabs alike that domestic life should
remain secluded from public scrutiny. However this may be, the
lack of domestic information tends to magnify Matoub's public
role.

Berberism

What exactly is the Berber cause to which Lounes Matoub devotes
his life? Despite the fact that Berbers are a sizeable minority in

Algeria, there has been no serious "Berber" problem, at least not at the level of elite politics. To be sure, Arabs and Berbers are aware of their distinctive identities and at times express hostility to one another. Many Kabyles consider themselves the original and by implication the "real" inhabitants of Algeria. Urban Arabs are often seen as unreliable persons lacking honor.

Individual Kabyles have played very important political roles in the national arena for the past fifty years, but not as spokesmen for Berbers as an ethnic collectivity. Although there was a brief Berber crisis in 1949 and the ethnic issue did play a role in the political conflict that broke out immediately after independence in 1963, Berber separatism has never been a strong political force in Algeria, the persistence of Kabyle hostility toward central authority notwithstanding.[10] There are some factors that might explain why a strong Berber movement did not emerge.

Kabyles had no written language of their own and, until their recent adoption of the ancient Tuareg script, had to use the Arabic and French scripts. The decentralized and politically fragmented nature of Kabylian society in the past, combined with strong local loyalties, probably helped them to survive as a minority but at the same time precluded the development of a sense of cultural and political unity. The Kabyles did not construct a national identity unlike, for instance, the Kurds who straddle several international borders. And finally, Boumediene, the second president of Algeria, and his successor Chadli Bendjedid employed a stick-and-carrot strategy, repressing overt Berber aspirations. There are indications of a politicization of Berber identity since the liberalization of politics and the erosion of the one-party state during the 1980s. Another important recent factor is the violent offensive of militant Islam in Algeria and the deepening crisis of the Algerian economy and state.

Let me now briefly sketch the development of the Berber Cultural Movement which has acted as the main stage for Lounes Matoub's cultural and political performances. The initial impetus towards a Berber movement came from Kabyle immigrants in France. In 1966 the *Association berbère d'études et de recherches culturelles* was founded in Paris. One year later a similar initiative resulted in the foundation of the *Académie berbère*, renamed *Académie Agraw Imazighène*, which played a role in the revolt of April 1980, since then known as "The Berber Spring."[11] The most important and theoretically nonpolitical Berber Cultural

Movement, based in Kabylia, was founded in 1976. All these initiatives by Kabyle intellectuals revolved upon the claim for the Berbers' language to be taught in schools alongside Arabic and gradually evolved into a more general Kabylian *réveil*, or awakening. Indeed, language is an extremely important way in which identity is maintained, asserted, and reproduced. One of its vehicles are the songs in Kabyle produced and performed by artists such as Matoub and Djura.

The events of the "Berber Spring" constituted a foundation for the Berber movement. Although Lounes Matoub was in France at that time, he gives a detailed account of the events in Tizi Ouzou in April 1980. Roadblocks had been thrown up on the approach to Tizi Ouzou where students and lecturers were on strike to press Berber cultural claims. A general strike took place in the Kabyle region. On April 20, the University of Tizi Ouzou was closed after students occupying it were removed by the riot police. Disturbances broke out and dozens of people were imprisoned. The extreme violence wielded by the security forces to suppress the Berber revolt is an invariable theme in Kabyle accounts of these events. Matoub thinks it a miracle that nobody got killed.

State repression of the "Berber Spring" provided the Berber Cultural Movement with the occasion for an annual commemoration in Tizi Ouzou, a focal point of the Movement. In October 1988, rioting erupted in Algiers over new austerity measures which caused prices to rise sharply. The government declared a state of emergency and deployed troops. On October 9 and 10, violence and demonstrations spread to Kabylia with serious disturbances in Tizi Ouzou, where economic complaints were linked to cultural claims. The economic failures and corruption of successive Algerian governments have sharpened a sense of a separate cultural identity among the younger generations in Kabylia. While handing out pamphlets, Lounes Matoub was gunned down by a policeman and seriously wounded. This event added to the aura of martyrdom that was being created around him. It certainly was a further step in the politicizing of the MCB and the radicalization of Matoub, who now plays an active part in the yearly commemoration of the "Berber Spring." One of the highlights of the MCB, in spite of internal divisions, was the staging of a demonstration of half a million Berbers in the streets of Algiers in January 1990.

A new phase set in with the escalation of clashes between the state and militant Islam. Berber activists, Matoub included, blame the Arabs in general and the Algerian governments in particular for the present crisis. At the same time, they have a deep mistrust of Islamism which they see as yet another manifestation of Arab expansionism. Caught between a repressive state and violent Islamic revivalism, a more radical wing is gaining momentum within the MCB. Said Saadi, the founder of the movement, is a supporter of the hardline *éradicateurs* in Algeria who call for a total war on all Islamists. Saadi, who argues that the MCB has become a resistance movement because of the Islamist threat, has called on Berber communities to arm themselves "because the government is failing to protect its people."[12] Matoub and many young followers share Said Saadi's political convictions (pp. 89, 153–155). The singer even calls him "the most courageous and honest man in present-day Algeria." The failed negotiations between the Algerian government and the FIS, along with Matoub's abduction, have strengthened the radical wing of the Berber movement. The longer Algeria's civil war and chaos continue, the more Kabylia could be pushed toward political separation.

A Female Counterpart

The author of *The Veil of Silence* belongs to the approximately three million French citizens of Algerian origin in France (apart from one-half million Algerians seeking asylum).[13] Djura was born in the late 1940s in a remote village in the Djurdjura. More or less rejected by her mother, she was adopted by the childless wife of a paternal grandfather. When this sterile woman took over the little baby, her mothermilk began to flow spontaneously. Local women considered this a miracle and for them Djura's grandmother had become a saint. A healer, guardian of oral culture, and singer and dancer at village festivals, this extraordinary woman became her grandchild's heroine and role model.

Djura describes an idyllic village world and a childhood among "a people who never submit, with an unfailing dignity, unwavering respect for traditional values, and a deep-seated attachment to the soil of their ancestors" (p. 5). The leitmotiv of her life story is summed up in the following statement: "Berber and rebellious, like the little girl I was, the adolescent I became, the woman I am" (p. 8). Throughout the book, she evokes not only her grandmother but also a mythical ancestress, the Berber warrior-queen Kahina, who fought the invading Arab armies in the seventh century. This is the female counterpart of Matoub's Jugurtha. In 1954, when the Algerian war of liberation broke out, her French-educated father decided to move with his family to France.

Djura recalls the hard life of immigrants in Paris, the first two years with six in a cheap hotel room before moving to a barracks in one of the desolate suburbs. She provides snapshots of immigrant life interspersed with reflections on family and gender. While on the one hand she glorifies Kabylia, its language and traditions, on the other she struggles against the controls and strictures of her family and rebels against the "outdated patriarchy" of Kabyle society in Algeria and France. Growing up, she felt "terrorized" by her father and brothers who disapproved of her "French ways." At age fifteen they sent her back to Algeria where she was kept secluded by her older brother. She succeeded in escaping back to Paris where her father forced her to stay at home. Nevertheless she managed to loose her virginity with a French filmmaker, with whom she traveled throughout Algeria to shoot material for a film about emigration (*Ali in Wonderland*, 1976).

Djura's mother divorced her husband who had become an embittered and violent drinker beating his wife and children. This meant that Djura, in the absence of her older brother, had to provide financial support for her mother and younger brothers and sisters. In 1977 she started the Djurdjura band, mingling "the riches of the Kabylian heritage with the resources of world music" (p. 113). Djura and her two sisters sang in Kabylian to the accompaniment of Algerian, French, and American musicians before a mixed Algerian-French audience. The band has become very successful and Djura, who also discusses the "Berber Spring" of 1980, became involved in political activities, participating in gala concerts for the benefit of Amnesty International, the League for Human Rights, and the Movement Against Racism. Her songs were banned in Algeria. In her own words: "The fact that my compositions were the vehicle for Berber culture was no more highly thought of than my 'feminism': as far as anything connected with the government was concerned, 'Berberitude' was considered synonymous with opposition, and many other artists have been permanently banned for having defended proud Barbary's cultural heritage" (pp. 129–130). While her professional career thrived, her relationship with her family ("the clan") which she increasingly perceives as "parasitical," rapidly deteriorated. Here we see a clash between a young woman striving for freedom and independence and her Kabyle family loyalty and obligation.

Djura's second book revisits and further elaborates the main themes of *The Veil of Silence*. She defines herself primarily as a feminist, with some sympathy for a modernized Islam, whose battle songs are dedicated to all those women who suffer from male oppression, racism, and Islamic fundamentalism. Apart from the self-portrait, brief sketches of strong women, mythical and real, who struggled for the emancipation of women in Kabylia and Algeria, are scattered throughout the book as role models. She situates her own life at the interface of Kabyle and French cultures, the northern and southern shore of the Mediterranean. She is rejected both by her own family and by Western feminism. Djura struggles to overcome her personal crisis by creating a new identity that is linked to a cosmopolitan multiculturalism. Her Berber background is only one, strongly idealized, layer in this multiplex identity. She also sees herself as a Muslim defining Islam as a valuable religion corrupted by reactionary Islamist forces. As an artist who sings in Kabyle, she feels part of both a local and global culture. As a fighter for female emancipation, freedom, and democracy, she places herself in an international intellectual movement. But she is also an immigrant *Parisienne* married to a Breton and mother of two sons. The name of her first son, Riwan, expresses this mixed Breton and Kabylian parentage: in the Berber language it means "child of music," in the Brittany of King Arthur "the king who advances."

Conclusion

The self-portraits of the two performers of Kabyle songs make an instructive comparison. They are at once alike and different, forming "a kind of commentary on one another's character" (Geertz 1968: 4). To begin with, their books are quite different: Matoub's self-portrait is very much a story *told* to a ghostwriter, whereas Djura's self-sketch is a literary account. Neither book is an autobiography in the strict sense of the term: they reveal the profiles of a man and woman just past their midlife who both have gone through violent confrontations causing an identity shock. They look back to the past in order to overcome their crises of identity. Both have an eye for the cultural and political constraints to which they are subjected. Matoub mainly sketches his public life, whereas Djura narrates her life in terms of the intersection of domestic and public domains.

Both Matoub and Djura identify themselves with ancient heroes of Kabyle culture, figures which give their lives shape and clarity. Their autobiographies are thus heroic and in a sense mythical. Both claim to act as a mouthpiece of collectivities: Matoub embodies Kabylian identity, whereas Djura represents the identity of female immigrants of Kabyle background in France, mainly the younger generations (*beurettes*). Both stress their intimate links with agents of traditional oral culture: Matoub with his grandmother, mother, and old village men; Djura with her grandmother. They thereby claim authenticity of voice and a rightful place in the chain of transmission of Kabyle culture. Their life sketches are mixtures of personal testimony written to pass on experience to future generations, didactic exemplars pinpointing how personal lives are embedded in collective identity, and implicit autoethnographic representations. Both relate experiences of exile which heightened their awareness of the multiple nature of their identity.

Their preoccupation with identity can be imputed to the ambiguous position they occupy. Although both try to be loyal to their Kabyle heritage, they are also part of a wider social and cultural configuration. They bridge the Mediterranean divide and in a sense mediate the local and global. Although both move back and forth between France and Kabylia/Algeria, their positions also differ. Matoub has his home base in the village where he was born, Djura in the capital of the Kabyle expatriates. Matoub represents the homeland, Djura the diaspora. Both are rebels: Matoub struggles against Arab repression and a totalitarian regime, Djura against male domination, oppressive tradition, and racism. Both search for self-awareness, autonomy, and freedom. In this struggle they act as exemplars and icons of creativity and resistance.

For the anthropologist, such life sketches are important additional sources for the study of identity formation at this particular juncture in time when political and cultural boundaries are redrawn and people's classifications are being thrown up.[14] They are written testimonies of informants who are cultural brokers and insider's outsiders. This particular perspective provides insight into the interplay of the personal and collective, the local and the global, and agency and constraint.

Notes

1. I wish to express my gratitude to Mahfoud Bennoune for his hospitality and for arousing my interest in his country and native region. Thanks are also due to Willy Jansen and to Deborah Reed-Danahay for making useful suggestions regarding content, grammar, and style. The Matoub case attracted considerable attention in the international media. For instance, see the reports in The *New York Times* (October 1, 1994, and October 3, 1994) and an overview in *The Economist* (October 15, 1994, p. 56). His autobiography appeared in 1995.
2. Djura's first book appeared in 1990 in France. It was translated into several languages, including Dutch.
3. See Houston (1964) for a brief description of the Kabylian landscape and settlement pattern.
4. See Quandt (1973) and Wolf (1973) on the role of Kabylia in Algeria's war of liberation.
5. See Sayad (1994). Ethnographic work on the Kabyles tended to reinforce these stereotypes. See Reed-Danahay (1995) for an analysis of Bourdieu's ethnographic work on the Kabyles whom he describes as an example of "traditional," "nonliterate," "classless," "undifferentiated" society. The irony is that Kabylia was the first region of Algeria where school education was introduced.
6. See Favret (1973). For a lively account of the educational system in colonial Algeria, see the autobiography of a Berber woman (Amrouche 1988). This remarkable woman was born in a mountain village in Kabylia, the illegitimate child of a widow. To save her from persecution, she was sent to a Catholic mission where she was baptized. Amrouche was one of the first Berber girls who attended French school. At sixteen she married a young Kabyle schoolteacher and bore eight children. Amrouche was devoted to Kabyle poetry and songs. At the request of her children, she wrote the story of her life in France in 1946. As an outsider she married another outsider and remained an outsider, "an eternal exile . . . the Kabyle woman who has never felt at home anywhere."
7. See Wolf (1973: 232–233) and Mahfoufi (1994: 33). While writing this paragraph, I received a letter from a young agronomist from Tizi Ouzou applying for a scholarship at the Dutch research

school in which I am involved. His Kabyle identity is explicitly mentioned in his letter (February 22, 1996).

8. The opposition involving mutual stereotyping between mountain dwellers and people of the plain is an ancient one in Mediterranean history (see Braudel 1976). The Berber-Arab opposition partly coincides with the mountain-plain dichotomy.

9. *Nif* means nose, an important part in the physiognomy of honor in North Africa. For instance, when he got into a conflict with his neighbor "my honor was tarnished by my neighbor's infamous insults *in the presence of my sister*" (p. 159, emphasis added).

10. See Quandt (1973) for an analysis of this problem. For an interesting case of an intellectual of Kabyle origin who negates his ethnic background, see Bennoune (1985). He wrote a very interesting personal account of the predicament of being an "indigenous" anthropologist in a developing country. He was born and raised in a peasant mountain village. At the age of sixteen, he was forced to migrate to the city in search of work. He then followed the footsteps of his brothers and father by joining the Army of National Liberation. He spent several years in jail where he received most of his basic formal instruction, but where he was also tortured. After independence he studied in France and the USA where he took a PhD in anthropology. Bennoune stresses the betwixt and between position of the Third World anthropologist: "Thus, he is subjected to a double alienation: from the majority of scholars who constitute the international anthropological community and from an authoritarian bureaucratic environment within which he exercises his profession in his own Third World country; an environment characterized by a systematic anti-intellectual attitude of the regime" (p. 363). In his political economy of Algeria (1988), he does not even mention Kabylia as a distinct region.

11. See Redjala (1994) for an overview of events.

12. See *The Economist*, 15 October 1994, p. 56.

13. I treat Djura's two booklets as one work. See Khellil (1979) for a general overview of the socioeconomic and demographic background of Kabyle emigration to France and the links between Kabyle immigrants and their home region. In France, many immigrants discover freedom and become politically

conscious. At the same time, they cherish nostalgic recollections of the warmth of the Kabyle home in their native village. Also see Lacoste-Dujardin (1992) on young North African women in the *banlieus* of Paris. Their experiences are highly diverse regarding relationships with parents and brothers, knowledge of Islam and their country of origin, activities outside their homes, attitudes towards men and sexuality, images of marriage and motherhood, and problems of identity. A common theme is the tension between individual aspirations as young women in France and their parents' desire that they become good women according to the traditional North African model. This tension is omnipresent in Djura's autobiography.

14. Most of the chapters in this book deal with similar themes. Also see Benson (1993).

Chapter 5

Leaving Home: Schooling Stories and the Ethnography of Autoethnography in Rural France

Deborah E. Reed-Danahay

> I finally realized that, without meaning to, but by living in schools, I had driven myself out of my natural environment
>
> Pierre-Jakez Hélias, *Le Cheval d'Orgeuil*

In an essay entitled "Homemaking," the novelist Jamaica Kincaid, a native of Antigua who now lives in Vermont, reflects upon the meanings of "home." As I read her essay for the first time while working on an earlier version of this chapter, one statement she made was particularly resonant: "Everybody who accomplishes anything leaves home" (Kincaid 1995). This sentiment has implications for anthropology, autobiography, and autoethnography, at least as practiced in the Euroamerican contexts in which I live and work. For the two French writers whose life stories I discuss in this chapter, the process of becoming educated leads inevitably to a departure from their rural villages. Their narratives center around the process of "leaving home." There are parallels in the process of becoming an anthropologist. It has long been a given in the field of anthropology that every *anthropologist* who accomplishes anything, in Kincaid's words, "leaves home." We ethnographers have, therefore, tended to locate fieldsites elsewhere, away from home. The concept of an "anthropology at home" (Jackson 1987; Messerschmidt 1981) has emerged as a recent preoccupation in our field, even though it is not an entirely new development. The growth of interest in home or native anthropology represents a questioning of the dominant thinking in anthropology that you must leave home to do good ethnography.

American anthropologists who seek academic jobs are also, however, subject to a related trend associated with home-leaving. As is the case with all academics, geographic mobility is expected for employment in our profession. Those who are not willing to move for jobs are often severely limited in their opportunities and may have to leave academia altogether. Many anthropologists find themselves living in unfamiliar settings where they have obtained teaching positions. The image of the academic in Ann Beattie's novel *Another You* (1995: 4), who finds himself "driving his car along a slick winter road in a place where he never intended to live," represents this common experience. The displacement of the intellectual in modern life has been chronicled by many.[1] Clifford Geertz (1983) writes of "the exit from Eden," a process in the United States through which Ph.D.'s are thrust from elite institutions into lesser colleges and universities where they get teaching positions, following a trajectory from center to margin. A similar process occurs in France, where intellectuals trained in Paris all too often get teaching positions in the "provinces" and yearn for the elite job back in Paris (cf. Bourdieu 1984). It is commonplace in contemporary life that "home" becomes a nostalgic term, perhaps even replacing "community" in its emotional importance.[2] Other factors of migration, such as poverty, war, or famine, also lead to the cultural displacement and exile associated with leaving home. Here, however, I am concerned with the cultural and geographical displacement associated with formal education and professional trajectories – an underexamined phenomenon.

Given our own dislocation as academics who have left "home" (however defined), it is not surprising that anthropologists are now turning to autobiography, to a search for origins and an explanation for the trajectory taken. Ruth Behar explicitly addresses this issue in her book *Translated Woman* (1993), describing how she began her anthropological career with an ethnographic and historical study in Spain. "There was no link between this topic and my life," she writes (1993: 331). Later, becoming more self-aware about the implications of her Cuban ancestry and ethnicity, Behar turned to the study of a Mexican woman that prompted reflections on the connections between their two lives.[3] Life stories, of anthropologists as well as of their "informants," have now moved toward the center of discourse within anthropology. The life history, while connected to images of "home" and of origins, has also become in the field of anthropology a search for "the past as another country" (cf. Foster 1988; Lowenthal 1985; and also Fabian 1987), perhaps reflecting the loss of traditional, "exotic" fieldsites in the contemporary world.

Kincaid's statement echoes a major theme in the two autobiographical/ethnographic texts from France with which I am concerned in this chapter. In both *Le Cheval d'Orgueil* by Pierre-Jakez Hélias and *Une Soupe aux Herbes Sauvages* by Emilie Carles, "home" becomes a key symbol. Education plays a major role in the narrative construction of "leaving home," and, in each case, the place that was left behind – "home" – becomes the object of the ethnographic gaze.

The Ethnography of Autoethnography

> The affectionate and touching portraits are not just of one family . . . but of a whole people . . . . Like that faintly sweet strong apple liqueur, this book should be savored slowly. . . .
>
> Neil Pickett, *The New Republic*
> (Jacket blurb for *The Horse of Pride*)

> A vibrant, uplifting account of a tough, independent woman's life . . . a personal hymn to a France that exists no more.
>
> *The Wall Street Journal*
> (Jacket blurb for *A Life of Her Own*)

Emilie Carles and Pierre Hélias, writing in a genre of French rural memoir, chronicle French folk culture as well as their own experiences growing away from these origins. By examining the differences as well as similarities between the two texts, the influence of region, gender, and eventual trajectory for these two figures in twentieth-century France can be traced. The overarching influence of the French educational system, and its ideological assumptions, can also be unpacked from these texts. They convey and encode important messages about what it is like to grow up in rural France and become an "educated person." Because Hélias and Carles position themselves as authentic, native voices for rural France, their texts, furthermore, display themes currently under debate in wider fields of scholarship about the authority of outsider vs. insider.[4]

Le Cheval d'Orgueil and *Une Soupe aux Herbes Sauvages* are not marginal texts by obscure regional authors, but, rather, mainstream popular books that have sold widely across Europe, North America, and beyond. Pierre-Jakez Hélias is a specialist in Breton folklore and a popular French radio personality who teaches at the University of Rennes. In *Le Cheval d'Orgueil*, he recounts his early life from childhood to young adulthood, setting it within the context of his family and native origins in the Bigouden area of rural Brittany. This book was immensely popular in France and became the subject of a feature-length film by Claude Chabrol in the early 1980s. In his forward to the English-language edition of the book, the late Laurence Wylie referred to *Le Cheval d'Orgueil* as both "an epic of peasant life" and "an ethnographic description" (Hélias 1978: xi). This underscores the text's position as part-autobiography and part-ethnography, prompting literary critic Philippe Lejeune (1989) to make a passing reference to it as an "auto-ethnology."

Emilie Carles was a primary schoolteacher of peasant origins from the Alps region of southeastern France, who gained much notoriety in later life as an environmental activist in her local region. Hélias and Carles are almost contemporaries: he was born in 1914 and she in 1900. While not enjoying quite the magnitude of fame that Hélias' book elicited, Carles' book was a best-seller in France and, like *Le Cheval d'Orgueil*, eventually translated into English and several other languages. *Une Soupe aux Herbes Sauvages* was widely disseminated as an offering of the French book club "France Loisirs" in the late 1970s and early 1980s. In a similar mode of writing to that of Hélias, Carles tells her own story but sets it very much within the context of rural life in her region, giving many ethnographic details. An important distinction between the two books is that Hélias was the sole author of his text, whereas Carles' book is constructed "as told to Robert Destanque." While written in the form of a first-person narrative, Carles' text was transcribed and edited by Destanque, a French journalist. While there was complete silence about Destanque's role in the text in the 1977 edition, later versions address this issue more openly (see Destanque's introduction in Carles 1988 and Goldberger's introduction in Carles 1991). In composing the text, Destanque follows many of the same conventions of popular life history in

France used by Hélias. His intervention in the telling of Carles' life is, however, impossible to truly assess.

In each of these books, the author is describing a way of life at the same time that he or she is telling us about events in a particular life. As such, they may be usefully analyzed as autoethnographies. They stand as ambiguous texts, with a dual ethnographic and autobiographical nature, hard to capture in a world where "ethnography" has been defined as a text about a people and "autobiography" as a text about a person. In conventional understandings of distinctions between these two genres, the author-ethnographer is *not* one of those people described, while the author of an autobiography is the main subject of the life portrayed. As autoethnographies, *Le Cheval d'Orgueil* and *Une Soupe aux Herbes Sauvages* invert many of the usual conventions of ethnography. In an inversion of the standard role of the ethnographer, who leaves home in order to study and record the lives of others, Hélias and Carles left home and then returned to record their own native "milieux." Whereas the ethnographer translates a foreign culture for members of his or her own culture, the autoethnographer translates "home" culture for audiences of "others." However, like most ethnographers, Carles and Hélias are bicultural, located in a border zone, or contact zone, (see Warren, this volume, and Pratt 1992) between cultures. Each writer has peasant origins, but has become an educated, literate cosmopolitan whose narrative expresses both desire and regret about leaving home. I will focus on these texts as "schooling stories" here, because the process of becoming educated is so intricately connected to the process of leaving home for these authors.

During the twentieth century in France, there has been immense popular interest in peasant and working-class life histories – called "temoignages," "memoirs," or "récits de vie."[5] While these flourished in the 1970s, a period of intense preoccupation with rural life on the part of urban French, they continue to appear in print. As Philippe Lejeune (1989) points out, these texts vary in authorship, from the "as told to" genre (as in the case of Carles' text) to direct authorship by the reputed author (as in the case of Hélias). My interest in narratives of education contained in such published autobiographical texts, especially those which circulate in the wider cultural space of the popular press, is based on the assumption that these both reflect and inform images of the "educated person." Like other types of personal narratives recently studied by cultural anthropologists – such as "thieving stories" (Herzfeld 1985), "hunting stories" (Rosaldo 1989), or "procreation stories" (Ginsburg 1987) – "schooling stories" form a culturally constituted narrative genre that shapes meanings about, and helps interpret cultural behavior for, those who tell and listen to such stories. My research on published texts represents a form of research best labeled "deskwork" (Driessen 1993) or "textwork" (Van Maanan 1995), rather than "fieldwork" in the conventional sense. This work constitutes an ethnography of autoethnography. In this phrase, the term "ethnography" refers to a method or practice (but not a field method – cf. Fox 1991) and "auto-ethnography" refers to a type of text. My working definition of ethnography as method is adopted from Geertz, who has defined it as an "enterprise . . . whose aim is to render obscure matters intelligible by providing them with an informing context" (1983: 152). More broadly, this enterprise can be viewed, in an inversion of Caroline Brettell's (1993) title: "When *we* read what *they* write!"

I was first prompted to consider Hélias' book as "auto-ethnography" in response to the brief remark labeling it as such by Philippe Lejeune mentioned above. A further influence shaping my understanding of these texts is Alice Deck's use of "auto-ethnography" in the context of Zora Neal Hurston's book *Dust Tracks on a Road* (Deck 1990; see also Lionnet 1993). Deck, who considers both Hurston and the Xhosa writer Noni Jabavu as autoethnographers, focuses on what she terms the "bicultural identity" of each, as well as their roles as "cultural mediators." This identity arose partly, Deck writes, through education: "both were educated first in predominantly black primary schools in their native villages and then continued their educations at white institutions" (Deck 1990: 241). Hurston and Jabavu consequently "developed and maintained an interracial and international lifestyle that fostered a bicultural perspective" (Deck 1990: 241). For Deck, autoethnographers are "indigenous anthropologists . . . as concerned with examining themselves as 'natives' as they are with interpreting their cultures for a non-native audience" (1990: 246–247). The autoethnographer, Deck asserts, already has indigenous status, and does not require the "validation" of other social scientists.

Hélias and Carles both present themselves as "indigenous

anthropologists" who, like Hurston and Jabavu, need not rely upon secondary sources in "the literature" for validation. They claim status as the native experts, who have participated in and observed first-hand, by virtue of birth, the sociocultural context described. Neither *Le Cheval d'Orgueil* nor *Une Soupe aux Herbes Sauvages* has a bibliography. Although the English translations of each of the texts received the validation of academia through an introduction written by an American scholar, the French versions did not. These academic endorsements only serve to confirm for an American audience, however, that these are "authentic" French peasant voices. At the same time that they "examine themselves as natives," both Carles and Hélias are aware of their distance from the social origins they record and interpret for a "non-native" (i.e., nonpeasant) audience, which is largely a result of the formal education they have received. Despite Hélias' own claims of a native voice, Carrard (1992) justly remarks that he is "no longer a representative of, but rather a spokesperson for his 'otherness.'"

A brief cross-cultural look at the different marketing strategies for these two books in France and in the United States underscores the cultural meanings specific to France that these books, and their wide popular appeal, represent. *Le Cheval d'Orgueil* and *Une Soupe aux Herbes Sauvages* appeared in French within two years of each other – the first in 1975 and the second in 1977. In France, these texts were marketed to a similar audience, and were presented as memoirs or life histories about "peasant life." Read mainly for their nostalgia value among the French, such values would not translate easily into contemporary American culture. While Anglo-Americans clearly participate in rural nostalgia vis-a-vis France, evidenced by the popularity of Peter Mayles' recent books on Provence,[6] the particular regional interest of *Le Cheval d'Orgueil* and *Une Soupe aux Herbes Sauvages* was downplayed in US marketing strategies. Two different publishers took diverse approaches in order to find a market in the United States. Significantly, whereas Yale University Press, the prestigious academic publisher of Hélias' book in English translation, lists it as an "anthropology" book, the more popular Penguin Books, publishers of Carles' text in translation, lists it as "autobiography" and targets a "women's studies" market. When I asked a representative of Penguin at their display at the American Anthropological Association Meetings held in Washington, DC in 1995 about the different possibilities for marketing Carles' book, I was told that autobiography sells much better than anthropology![7] The time lapse between the translations appearing in English is an important factor in the different marketing strategies. Hélias' book was translated in 1978, only three years after it was published in France. By 1991, when Carles book was finally translated, the terrain of scholarship had shifted, with a growing field of women's studies and heightened interest in women's autobiography. The different translations of these texts signify their ambiguous nature as anthropology/autobiography and the ways in which this was treated in each case. Hélias' title was translated almost verbatim into English: *Le Cheval d'Orgueil* became *The Horse of Pride*. The subtitle was, however, changed: "memoirs of a Breton from the Bigouden countryside" (a verbatim translation of the French subtitle) became "life in a Breton village." The new subtitle de-emphasizes the autobiographical nature of the book and highlights its "ethnographic" interest. Carles' book title was, in contrast, changed dramatically when it appeared in English. The original French title, which would literally translate as "a soup of wild herbs" and had no subtitle, was changed in English to *A Life of Her Own: The Transformation of a Countrywoman in Twentieth-Century France*. Here, the ethnographic interest of folklife evoked in the original title is substituted with a more global, gender-based slant. The introduction to the English version is by Avriel H. Goldberger, a French professor who framed the story in a feminist, literary perspective – hence the title's echoing of Virginia Woolf's *A Room of Her Own*. In his introduction to Hélias' book, Laurence Wylie used a very different framing, accentuating particular French themes and regional ethnographic interest. Another significant difference between the two texts is that Hélias' masculinity is not "marked" by his title as is Carles' gender, and his story is not pitched as one of self-discovery and transformation as is Carles'.

The repackaging of Carles' book, as illustrated through the different jacket designs in a French and English version, is most striking. The 1977 cover of *Une Soupe aux Herbes Sauvages* depicts a close-up photo of the weathered face of a "peasant woman" with unkempt hair and in modest dress: Emilie Carles in old age. She looks happy and peaceful; she appears as the French stereotype of an unpretentious (*simple*), down-to-earth rural person. The Penguin paperback version of 1991 conveys a very different tone for the book titled *A Life of Her Own: The Transformation of a Countrywoman in Twentieth-Century France*. Its cover shows snow-peaked Alps in the background with a small insert photo of a young woman standing on a hillside, looking down in a pensive stance. She is wearing stylish but casual 1930s clothes. The reader presumes that this young person is the "countrywoman" whose "transformation" will be chronicled in the text. On the back cover, a small cameo photo of an older Emilie Carles shows a much more urbane woman than does the French cover photo. Her hair is stylishly coiffed and a sophisticated scarf is draped around her neck. The contradictions between these two versions of Emilie Carles are provocative and tellingly reveal the growing commodification of lives in Euroamerican economies. They also signal Carles' ambiguous bicultural identity – as both French peasant and educated intellectual.

Leaving Home

Le Cheval d'Orgueil and *Une Soupe aux Herbes Sauvages* are both written from the perspective of later life, yet differ in their attitudes toward what is viewed as a lost past. Whereas Hélias regrets what he views as the inevitable changes associated with modernization in the twentieth century, Carles takes a negative stance toward peasant culture and views many changes as positive. As such, the books are almost mirror images of each other, expressing the historical tension and shifting images in France about "the peasant" (see Rogers 1987). As a schoolteacher who eventually returns to teach in her native village, Carles adopts the attitudes and criticisms typical of French teachers toward peasants – that they are "backward," "patriarchal," and "superstitious" (cf. Favret-Saada 1980; Reed-Danahay and Anderson-Levitt 1991). A professor of Breton folklore, Hélias is in a different position and sees himself as a protector of, and advocate for, peasant culture. In a more recent memoir (1990), Hélias refers to himself as a "memory collector," evoking the collection of his own personal memories but also of the collective memory of Brittany.

Another important difference between the two texts lies in the authors' use of the symbols and meanings of regional identity. Breton identity, emphasized by Hélias in his narrative, takes on a much stronger and more coherent set of meanings in the French imagination than does Carles native region of the southeastern Alps. Brittany is a region with a long history of regional activism and of established regional stereotypes well known to most French citizens (cf. McDonald 1989). The southeastern Alps region lacks such a strong regional identity on the national level. Although she is firmly rooted in what she calls her Briançon *pays*, Carles does not make much reference to a regional identity or to a distinctive regional culture. French was spoken at home when Carles was a little girl, so that she did not experience cultural otherness associated with language difference to the same degree as did Hélias, for whom Breton was the language of home and family. When Emilie Carles first went to school, she could speak the language she used at home; for Pierre Hélias, attending school meant learning a new language. Carles makes reference to a more "generic" French peasant culture, not one rooted in distinct opposition to French national identity.

A distinct Breton culture, as a particular regional version of peasant life, permeates all of Hèlias' early experiences. His Breton and Celtic heritage form a vital symbol, one reaching far beyond his natal village and carrying a great deal of cultural capital. These differences in the symbolic weight of regional culture and cultural distinctiveness in the two books affect the relative mix of auto-biography and ethnography in each text. Carles' life story reads more like a standard autobiography, with a backdrop of what is portrayed as a stifling and backward rural lifestyle peopled by uneducated peasants. Her negative stereotype of the peasant stands in vivid contrast to her own identity and to the model of the peasant used by Hélias. *Le Cheval d'Orgueil*, more ethnographic, celebrates Breton folklife and culture, and adopts an image of peasant-as-colorful ethnographic object. The author merges his identity in important ways with such characters. Hélias and Carles are both cultural translators. However, whereas Carles tells about her native culture in order to point in the direction of progress and civilization, Hélias tells about his native culture in order to mourn its inevitable passing. Carles is proud of her active role in the transformation of the French countryside; Hélias ascribes a more passive, almost unavoidable, role to himself, about which he is uncomfortable.

For both Carles and Hélias, the *pays* is "home." This French term can be used broadly to refer to France as a whole, but is more often used to refer to one's particular subregion of origin within the country. The phrase *"mon pays"* is heavily laden with emotion for the French, and when evoked in these two texts, provides a shorthand to symbolize the strong attachment to place in French cultural ideals. Carles preoccupation with the *pays*-as-home becomes linked to her eventual return, after some years of absence, as a schoolteacher who can help to transform and modernize the region. Her *pays* is the village where she grew up and the countryside around Briançon. For Hélias, who has traveled farther both in space and in professional credentials than has Carles, *pays*-as-home is linked to a nostalgia for a world that has been lost. The Bigouden subregion of Brittany is Hélias' *pays*, not Brittany as a whole.

In each book, schooling looms large, representing a form of "otherness" to the author during childhood. The transformation from the experience of strangeness to that of familiarity with education deeply marks the lives of these authors. In French schools at the turn of the century, the Ferry laws established mandatory and free secular education for all primary school-age children, and schools were built in each township. The self-ascribed "civilizing mission" of teachers in the national educational system brought the French language to non-French speakers and tried to spread middle-class values of citizenship and morality to peasant households.[8] The school represented forms and styles of behavior and meaning that were often foreign to rural folk. Carles informs the reader of attitudes toward education among her people: "they had a morbid distrust of school – school took away their farmhands – so in self-defense they said it was a waste of time, and you only learned nonsense; but it was obligatory so clearly they had no choice" (1991: 37). In Carles' village, there seems to have been only one school – the public school. But in Brittany, where Hélias grew up, there were always two schools – the Catholic school and the public school. Which one the family sent their children to indicated political allegiances of either White (conservative, Catholic school) or Red (Republican, public school). Even though his parents were Catholic, Hélias was sent to the public school, where he learned French for the first time. He vividly portrays his experiences in school: "The first day of school was, of course, approached with apprehension. We would have barely crossed the threshold and there we were, in another world." (1978: 143)

Schooling facilitated the distancing from social origins that allows the life stories of both Hélias and Carles to become ethnographic. A crucial moment in each story is when the choice is presented for the child to continue schooling beyond the obligatory primary-school level. Whereas primary schools were established in each township by the national educational system, secondary schools were located only in large towns and cities. To continue schooling, for the French rural child, meant leaving the village. To enter secondary schooling was, quite literally, to "leave home." Carles and Hélias tell the story of their schooling differently but share several themes. Both authors describe the possibility of secondary education as having been offered from "above," from educational authorities who recognized potential in each child and came to their parents to present this opportunity. Yet their gender, region, and family circumstances differently affected family attitudes and strategies toward higher education. Hélias' father was a clog-maker, who had gone to school himself. The eldest child in his family, Hélias was encouraged by both his parents and his grandparents to attend school and to do well. Although Hélias himself never explicitly acknowledges this factor – that there was no farm to pass on in his family, since his father and paternal grandfather were artisans – it must have been an important influence on the family's support for education. He describes his early schooling in a village torn between the Reds and the Whites. Since his father supported the Reds, young Pierre was encouraged to attend the public school and to learn to speak French. Despite his family's urgings, however, Hélias portrays himself as a child who was reluctant to learn French in a local region of Breton speakers.

Hélias writes that when his grandfather told him of the opportunities he would have when he left the village knowing how to speak French, he replied: "But all I ask is to stay here, Grandfather." The old man answered back: "Exactly. Because you still don't know any French. The day you speak it as well as Monsieur Le Bail [the mayor], you'll want to go somewhere else" (1978: 134). Hélias portrays a scene in which the local priest and the local mayor each lobby his parents about his future education. Hélias' father, influenced by the mayor, had already decided that "the only proper ambition for a Red was to be a teacher" and knew that Pierre would receive a scholarship to attend high school in the city. In telling about this period of his life, Hélias denies much agency on his part about leaving and describes the process as one in which he was inevitably swept up. Later in the narrative, long after having been educated up through the university level in the French educational system, Hélias expresses nostalgia and regret for his estrangement from his origins. Only on rare occasions in the book does he hint at his own desire to leave. At one point, speaking in veiled terms of "others" from his town, he writes: "One couldn't always withstand pressure from a society whose main ambition . . . was to continue precisely as it was. Anyone who didn't like it had only to leave; a train was soon to come through the town every day" (1978: 289).

In the last chapter of the book, entitled "The New Testament," Hélias returns to the theme of his experiences away at school and tellingly speaks of his dual identity, the "bicultural" identity associated with autoethnography. He writes:

> I was then leading a double life and I expect that I always will. I spent three-quarters of the year at the lycée – first as a student, then as a supervisor, a tutor, and a professor, or else I worked at various jobs at night so that I could get my master's degree. The last quarter of the year I spent in my village: I would go back to my mother tongue; I'd cast off the clothes I had been wearing as an intellectual and slip into my peasant surroundings as one slips into a clean shirt . . ." (1978: 309).

Later in the same chapter, Hélias expresses his guilt and ambivalence about having "left home."

> There was one sure thing: the whole region was in flux. And we were responsible for all the agitation, we who were studying elsewhere and would come home for our vacations behaving like strangers, bareheaded, wearing knickers, and making the kind of revolutionary remarks that bewildered our childhood friends, who were still making every effort to stick to the rules (1978: 313–314).

Hélias' earliest struggles with education occurred at school itself, and he describes harsh schoolmasters and the problems of being a country boy in the urban secondary school. He emphasizes the trauma of schooling, even while he succeeds in the system. Hèlias tells of a teacher who "in moments of rage . . . would grab you roughly by the hair on your temples and at the same time call you every unpleasant name he could dig out of his vocabulary" (1978: 142). At secondary school, in the city, he became acutely aware of his marked status as a rural child, denoted by his different clothing and uses of language.

Emilie Carles tells a different story – her struggles to become educated lay in her family's attitudes rather than in the school itself. She describes the intense enjoyment she experienced as a girl with the acquisition of literacy skills, of learning to read. Carles is deliberate in telling of her early desire to flee the restrictions of village life. Commenting on the drudgery of peasant life, especially for women, she reports that "almost every girl from around here was condemned to a life she had not chosen" (1991: 8). Whereas Hélias distances himself from those who might have desired to flee from the restrictions of village life, Carles places herself squarely in this camp. Motherless from an early age, Carles came from a farm family with several children. Her family was not easily convinced that education was desirable for Emilie. In contrast to Hélias' father, who supported the public schools, Carles' father listened to the local priest, who was distrustful of state secondary schooling. Lacking an education himself (again, in contrast to Hélias' father), Carles' father discouraged her from her desire to become educated. For her part, Carles tells the reader: "I liked school right away." So zealous was young Emilie as a pupil, according to Carles, that she was even chastised by her school-teacher:

> It made my teacher sick to see me reading while the other children were at play, it drove him crazy. He'd come over to me from behind and snatch the book out of my hands. "Go play with the others," he'd say. "You have plenty of time to read later" (1991: 43).

When Emilie performed well in school, the educational authorities came to her house to convince her father to let her go on in secondary school. But her father refused. According to Carles, the principal of the school pleaded with the farmer: "But you have no right to keep her home . . . your little girl does remarkable work and if she goes to school, you will be helping her to get a good position in life" (1991: 44). With the help of other family members, more open to the idea, Emilie and her teachers finally prevailed. She went on to become an educated person, a primary school-teacher. Education has long been one of the main avenues of social mobility for peasants, making Carles' trajectory a familiar story in rural France. Carles describes her strong desire to mold young children. After years of schooling and early posts outside of her native village, she eventually returned to instruct generations of children there before her retirement.

The early distancing from the others at school and in the village which Carles illustrates through the anecdote about reading at school, is a theme lasting throughout her narrative. Hélias writes a different story. He portrays himself as part of the gang of children, and as part of a cohort who left, describing his distance from his origins as a gradual process with which he had some regret. Carles always speaks of "the peasants" as different from herself, and does not portray herself as a peasant in the narrative. While Carles underscores her differences from others who grew up in her village, Hélias tries to downplay his own distance from his social origins. Carles' attitudes toward "the peasants," exemplified by her own father, illustrate her attitudes. In describing her regret that so few peasants took the trouble to read, Carles tells the reader:

> The father I adored was of that race; he had never read a book in his life or even a newspaper. I remember at the time of my marriage, that was one of the things he didn't like about Jean, and he said in all sincerity, as the ultimate proof that Jean was not for me: "He reads too much," thus revealing the source of his fear and distrust. How could they think for themselves? . . .. That's what our peasants were like here; and to all practical purposes, nothing is different, for there have only been material changes . . . (1991: 184).

This attitude towards peasants is reflected in Carles' many statements about her attitudes toward teaching. On the subject of her return to teach in own village, after many years away, Carles tells the reader:

> For me, teaching the children of my own village was the culmination of all that I had dreamed of since I was a little girl . . .. In a backward region like ours, considering the life I led, what seemed indispensable to me was opening their minds to life, shattering the barriers that shut them in . . . (1991: 225).

Despite her cultural and social distance, and long periods in which she lived outside of the region, Carles makes the remarkable statement in her introduction that "All my life I have lived where I was born, in the mountain country around Briançon" (1991: 2).[9] While not entirely accurate, this statement positions her in the beginning of the text as an authentic voice for this region and is meant to lend authority to her autoethnography. Presenting herself as an active agent for transformation from darkness to light through education, Carles identifies with the "civilizing mission" of the school and leaves home in order to join the legions of schoolteachers who themselves perpetuate the distancing of social origins associated with becoming educated in France. Self-righteous in her mission, Carles lacks the self-deprecating humor and ambivalence about leaving home that so marks the voice of Hélias in *Le Cheval d'Orgueil*. Hélias' narrative enfolds as if his life story followed the same trajectory as other changes occurring in Brittany. He describes his education and academic profession in terms of inevitable forces by which he was carried along, rather than as deliberate choices. He thus absolves himself from responsibility for the changes, for the loss of traditions, and is thus able to take on a role of protector and keeper of tradition – a native, indigenous Breton, whose autoethnography is more authentic than the ethnography of the outsider.

Deeply attached to "home," to place, to *pays*, Carles and Hélias adopt opposed stances toward this place of origin. As such, they illustrate the important theme of ambivalence toward rural life characteristic of French culture for centuries. The tension between regional identity/peasant identity and French national culture remains unresolved to this day.[10] Issues of gender cross-cut these other issues in the texts. Carles' story adopts a negative view of the drudgery associated with female farm labor, and she asserts her preference for what she sees as the easier and more fulfilling life of teaching. Written at the height of the woman's movement during the 1970s, *Une Soupe aux Herbes Sauvages* reflects the feminist sensibilities of the time. While this text, in its portrayal of Carles as an ecologist-activist, supports the pro-rural movement also evident at that time, its heroine is shown to be no defender of peasant sensibilities. This text is pro-rural but not pro-peasant. Gender is the main reason, as the life of farm girls and women in Carles' *pays* was perceived by her to be highly undesirable. Carles preserves her femininity in the role of nurturant schoolteacher who returns to the village, but rejects that of *paysanne*. For Hélias, a male who has, in effect, rejected the manual labor of artisanal and peasant life associated with masculine identity, home takes on a different meaning. His text is both pro-rural and pro-peasant, romanticizing the world he has lost. Unwilling to openly reject the lives of his male ancestors, Hélias finds a way out by embracing Breton regional identity and language, and by sentimentalizing his mother and grandmother. For Hélias, the academic and folklorist, masculine authority is preserved through his role as keeper of traditions. An important difference in these texts is that, whereas the role of gender in Carles' relationship to home and peasant life is made explicit in her story, the role of gender is submerged in that of Hélias. The opposite can be said of the role of regional identity in their stories: Hélias is a "Breton"; Carles, the female schoolteacher.

Conclusions

The term "autoethnography" has sometimes been used to refer to a category of counter-narratives, politicized texts that resist ethnographic representation by outsiders (Ashcroft et al. 1989; Deck 1990; Driessen 1993; Pratt 1992). The native voice is privileged as more "authentic" than that of outsider. Lejeune criticizes what he calls the "screen" of ethnographic representation, a problem that, he suggests, can be minimized in life history. He even goes so far as to suggest that by using video recordings of indigenous peoples, we can avoid any obfuscation associated with the written word. Lejeune writes in glowing terms of the *eco-musée* in Creusot, which has been collecting video recordings of French farmers and other locals. Such an emancipatory enterprise, Lejeune writes, will "neutralize the ethnological relationship" (1989: 215).

Perhaps so. But in my examination of the texts of Hélias and Carles, I have not been looking for, nor did I expect to find, an "authentic voice" for French peasants. Despite the self-presentation as authentic, native voices offered by these two autoethnographers, I am skeptical of their claims and of the search for authenticity by readers of such texts. I do not expect that I would find an authentic peasant voice in *any* published life history written by a person of rural French origins that had become a best-seller. Hélias and Carles have much more in common with middle-class academics, I suggest, than with French peasants. And this helps explain the popular appeal of their texts. They illustrate the ambivalence associated with distance from social origins, a preoccupation specific to those who have left home. The attitudes of Carles, the teacher who wants to enlighten her pupils, and of Hélias, the professor of folklore who wants to protect local customs, convey middle-class attitudes about rural life. This does not necessarily detract from their interest either to the general reader or to the scholar. But it is important to see that these are texts mediated by a whole host of conventions of discourse associated with images of education and of rural life.

My ethnographic interest in such texts is located more in the possibility of locating the relationships of power associated with education and literacy in France, than in finding truth in "realist" accounts of peasant life written by former peasants. Schooling narratives in French life histories are associated with the dilemmas and attractions of leaving home. The educational system is so organized that a student who continues in secondary school and beyond *must* leave for the city, *must* be geographically mobile. This geographic mobility is connected to class mobility. The associated themes of both desire and regret about leaving home are central to the stories told by Hélias and Carles, even though they lived at opposite ends of France. That one could find related themes of education leading to social distance in such diverse American texts as Richard Rodriguez's *Hunger of Memory* (1981) or Hurston's *Dust Tracks on a Road* (1942), underscores the universality of these issues in the twentieth century. In the recent posthumously published autobiographical novel *The First Man*, Albert Camus (1995) writes of the attractions of schooling for a poor French boy living in colonial Algeria:

> Only school gave Jacques and Pierre these joys. And no doubt what they so passionately loved in school was they there were not at home, where want and ignorance made life harder and more bleak, as if closed in on itself; poverty is a fortress without drawbridges (1995: 145).

A different perspective to that of many minority writers on education, a call to resist assimilation to dominant culture when acquiring an education, is offered by bell hooks, who describes her own distancing from her family when she went off to Stanford. She writes: "I do not know that my mother's mother ever acknowledged my college education except to ask me once, 'How can you live so far away from your people?'" (hooks 1993: 110) Hooks urges fellow academics to maintain ties to "familial and community backgrounds" and suggests that "education as the practice of freedom becomes not a force that fragments or separates, but one that brings us closer, expanding our definitions of home and community" (1993: 111). I bring in hooks' perspective here to counter the more common, pessimistic view of the dilemmas facing those who, through education, leave home. The educational narratives of Hélias and Carles cast the experience of becoming educated as one that necessitates the estrangement from one's native "culture," whether or not this is viewed as a negative. According to hooks, this is precisely the view fostered by ruling groups – that assimilation is necessary. She attributes the popularity of Richard Rodriguez's *Hunger of Memory* among white people in America to this assimilationist perspective. Like Hélias, Rodriguez chronicles the distance from home culture that comes with education in the dominant language, Emilie Carles' story offers an enthusiastic embrace of dominant French culture, which she sought to acquire through education, and, consequently, more obviously supports a mainstream view than does Hélias'. However, even though Hélias bemoans his estrangement from Breton culture and writes of his "double identity," he offers little insight into the possibilities for resistance to this process. Each text, in its own way, underscores the inevitability of leaving home and presents a binary choice (either stay with your people or become educated and leave) for the individual from a culturally subordinate group.

The attitudes and values conveyed by those who have become educated persons and returned to the village in their memoirs, often construct dominant, master narratives of schooling and schooling experiences – *not* counternarratives of resistance. Those children who stayed behind in the village, either by choice or by circumstance, would no doubt tell very different stories from those of Carles and Hélias (cf. Reed-Danahay 1996). The problem for anthropologists is that "those who do not write" (Lejeune 1989) do not write autoethnographies. Their autoethnographies, which may be oral narratives, may very well form counternarratives, as well might those autoethnographies associated with nativist movements or ethnic activism (see Warren on Montejo, this volume). But best-selling published life histories, the auto-ethnographies by people like Hélias and Carles, represent the kinds of stories that educated, literate people like to tell themselves about the meaning of education and of rural life. So here I return to our *own* preoccupation of late with autobiography that I mentioned in the beginning of this chapter. In the current search for authentic voices, it is important to recognize the existence of multiple native voices, colored by social position, location, and gender. It is not only in anthropology that the blurring of boundaries and blending of voices (see Brettell, this volume) occurs; the blurring of the boundary between native and outsider is also present in the autoethographies by Carles and Hélias considered here.

Notes

1. In his recent book on *Representations of the Intellectual*, Edward Said (1994) sees many advantages to exile for the intellectual, particularly in his chapter on "Intellectual Exile: Expatriots and Marginals." See also Gilroy (1993) on African-American intellectuals living in Europe, and Tokarcyz and Fay (1993) on working-class women in the academy.
2. Several recent interdisciplinary, edited collections have taken up the theme of home and identity. For example, *Names We Call Home: Autobiography on Racial Identity* (Thompson and Sangeeta 1993); *Traveller's Tales: Narratives of Home and Displacement* (Robertson et al. 1994); and *Displacements: Cultural Identities in Question* (Bammer 1994).
3. A similar experience is related by Greg Sarris (1994), who underwent a process of self-discovery when working to collect the life history of a Pomo basket-weaver. I would like to thank Ken Roemer for this reference.
4. All of the papers in this volume deal in some way with the issue of native vs. outsider voice and its delicate complications (see Motzafi-Haller, Herzfeld, and Warren in particular). The recent controversy between Sahlins and Obeyesekere, and its wide appeal within anthropology, encapsulates the dilemmas (see Obeyesekere1992, Sahlins 1995, and Geertz 1995).
5. Mary Jo Maynes (1995) has recently drawn from this rich corpus to discuss the formation of working-class identity. In my own research, I have uncovered over fifty regional memoirs written within the past few decades dealing with rural childhoods.
6. Mayle's best-selling titles include *A Year in Provence* (1991) and *Hotel Pastis* (1993).
7. It was interesting for me to see that both of these texts were on display at the AAA meetings in 1995 when I first delivered a

paper upon which this chapter is based, indicating a continued market for them among academics.

8. There is a significant literature on the nineteenth-century history of French rural education. Classic works include Furet and Ozouf (1982), Heywood (1988), and Weber (1976); see also Reed-Danahay (1996) for a local study.

9. This is similar to claims made by some Corsican writers (Jaffe, this volume).

10. See Reed-Danahay (1996) and Rogers (1987).

Chapter 6

Narrating the "I" versus Narrating the "Isle": Life Histories and the Problem of Representation on Corsica

Alexandra Jaffe

Introduction

In this chapter, I explore the social context of first-person narrative on the French island of Corsica. The works that I consider do not fall neatly into any one genre: some are autobiographical, some are fictional autobiography or biography, some are simply ambiguous. The authors' intents are no more homogenous. While some may have set out to write an "ethnic autobiography," for others, the ethnic dimension may have been subordinate to the urge to recount a particular life or to give artistic voice to the universal, rather than the particular. Of course, individual texts may be written with more than one of these aims in mind.

Given the heterogeneity of the format and purposes of these texts, this analysis is not so much about different ways of representing the social as it is an examination of the tension and interplay between the individual and the social in Corsican writing about the self. The focus, in this chapter, is on the politics of self-representation in Corsican texts. As Reed-Danahay points out in the introduction to this volume, this facet of "autoethnography" flows out of the postmodern abandonment of the idea of pure objectivity, and recognition that all writing is "writing for" (a purpose) and "writing in" (a particular social, cultural, and political framework). It therefore involves the study of both the production and consumption/reception of writing: in the Corsican case, I examine the ways in which meanings of texts are forged and debated by both authors and audiences. Thus I will explore, in these various texts, how the social/political pressure on the Corsican writer to be culturally "authentic" and representative, conflicts with and sometimes mutes or devalues the complexity of multiple, ambiguous identities that is an inevitable part of the experience of "minority" identities. While, as Reed-Danahay points out, autoethnography has been sometimes seen as an alternative to a stance of ethnographic realism, this chapter also serves as a useful reminder that native ethnographers and writers are no less subject than outside anthropologists to representational politics and dilemmas.

This pressure exists because the issue of Corsican identity is charged with cultural and political significance. As a French ethnic minority, Corsicans are extremely sensitive to how they are viewed from "the center": mainland France. French images and stereotypes about Corsicans have been largely negative, and even among those Corsicans who resent and would like to resist the negative social and economic consequences of their status within the dominant culture, there still seems to be a strong desire to rehabilitate the negative image. Secondly, there is the influence of Corsican nationalist/autonomist ideology, since nationalist claims for greater political autonomy are based (in keeping with a long European tradition) on the assertion of a unique and authentic cultural identity. Finally, the very smallness of Corsican literary production (particularly in the Corsican language) intensifies the social significance of individual texts and the way in which they represent Corsicanness to both the outside and the inside.

Four Brief Stories

ONE: Summer, 1994, at a meeting of the jury that had chosen that year's Corsican literary award winners. Not surprisingly, the assembled writers, academics and other "*culturels*" were discussing the health of Corsican letters. Marie-Jean Vincinguerra, president of the jury launched the question: Was there a real Corsican literary criticism? Now that they had a certain corpus, were they poised to be more ruthless, rigorous in their assessment of Corsican texts? A literature, he said, was not just anything anyone writes, there was an issue of quality. Called on to comment, a literary journalist immediately disqualified his texts as true literary criticism, saying all he did was write a short description, followed by some extracts that rendered the sense of the book, and a few more or less bland compliments. "It is not," he said, "that I do not mean what I write, but after all why go out of your way to hurt someone in an almost familial circle?" "That is the problem," interjected Vincinguerra, "a literature and its criticism must be the voice of the people; it should be a voice that can say anything. The unsaid that hovers in the background of both the production and review of Corsican literary works is one of the things that will stop us from ever having a real literature."

TWO: 1989. A prolific poet and editor of the island's first literary journal published a Corsican translation of Jules Romains' book *Knock*. He had picked this text, as he made explicit in a later interview (Franchi 1992), because it was well-known to every schoolchild. This insured its pedagogical value in the teaching of Corsican: as they read the Corsican version, readers would be able to compare it to the ghost of the French one they carried in their heads. This would highlight what the process of translation has highlighted for him: the cultural and linguistic specificity of the Corsican language. He was clear: the French text is a "pretext" for an exercise in linguistic awareness.

But the translation was not read in these terms. In one review, all translation was interpreted as:

> a dangerous symptom of a serious psychological complex that keeps Corsican literature in a state of infantile dependence on its French "big sister" . . . a destructive force which prevents it from finding its unique voice . . . with Corsican creation in crisis, translation is an evasion of the facts: the language is moribund. It is premature to waste time and energy on translating foreign works while Corsican literature is only in its first stammerings (1989: 52).[1]

In a letter to the editor of the magazine *Kyrn*, which reviewed the book, an angry reader wrote in to amplify on this theme, stating that the "soul of the nation" was best served by documents created in its own language, and called translation "imported foreign philosophy, the reproduction of outside identity." He concluded: "If Corsican culture is sterile, then better not to deceive ourselves with translations, and to wait with patience for future literary harvests of genuine identity" (*Kyrn* 1989 293: 1). The editor of the literary page in this same magazine also suggested that most translations from the French were a "trap" into which minority languages in "diglossic" situations were often lured. Like the other critics, he assumed that the primary motive for translation was to prove the value or raise the stature of the language in the idiom of power. *"Scrivi tu è scrivi toiu, ô Ghjuanghjasè,"* (Write of yourself and of your own, oh Jean-Joseph) he wrote, advising Franchi not to waste his considerable creative talents on more translations (Fusina 1989: 61).

THREE: Francis Aïqui, half Corsican, half Scottish, born in Paris and educated in London, is a playwright and director in Ajaccio. One year, he adapted two plays by John Synge. The first was *Riders to the Sea*, which he transplanted to the Corsican peninsula and performed in Corsican. The Irish keeners were replaced by Corsican women singing the traditional funeral *lamenti*. The second was *The Turkish Wedding*. He had been struck, while in Scotland, with the unique character of Scots English and wanted to put on stage its Corsican parallel: Corsican French. He commissioned several writers and linguists to translate Synge's dialog into a French that had Corsican sentence structure and idioms. On the nights of the performance, his audiences were not attuned to the cultural and linguistic subtleties of these adaptations. One set of people came for the Corsican play and then left. Another set showed up only for the play in French. These divided audiences always found room to take him to task. "Why don't you do more plays in Corsican?" one would ask. "Why do you do so many plays in Corsican?" said the other.

He told me that his repertoire, even if it was not in Corsican or written by Corsicans, was almost always relevant to the island, although there had been an exception. This was his performance of *The Dumbwaiter* which he did, he said, just because he wanted to do it. But he was amused to see that in one of the nationalist newspapers, *U Rimbombu*, the reviewer wrote about how relevant it was to the current situation. Of course, he said, it was in the sense that the play deals with universal themes: alienation, loss of meaning, love, hate, war, etc. But there you had it. "Corsica isn't the world," he said, "but Corsicans react as if it were."

FOUR: 1989. I had been on Corsica about a year when I got a phone call from the president of the CCECV (the Corsican Regional

Assembly's Council of Communication, Culture, Environment, and Quality of Life). The star of the television show *"Du Coté de Chez Fred,"* Frédéric Mittérand, who often vacationed on Corsica, had decided to do a special program on Corsican language and culture. One of his producers, a Corsican, was on the island rounding up the cast, and I had been designated as the representative of university students of Corsican. When I hesitated, uncomfortable with taking the place of a Corsican student, the CCECV president told me that he had cleared this with the student union, which was originally against the idea but had been convinced that sending me packed a worthwhile symbolic punch. So I went. I flew to Paris with the rest of the group and dutifully discharged my appointed role, with no illusion that it had anything to do with me personally. An outsider – particularly one from a country with a language and a culture of power – who had taken the trouble to come to Corsica and learn the language, legitimated the language and its study to a French audience. It was the reception by this audience that occupied the Corsican organizers' thoughts from the outset.

I knew this, going in. I also knew that the fact that Mittérand was sympathetic to Corsica in general was important. This sympathy was evident in the format of the show and its questions. The atmosphere was convivial, positive. But I could not help but be struck, during the broadcast, by the profusion of outdated and stereotypical images of bandits, women in headscarves, donkeys – during one break in interviews with guests, a clip from a very old film on the vendetta was aired. I wondered to myself what people would say about all of this. I anticipated a vigorous and critical response, given how much of a stake people seem to have in the nature of this representation of Corsica.

When I returned, I heard nothing. Not from my friends and neighbors, not in the press, not in academic circles. The prickly sensibility of this island, always vigilant to spot the smallest slight from the continent, was nowhere in sight.

The Politics of Representation

In all of these stories, what is at issue is the politics of representation in a small, minoritized, stigmatized culture with a tiny core of literati. Their messages seem at first to be contradictory, irreconcilable. You can write *anything*, and no one will say anything bad. You *can't* write anything without someone criticizing how you represented Corsica.

What they have in common is this: in the public analysis of representations of Corsica, polyvalent texts are made monovalent; the multivocal is interpreted as univocal. And the one story that they are allowed to tell is not a nuanced, individual one. It is collective. In Story One, a piece of literature could not just be written off because it contributed to a such a small corpus, because it was a resource in such short supply. At this point in the short history of Corsican letters, it is hard for anyone to feel that they can afford the loss of one author, discouraged by harsh criticism. In Story Two, the social meanings attributed to the translated text had nothing to do with the text itself or the effect that reading it might have on the linguistic or cultural consciousness of its readers. The key, and only, framework within which it was evaluated by other cultural militants was the extent to which it did or did not assert a literary identity for Corsican which was independent from French criteria of value. The translator Franchi was criticized for the very same reason that some authors are spared: building up a Corsican literary corpus was seen as the key to establishing status and legitimacy for Corsican as a written language. As such, it was a moral imperative. Franchi, himself, was a scarce resource: as an author who can write, and write well, in Corsican, he was enjoined to use his talent for what was seen as the public good. In the case of the playwright Aïqui, it was the choice of the language of production that served as the primary or sole criterion of judgment by a certain sector of his audience. For some, the exclusive use of Corsican in public domains dominated by French was the same kind of moral and political imperative as building a Corsican literary corpus. Like the translator, Aïqui was seen as a traitor when he strayed from this narrow path. And his story also shows the extent to which all art on Corsica is assumed to be self-referential; Corsican particularity weighs so heavily in the popular consciousness that other possible artistic messages are occulted. In my own experience on the TV show, the political symbolism of me, an outsider in the French context, completely overshadowed my ambiguous status in the Corsican context. And, the positive overall tone of the program was yet another valuable and scarce resource that drove all other possible readings off the public stage.

The Social Bases of Representational Demands

These stories allow me to suggest that there are few narratives in Corsica that cannot be considered autoethnographical. You cannot write the "I" without that "I" being read as the "Isle," as a representation of the collective, cultural identity. This is particularly true of autobiographical works, but it is also the case for other genres (fiction, history, poetry) that do not make any explicit social-scientific claims. Ottavi sums this up nicely:

> the critic and the writer are both viewed as spokesmen, whether or not they want to be . . . in the case of Corsica, any piece of writing that evokes Corsica is immediately fixed and evaluated by a community that is extremely concerned about what is said about it . . . the novelist who writes about Corsica or even who situates all or part of the novel in Corsica will be perceived as someone who is speaking on behalf of the island. From this moment on, he is no longer heard as an [individual] consciousness reflecting a personal sensibility and point of view, but as a public voice of a community which does not have, or has not made use of a public voice (1992: 8).

The politics of representation faced by Corsican writers is rooted in a set of social expectations and experiences that structure the way that Corsicans think and talk about their identities.

A Visceral Bond

The following excerpts give a sense of the intimate and exclusive bond between the I and the Isle that permeates most Corsican narratives, both literary and informal – even those that do not paint an idyllic picture of the island. In many Corsican texts, the I and the Isle are inseparable: "But if there is more than one way to get out of a city, you cannot fool an island – if you do tear yourself away, it is never without irreparably breaking something deep within you" (Rinaldi 1974: 204). This attachment is often presented as a visceral, even sensual kind of identification with the physical space of the island, the *Terre*:

> The maquis is lodged in me. It encircles and isolates me in this tower . . . only the sea is outside of me . . . My *terre* too is unable to escape what is woven in me when I imagine her, she too, like a terrible

set of shackles that envelopes me in chains so tight that I cannot undo them. In contrast to the sea that will never be able to seize me (Mitchell-Sambroni 1991: 11).

Elsewhere, the same author writes: "If I have been able to get far away from [the island], I have never been able to take a step forward without conserving its image in me . . . everything I wrote was a path that I took, despite myself, to get back to the island (Mitchell-Sambroni 1992: 124)." Poli writes:

> It (*la terre*) becomes indispensable for [the Corsican]. He does not say that it belongs to him, he says he is "of" it. Look at what happens off the island when two Corsicans recognize each other, hurry to invite each other over for get-togethers that give them great pleasure but often do not prolong their relationships once they are back on the island . . .. What are they looking for, these people of the diaspora – in these spontaneous gestures? Corsica. Yes, Corsica. They are not meeting some Corsicans, but Her, their island (1991: 62–63).

And Desanti comments that: "A transplanted Corsican will never say, speaking about Corsica, 'I was born *là-bas*'" [there]. He will simply say, 'I am a Corsican, that island is my place' (Desanti 1990: 12).

The intertwining of I and Isle is also dramatically and graphically encoded in a short dramatic piece by Vincinguerra, in which the dramatic voices are labeled "*il*", "*île*", "*îles*" and "*lui*." The fact that the first three are indistinguishable in pronunciation sets up a fundamental ambiguity: in the reader's imaginary ear, it is impossible to distinguish between the "he," or subject, and the island, as well as between the island (singular) and the islands (plural). Even gender is made ambiguous: on one line the feminine "*île*" (island) declares "I dream that I am androgynous." The existence of the "*il*" and the "*lui*" also suggest an unresolved and dual sense of identity for the subject. This symbolic ambiguity is echoed in the content of the text, in which the voices rise and blend, sometimes in conflict, sometimes in harmony, in unpredictable patterns (Vincinguerra 1992).

Geography and Being: Exile and Otherness

This intense connection comes, in part, from the nature of island-ness: the way in which symbolic and geographical boundaries coincide. As Desanti writes, Corsicans are "unified by the sea which defines our boundaries." Corsican soil becomes a "place of refuge," (1984: 17,18) a locus for an "intense intimate life" (Codaccione-Meistersheim 1989: 106). According to Franzini, "the contours of the island provide a real frontier to the imaginary natal soil, sacred ground. This collision between the real and the unreal, is it one of the causes of the unique attachment of islanders to their land?" (1991: 35) The idea of safety and refuge is linked to other potent images of motherhood: hence the recurrent theme of the island as the *"terre mère"* (mother-earth) (Codaccione-Meistersheim 1989: 110; Giudicelli 1984: 190).

The attachment to the island is also intensified by a collective history of departure: since the beginning of this century, Corsicans have crossed the sea to seek education and employment on "the continent" or in the French colonies. In the literature of "exile," the place of the island carries all of the symbolic weight of Corsicanness. In his preface to a book by Maroselli-Matteoli, Desanti writes of his own education in Marseille: "Although not uprooted in a banal sense, I was in a profound way: I was a person who comes to miss the depth of the earth, but who keeps within the form of what he is missing: this substantial and significant something is insularity" (Desanti 1990: 11).

Exile also intensified Corsicans' awareness of their "otherness," since the movement of people from the island to the continent and back brought Corsicans into contact with the images that the rest of France held of them and heightened their awareness of cultural differences, both real and imagined (see O'Brien 1993 for a similar phenomenon among civil servants in North Catalonia). As Culioli points out, continental French discourse always describes Corsicans in extreme terms:

> Heroic or good-for-nothing, with a slothful or aristocratic soul, bandit or man of law, the Corsican has never succeeded in finding his just place on the continent, that of a person like any other, with his specific culture, and good and bad like all the inhabitants of the earth (Culioli 1990: 16).

If anything, the "good-for-nothing" outweighs the heroic in French discourse about the island. Mezzadri (1991: 57) writes that "Our metropolitan neighbors . . . laugh . . . at the archaisms they see in us, sticking to us permanently like manure." During the three-month strike of 1989, in which Corsican civil servants protested the lack of compensation for the high cost of living on the island, some of the intensity and duration and extent of popular support for the strike among Corsicans was a response to reactions from the French government and press that Corsicans identified as part of a history of prejudice. The Corsican monthly *Kyrn* (1989, 248: 17) compiled a list of quotes from the national press entitled "Common Racism." A few of these illustrate the dominant tone:

> "If the cost of living is higher on Corsica, it is because the little thugs racketeer distributors" (*Minute*, 30 March 1989).

> "Corsica will have cost us the skin off our butts . . . our first mistake was to buy it from Genoa . . . let it be independent" *Le Monde*, March 30, 1989.

> "It's an intolerable island – you forget it for a few moments, 55 million people are not by its bedside, and it runs a fever" *Le Monde*, March 19, 1989.

A Political Context

And finally, the sense in which the personal is infused with the collective has been magnified in the last two decades by the political context of Corsican identity. It is political in two senses: first, in that cultural identity – difference or sameness – has been the primary grounds on which actual political and economic relations with the French state have been played out. It is on the basis of an appeal to cultural particularity that Corsican politicians have successfully lobbied for exceptions to France's inheritance laws; it is on this same basis that they have a special statute and were given the first Regional Assembly in France. Secondly, Corsican identity is political in that the nationalist movement has made culture, in general, a prized resource in the battle for increased autonomy. There is no linguistic or cultural activism on Corsica that is not framed, implicitly or explicitly, by the political movement. My original stories show how this political backdrop establishes and demands certain modalities of representation as part of a campaign of resisting France and French, and empowering Corsican.

Exported Images Under Fire

It should be clear that for a Corsican readership, no piece of writing that concerns the island can be neutral. Writers cannot escape the intimacy of their relationship with the reading public, an intimacy born out of a shared relationship to the island. They do not own their representations of the island.

Any representation is subject to this scrutiny. But images that are exported to the French continent, particularly by "exiled" Corsicans, carry an additional symbolic and political weight (as the story about the television show, above, illustrates). Marie Susini and Angelo Rinaldi are two Corsicans who live in Paris, and whose works are a source of permanent discomfort and debate within Corsican literary circles because of the way in which they represent Corsica and their own relationship to it. One of Susini's books is called *La Renfermée, La Corse* (The Closed-in One, the Corsican Woman) and is semiautobiography, semisocial critique. As the title suggests, Susini represents Corsican society as suffocating and oppressive, particularly for women. "I have never been homesick," she writes, "as soon as the plane closes in on the island, I have an immediate desire to flee" (1981: 30). For both Susini and Rinaldi, personal identity is crushed on the island and realized on the continent. At a very straightforward level, Susini in particular violates the requirement for perfect fidelity to the island that requires, as Ottavi writes, that one "only speak about the island in a positive way, therefore the evocation of one's past must be with regret. It is like a shared reservoir that one cannot attack without betraying one's own" (1992: 11). In the preface to her book, Mitchell-Sambroni (1991: 8) presents an imaginary conversation between herself and her big brother that lays out the implications of Susini's failure to claim a visceral link with Corsica:

> "Tell me Mathieu, what is an island?"
> "It's a big rock surrounded by water that will punish you if you disobey it."
> "And what do I have to do not to disobey it?"
> "You have to stay on the rock. You are part of our *terre*. Understand that she loves us with an exclusive love, and that she fears your death less than she fears your betrayal."

At the heart of the betrayal is the issue of continuity of personal and cultural identity in the face of "exile" which touches so many

Corsicans who have left, as well as the family members who stayed behind. The ideal narrative, from one who leaves, acknowledges that departure is betrayal, while affirming that it is not really a rupture of the essential link. For example, Lovichi recalls keeping away from his village for ten years after his relatives died, for fear that he had lost a social history and all grounds for acceptance. But when he finally returns, his welcome makes him feel that it was "as if he had just left the day before." He writes: "Now I am in a position to say to all those who are still in my old situation: Come back! Come back! You can go home, the *pays* never forgets" (1992: 183). From this perspective, we can understand not just the response to Susini, but also why the accounts of Corsicans of the diaspora are so important to the island as a whole: if leaving for any reason is betrayal, then the steady flow of Corsicans towards the Continent and the colonies is a collective history of betrayal. It can be downplayed by insisting, as many do, that the departure was exile: since it was forced, not chosen, it has no effect on individual or collective cultural identity and unity.

Thus it is very important for Corsicans who live elsewhere to be represented and to represent themselves as being authentically Corsican, as sharing the deep connection with the *terre* that they unfortunately do not inhabit. This is the image of identity promoted by some of the works cited above; it is also the dominant theme of representations of the diaspora in the press. "Diaspora?" wrote one journalist, "not in the etymological sense of the term. Corsicans have never felt dispersed since they have always grouped together in communities abroad" (*Corse Matin-Nice-Matin* June 16, 1991). Expatriate associations (*"amicales"*) are also often the subject of Corsican newspaper reports. A typical article about a Puerto Rican group said that it was "making enormous efforts to insure that our compatriots who arrived there several generations back, do not lose their identity" (*Corse Matin-Nice-Matin* June 5, 1991). In newspaper and other accounts of faraway Corsicans who return after a prolonged absence or who visit the island for the first time in their lives, there is often an emphasis on the instant cultural empathy these people feel. I was told, for example, about a Corsican of Puerto Rican birth who had never been to Corsica, but was nurtured on the image of his grandfather on his deathbed, clutching a bottle of water from his native village of Macinaggio. As a young scholar, he returned one summer to the island, was enchanted, and came back to teach at the university for two years. For several years, there was also a very popular radio program called *"Décalage Horaire,"* (referring to changes in time zones) which was a live broadcast of parts of conversations between Corsicans living in faraway places and their relations on the island. The accent, once again, was always on the continued Corsicanness of faraway kin.

To Be "Real" and "True" as a Corsican Text: Critics' Voices

Susini's work is criticized because it cuts too close to the bone: it lays bare the cracks in the collective image of exile and cultural continuity that are far from invisible to other returning Corsicans. There is the pull of the continent, the intense desire to leave which is described below. And then there are the ways in which departure does alter people – the fact that the achievement of an acceptable identity on the continent requires, at some level, an abandonment of the contours of self valued on the island. And finally, there is the fact that the open embrace by those who stay, described by Lovichi, may hide more private boundaries which may in fact exclude the ones who leave. To the extent that the public demands a simple and unambiguous story of the link between exiled Corsicans and their island, Susini and Rinaldi's work draws criticism, because their relationship with their culture of origin is conflicted.

When these authors are evaluated from a politicized intellectual and literary standpoint, they can be criticized for not writing works that present Corsica in greater complexity. Gabriel Xavier Culioli, another Corsican author, has written that:

> Without in any way casting aspersions on their talent, [their success] can be explained by the fact that their vision of the island is particularly attractive and reassuring to continentals. They [Susini and Rinaldi] do not show a combatative Corsica, nor its contradictions, nor the deep causes of its problems. The solipsistic vision – the contemplation of one's navel – that does not disturb anyone (Culioli 1992: 45).

Elsewhere in the same essay, Culioli makes an argument that parallels Vincinguerra's comments about criticism in the opening stories. He writes that "Islanders have a need to be accepted by their community. Now a literature, and in particular, the novel, does not necessarily cast a positive light on the society one belongs to. All of this has to change, or there will not be a Corsican literature" (1992: 44). For this reason, Culioli stops short, in this quotation, from censuring these authors because their images are unflattering. However, if we unpack his last comment about "navel-gazing," he is in fact delegitimizing the purely self-referential text. Such a text, he suggests, deforms the image of Corsica that is projected to the rest of the world because it discourages readers from grasping the connection between the particular of the text (and the particularity of the island) and the universal. It is only in the inclination towards the universal that readers can develop a real empathy with people facing problems of a nature that concern them as well; in its absence, a Corsican text may produce nothing but the titillation of the exotic.

The text that represents only one individual consciousness is also politically defective, according to Culioli. Implicit in his remarks about presenting a picture that colludes with dominant images of Corsica is the knowledge that in the French imagination, what he considers the idiosyncrasies of these authors' personal visions will be taken as representing all Corsicans. From Culioli's perspective, Susini and Rinaldi do not adequately represent what he takes to be the "true" Corsica: a complex, militant society facing problems with multiple and complex causes that include French domination.

Ottavi pursues a similar line of reasoning when he reproaches all the Corsican authors who have written sentimental accounts in which village life is represented as a lost paradise: these accounts fail to express the complexity of the contemporary Corsican experience (1992: 10). Ottavi holds both Corsican authors and Corsican society accountable, for he recognizes that the attraction of the past is forged out of the insistent demand of the collectivity – the island – for total fidelity, total solidarity. The result, he writes, is a sterilization of inspiration and a stifling of the author's "right and sometimes responsibility . . . to rise up against his origins, against his own, against a part of himself (11).

Both Ottavi and Culioli defend the author's right to a personal voice at the same time as they implicitly argue for a set of restraints on that voice by setting up their own, particular criteria of authenticity. Even though these academic views of the nature of the "real" Corsican reality may differ from the simpler popular injunction to write a positive account, they share the conviction that cultural authenticity can be taken as a constant, as a clear and concrete entity with contours that are as tangible and clearly recognizable as those of the island itself.

Complex and Ambiguous Lives

This image of what is real and true in fact conflicts with the way that Corsican identity is often represented in texts about Corsican lives (Susini's and Rinaldi's included). To the outside reader – myself – the thing that emerges most clearly in this literature, is the perpetual tension of Corsican identity – the push and pull between competing images, models of value and self. One of the places in which this is evident is in the attraction and repulsion exercised by the sea (as a symbol of departure) and the continent itself. For example, in his description of his student days in Marseille, Desanti compares the city of Marseilles to the sea: both are "sterile spaces" that he only crosses to get somewhere important (1990). For Mitchell-Sambroni, too, the sea is the cold antithesis of the *terre* and its consuming and jealous love. At the same time, she writes that sometimes "I wanted the sea to take it all away. To rise up and assault our island and swallow it. My *pays* would be nothing more than a simple stone at the bottom of the water" (1991: 13). It is the sea that promises escape from the bonds of identity that are as suffocating as they are reassuring. "The island is without a doubt a womb that is protecting and devouring" (Mitchell-Sambroni 1992: 121).

Even though the word that Corsicans often use to describe their life off the island – "exile" – connotes involuntary departure, the literature about exile clearly shows that the pull of the continent is very powerful. Desanti writes that,

> In my childhood, what we called the "continent" was an "elsewhere." We wanted to go there, sometimes with a violent desire . . . .. We knew, without really being able to conceive of exactly why, that what we were living here depended to a great extent on what happened *là-bas*, on the other side. We had the feeling of dependence and rupture and thus of abandonment and confinement. Then, when the time came to leave, everything was reversed. The relation of the here and the there was turned upside down. The continent, place of "exile" became the "here:" a here that was real and heavy: but it carried the mark of the "elsewhere" that it used to be (1990: 11–12).

In another short biographical account, the author's grandfather finishes high school and spends an idyllic summer working his father's fields and putting off the decision about whether he should continue his schooling or stay to help his father, whose health is failing. In the end, he decides to leave, and enrolls in medical school. The author jumps ahead sixty years, and describes himself as a young man, sitting on a low wall talking with one of his grandfather's companions. He writes, "like many Corsicans of the time, I was attracted to the Continent, people said that you could get good jobs, you got paid every month, our elected officials would find work for us – we said to ourselves 'Laschia corre' and off we went" (Brunati 1992: 42). Graziani, whose nostalgic representations of his Corsicanness are cited above, also describes in detail the attraction and value held by the continent: "My back to the mountain, I looked beyond the sea, towards the continent. I would have to follow my relatives there . . . was it not there that you established a career . . . where the future held out the promise of wealth?" (1986: 17) Success took place on the continent. Corsica was a place of affection but, in the hierarchy of things, affection was subordinated to social and economic advancement. Once on the continent, Corsicans fed their nostalgia in Corsican *amicales*. But they did not in any real way wish to live the life that they had fled.

Just as the island repels and attracts, life on the continent is ambivalent for many Corsicans. The continent is where you can escape the bonds of a small society, escape being somebody's son or daughter, from village X, from party Y. The continent is where you can live, and write, without being "under surveillance." (Susini's theme in *La Renfermée, La Corse*). The experience of Corsicanness can also be more immediate, more emotionally satisfying, less complicated away from the island: the quality of that identity can be constructed far from the exigencies and troubles of everyday existence. The Corsicans who seek each other out and organize dinners and language classes and other events that remind them of "back home" collude in making their brief, recreational representations of the island warm and positive. The continent is where you can live, and write *as an individual* while maintaining and managing your collective identity.

But sometimes, you cannot manage it. In the same way as the sea crisply demarcates the frontiers of the island, images of alterity from the dominant culture circumscribe Corsicans' identity in

France. Graziani writes that "on the continent, a Corsican child remained just that: he was never really from the neighborhood, fully part of where he lived . . . the other children never forgot to remind him that he was Other. 'you're a pal, but you aren't like us'"(1986: 19). Mezzadri writes that even Corsicans who have been in Paris "forever" are "forever strangers. At least, we feel like strangers. Neither from here, nor from there or elsewhere" (1991: 57). Growing up on the continent, for Acquaviva "made me lie, Corsican among the French, French among the Corsicans, and always a stranger" (1984: 40). So, the cost of individual identity is the loss of the link with place that weighs so heavily in the collective representation of Corsicanness. Both Desanti and Mezzadri, above, express this sense of dislocation and personal alienation. What they have in common is the shared sentiment of not knowing who they are, of feeling that they belong nowhere at the same time as they feel that the only place that they belong is on the island. And the fact remains, that despite the approved imagery of a primordial and unassailable Corsicanness, they also live with the fear of being rejected as culturally inauthentic or incomplete by the island community. In their lives on the continent, the specter of rejection by Corsicans is coupled with the tangible stigma of Corsicanness. The achievement of an acceptable social self on the continent requires, at some level, an abandonment of the contours of self valued on the island. The cracks in the collective collaboration in the myth of exile and cultural immutability are not invisible to the returning Corsicans. Mezzadri (1991: 57) writes that "Our village cousins . . . gratify us with a silence of reproach for not being there with them on the island. Their muteness is a pain that strangles the words in its force . . .. It is true, we are deserters." Even if there is no alteration of the signs of Corsicanness, the achievement of modern, isolated identity engenders a set of habits and reflexes which in themselves create a rupture with the society of origin.

These are the complex stories – full of desire and regret vis-à-vis departure – that get read out of the public transcript. Delavalle's fictional autobiographical work *La Terre Partagée* shows how this can affect not just the writer, but the very experience of self. In this book, the protagonist, Antoine, grows up in Algeria. Like most Corsicans, his family returns to their natal village every two years or so in the summer. They return for good when Antoine is an adolescent. He is haunted by the images and memories of his

Algerian childhood, but he finds that they have no place in the here and now of his Corsican life, in which he suffers from a constant sentiment of being different, and somewhat detached. What he has discovered is the silence (*"le non-dit"*) in the collective narrative of identity. Life elsewhere is unspoken, erased from the record. In my own fieldwork, people often represented life away from the island as a parenthesis, closed without comment upon return. This was brought home to me dramatically one day when I was interviewing an elderly couple. I asked the man if he had ever lived away from the island and he said no. His wife jumped in, "What do you mean, no? What about the 25 years you spent in the Army?" "Well," he replied, "I didn't consider them a *habit*."

In the collective narrative, the substance of life elsewhere has no value in Corsican social exchange. Diplomas, titles, rank, prestige – all those can be imported, they are the prizes gleaned from exile. But life elsewhere is nowhere valued as a source of personal identity. Once on the island, one either belongs or does not belong. In Delavalle's story, Antoine grasps this fact, and embarks on a quest for inclusion. The first thing that he does is abandon his social ties with other *pieds-noir* [repatriated former Algerian colonials] and contacts even distant relatives. Hearing them tell about the past, he tried to weave the affective and cultural link with his ancestors that he had been deprived of. But he was unable to shed his Algerian memories. He lived a double identity and remained a prisoner of what seemed to him to be an insoluble contradiction. His efforts to imagine a Corsica he had never known got mixed up with his reminiscences of Algeria, and this disorderly mass of thoughts gave him the unhealthy feeling of being from nowhere (28).

Antoine ends up getting a white-collar job in Ajaccio, where his next strategy in his bid to connect with his Corsicanness involves a voracious consumption of books about the island's history and culture. In one scene, he is pictured in his lonely apartment, reading the ethnographic text *Bergers Corses*, by G. Ravis-Giordani. Alone in a city, engaged with a text about culture, Antoine could not be further from world of the shepherds he is reading about.

Antoine's story dramatizes the way in which a real personal trajectory – a complicated story that spans three different cultures – is stifled, because despite the fact that it is a story that he shares with many Corsicans, it is not one of the authenticated stories of Corsicanness of the collectivity. He has a polyvocal life, but access only to a univocal text to tell and understand that life.

Complex lives, Complex Texts: Toward a Synthesis

How can individuals in their lives or authors in their work succeed in telling a complicated story of Corsican identity? I return, for one example, to the playwright and director Aïqui whom I described above. Although Aïqui cannot escape the desire of his audience to categorize what he does as either "Corsican" or "Not Corsican," he relentlessly refuses those categorizations and tries to keep his audience guessing. He also presents a wide range of themes and modes of representation as "authentically" Corsican. In particular, he stages hybrid linguistic (and by extension, cultural) identities. In his choices of plays that have no particular relation to Corsica, he also insists that Corsicanness, although an omnipresent issue, is not the only thing that might concern Corsicans in their artistic expression.

My second and final example is Jacques Thiers, an academic and author who balances the I and the Isle with great adeptness. In his book *A Funtana d'Altea*, Thiers confronts and confounds both the politics of identity and the politics of expression in ways that confound standard readings. First, Thiers has refused to assign a particular genre to this book, a refusal which one analyst views as a "desire to affirm oneself [as an author] solely as one's essential self" (Fusina 1992: 18). Secondly, he has published the book in three languages: a Corsican original, followed by a self-translation into French, followed by a translation by someone else into Italian. In doing so, he symbolically evacuates the debates that have gone on in Corsican literary circles about the authenticity or value of Corsican literature in French. Thiers presents both the Corsican and the French texts (and by implication, Corsicanness and Frenchness in himself) as equally authentic. He also dedramatizes the political context of reading: Corsican literacy is not presented as a litmus test of political commitment or authentic identity. At the same time, he achieves what is for him an important political goal of presenting the Corsican text as the primary one. The addition of the Italian translation adds another symbolic nuance: by evoking a non-Corsican audience, it suggests that the book has a transplantable theme, that it has both particular and universal significance.

The book is a monologue, a series of conversations, real and imagined, that the protagonist Brancaziu has with an Italian woman journalist, whom he links and fuses in his memory with Altea, a love from his past. As Brancaziu reflects on his life and career as a poet, responding to the real and imagined interrogation of a stranger, he reveals himself as a mass of contradictory and passionate convictions and sentiments. He is, as the author commented in an interview for the journal *Etudes Corses*, dominated by a discourse that he does not master. It is his investment in the discourses of others that allows the conflicts and paradoxes of his nature to emerge (1992).

What is interesting here is that Thiers displaces the authority of the writing "I" by creating a character who demonstrably does not control discourse. Or, put another way, Brancaziu's loss of control of his discourse allows Thiers to rhetorically include himself among those who do not "master the word" – to distance himself as an author from any pretensions of ownership or authority in regard to the representation of Corsican identity. His rhetorical strategy also includes the reader. The underlying message of Brancaziu's struggle to negotiate a self in the eyes of others is that everyone shares in the problem of being "invested in other's discourses." Thiers emphasis on the social construction of identity deculpabilizes Corsicans' inevitable investments in dominant discourses, in French identity. Corsicanness is not primordial, it is not a thing, it is process and movement between various poles of value.

Another way in which Thiers legitimizes a complex and mixed identity in which both dominant and minority models are intermingled, is in his representation of Brancaziu's poetry. Brancaziu characterizes himself as a "dialectal poet." His allusions to his poetry (which is not part of the book) allow the reader to imagine that it is of a sentimental sort, replete with archaic images of pastoral purity. As Thiers remarked in his 1992 interview, this poetry is the exact opposite of the kind of militant literature that he values. Brancaziu disparages Corsican, the language that he writes and speaks in. He is thus the embodiment, Thiers tells us in the interview, of a "dialectal consciousness – slave of hegemonic values." An engaged, or militant writer, says Thiers, must do everything that Brancaziu does not: he or she must "escape the imprisonment of personal memories . . . exorcize nostalgia and particularism in a general definition of corsicanness"(Thiers 1992: 64). Summarized in his later comments, this may seem to be a rather heavy-handed didactic use of Brancaziu as a negative example. But, in the book, Brancaziu is also a sympathetic character. The reader is not led to pity or scorn him; rather, his weaknesses are represented as every person's weaknesses, the author and reader included.

In much Corsican literature, the island – often as an embodied, physical presence – stands in the path of the narration of a truly independent self. In Thiers' work, it is through the narration of a collective life that Thiers as an author seems to find a personal equilibrium, a space within which to have an independent "I". The island is always present in Thiers' account, but individual identification with it is not focused obsessively on place as an embodiment of self, identity, and desire. Rather, the Isle is present in Thiers as a shared process of constructing the self out of both dominant and minority cultures and their competing systems of power and value. Thiers tells a story in which the tensions and contradictions of Corsicanness are not censored out of a sense of social or political obligation, but rather, form the basis of a collective identity in a movement that recalls Frankenberg's elegant analysis of a dialectal play in a Tuscan rural *comune* (1993). In the Tuscan play, in Aïqui's work, and in Thiers' book and translations, authors, directors, and players tap into the power of expressive culture to evoke and manipulate ambiguity while evading single and reductive readings and resolutions.

Note

1. All translations of French are my own.

Part Three

Voice, Representation, and Genre

Chapter 7

The Taming of Revolution: Intense Paradoxes of the Self

Michael Herzfeld[1]

Intersecting Trajectories

Fieldwork brings anthropologists into contact with many styles of self-narration. Those idioms of selfhood that we choose to highlight in our own narratives, or ethnographies, are not necessarily the models that we would choose for ourselves. Indeed, they may celebrate the attraction of opposites or the fascination of the bizarre. Yet they shadow our personal trajectories in ways that can be mutually illuminating. They may have most to teach us when they force us to confront the inevitable dissonance within ourselves at a particular and recognizable type of moment: when the empathy that we feel toward our hosts overpowers our awareness that their most salient values would cause us acute distress at home. I pursue this theme here through three stages of my personal trajectory. Although I have worked with many people in Greece, I choose here to intersect three categories of "field" acquaintances: shepherds addicted to stealing each other's sheep; bureaucrats of various kinds; and a Cretan-born novelist, Andreas Nenedakis, whose biography I have explored as a counterpoint to the more conventionally ethnographic work that I have carried out in Greece (Herzfeld 1997).

This may seem an odd combination; but there are some surprising linkages here. The differences among the people discussed here are constantly subverted by the cosmologies they share: they inhabit the same, or at least overlapping, symbolic universes. In this way they challenge our propensity – which they, too, display in ways specific to their own interests – to seek taxonomic order in the confusion of human experience. What links them is a bloodline – not common descent itself, but the view that common descent is what matters. The impersonal rhetoric of the nation-state as well as many of the behind-the-scenes manipulations of the bureaucrats follow a logic of patrilineal solidarity that also informs the lives of both the novelist and the shepherds whose way of life the novelist's own father had left behind him.

Is this common grounding of the bureaucratic state and its unruly citizenry any more surprising than finding the very same symbolic connections between the principle of the purity of Christian blood (*pureza de sangre*) so jealously guarded by the Holy Inquisition in fifteenth-century Castile and the genealogies of that godless invention, the Darwinian theory of evolution? For that is the shared basis that Davydd Greenwood argues in his magisterial *The Taming of Evolution*. Such disruptions of the conventional separation of rationality from the symbolic and religious possess the capacity for "disclosure" that Crick (1976: 135) attributes to metaphor. I would place my own tracing of both analogy and genealogy between social anthropology (a discipline) and Greek nationalism (a political ideology) – in this case grounded in a common concern with the demarcation between Orient and Occident – in the same conceptual space (Herzfeld 1987). The present essay, in which I explore the grounding of what initially struck me as contradictions or inconsistencies in the self-construction of people I encountered in the course of fieldwork, consequently has its own distinctive genealogy. Experientially, I link it to these larger disruptions of rationalist convention through my own unease: people I liked, I thought, should not hold such unpleasant views, while as an anthropologist I should not feel so repelled by these views – especially in people I liked.

But radically opposed views may indeed share a common genealogy. Disruptive linkages such as Greenwood's tracing of evolutionism and Spanish blood ideologies to a common source show that our personal embarrassment reflects an encompassing intellectual and ideological history. The rationalist defense against these embarrassments is to deny the common history altogether or to place it in the framework of an evolutionary view of social scale. Thus, for example, ethnonationalist strife becomes the expression of irrationality (e.g., Connor 1993; Huntington 1993), a view that completely ignores the common history of modern rationalism and the very imagery of blood on which such arguments depend (see Herzfeld 1992; Lloyd 1990; Tambiah 1989). The rationalist argument ultimately founders on two immovable objects. One is our informants' disconcerting conviction that they, and they alone, are the only true, full representatives of humanity. That conviction mocks our own sanctimonious version of the very same attitude – a version we might call *humanistic fundamentalism* – by exposing the incompatibility of relativism and rationalism, both concepts born of the same Enlightenment impulse to universalism. The other immovable object is the intellectual genealogy I have sketched here: the common ancestry of supposedly incompatible ideas lies in the concept of genealogy itself, symbolized by blood and grounded in the patrilineal, even Abrahamic (Delaney 1990, 1995), models that have given us nationalism *and* the popular models of procreation that continue to dominate much popular science. We cannot afford to be sanctimonious when we meet in others substantial traces of the ideological histories of which we have tried to cleanse ourselves.

Were this simply a matter of self-examination, it might perhaps not take us very far beyond what has already been written about anthropological reflexivity. "Often condemned as apolitical," however, "reflexivity, on the contrary, can be seen as opening the way to a more radical consciousness of self in facing the political dimensions of fieldwork and constructing knowledge" (Callaway 1992: 33). Moreover, if reflexivity "obliges us to confront the moral and political responsibility of our actions" (Okely 1992: 24), by the same token it should give us a more generous understanding of the dilemmas and paradoxes that our informants share with us, and a clearer understanding of how eminently likeable people may entertain ideological positions that repel us. Nowhere is this clearer than in confrontations with official power and especially with the bureaucratic practitioners of nationalistic logic. Awareness of the paradoxes of our own responses to state authority is surely one of the keys to a more comprehensive understanding of the nation-state, that curiously prevalent modern symbiosis of authority and identity that we, like most of our informants, inhabit.

For our ambivalences reproduce those underlying the historical genesis of the nation-state itself. The nation-state is often situated on the cusps of a dilemma that is directly related to the tension between selfhood and authority: founded in revolution against authority, the official national entity must now impose an authority of its own. Whether American "rebels," Greek *kleftes* (literally "thieves"), or Italian *Carbonari*, the mythologized figures of revolutionary zeal must be tamed, lest they give moral force to new forms of insurrection, from petty illegality to political violence against the state. Cooptation is often achieved through a discursive absorption of potentially discomfiting origins: in Greece, the patrilineal organization of the revolutionary guerrilla bands has become a metaphor for the entire people, defined by the common "blood" (Just 1989) that is said to infuse the national character with a spirited love of independence. It is thus precisely as the nation-state discursively translates local-level social discord into national revolution that it tames the internal forces responsible for its very existence. Over two centuries ago the philosopher Giambattista Vico (1744; see Herzfeld 1987: 23–25) showed how the state is always hostage to its own popular, and often violent, origins. These sources of its legitimacy may turn against its leaders when they forget the conditionality of their power. Thus, when the state becomes the source of intolerable brutality, it can be called to account by recastings of the same discourses that it had employed to legitimize itself. Andreas Nenedakis, imprisoned by repressive régimes in Greece, deployed many of his writings to that end; so, too, do some of the Mayan writers described by Kay Warren (this volume).

Intense Paradoxes

Such transformations often display the extraordinary versatility of what Mary Douglas (1970), with a mischievous sense of paradox, has called "natural symbols." Nowhere is this more apparent than in the Greek (and more generally European) symbolism of blood. Blood is one of those material images whose meaning people take for granted. Here the Cretan mountain shepherd, the evolutionary scientist, and the Grand Inquisitor of Castile are on common ground: blood is the single substance through which (usually agnatic) kinship is brought into full substantial existence; this is a secular miracle of transubstantiation, perfectly adapted for the extraordinarily nasty butchery and political repression committed in its name.

In similar vein, Kapferer (1988) has asked how a pacific creed like Buddhism could beget the horrendous violence seen in Sri Lanka, and how ideological egalitarianism could spawn the idiom of racism that prevails in some sectors of Anglo-Celtic society in Australia. Not only does a set of symbols appear to stand for two different things in each case – no surprise, that, in an age where endemic cynicism would probably lead us to imprison a fixed signifier in a museum of curiosities – but it conjoins opposites in a common logic. That logic appears to allow context to turn a principle of human fellowship into destruction, of respect into viciousness, and liberation into repression.

I want here to suggest a specifically ethnographic way of examining, through the conventions governing the narrative construction of selfhood, the *processes* that engender this alchemy, a process through time that, when flattened as a moment of self-identification with multiple pasts, generates an intense sense of paradox. I propose to do so by tracing the trail of blood, as Davydd Greenwood has done from Basque egalitarianism to Castilian *pureza de sangre* and on to neoevolutionist theories of essential descent, from the Cretan highlands to the sophisticated salons of the Athenian literary and art world. In so doing I shall complicate matters still further, for my story is not one of a necessary descent to violence; rather, I hope to show that there are other possible paths.

This is an important move: we must break out of the moral and epistemological determinism that both the logic of the bloodline and some of our more pessimistic projections and experiences – inspired, perhaps, by the horrors of the Bosnian bloodletting – might otherwise seem to require. My purpose, then, is to reconstruct something of the range of the choices open to the agency of the self.

In the process we shall perhaps begin to get a glimmer of how revolutions are tamed, or, rather, routinized, to adopt a more Weberian terminology. Conversely, however, we shall also see how certain individuals rediscover for their own ends the disorderly delights on which the state's projection of an orderly society so precariously rests. Like professional anthropologists (who are often insistently marginal social ritics at home), these autoethnographers find themselves dislocated in a variety of ways from the normative structures of their familiar contexts. I have already noted how the Cretan highland shepherds, famed throughout Greece for their institutionalized practices of feuding and animal-theft, find in their constant opposition to official authority a powerful incentive to decode and manipulate its discourse for their own purposes – a situation that makes them effective and perspicacious theorists of social and cultural life (Herzfeld 1985: xi–xv). Opposition to an official presence makes social theorists of us all. Andreas Nenedakis, a patriot exiled to arid prison islands by régimes whose brutal practices gave him profound insight into the relationship of the inner self with the official state, acquired thereby a truly ethnographic sense of critical distance. This sensibility informs his analytical skill both in decoding the state's excesses of classificatory zeal and in describing the human dilemmas that it conceals.

This, then, is the encouraging paradox of state brutality (or sheer insensitivity): that the internal contradictions, born of a failure to place the state at the service of ordinary people, provoke a sense of categorical failure. In such situations, the state becomes the casualty of its own deep concern with classification. Even when the state is relatively benign, those who – like the highland Cretan shepherds – find themselves opposed to its hegemony for any lasting reason, become adept at the analysis of its discourse. Other alienations (the racism of immigration politics, for instance) provoke the emergence of related semiotic sensitivities. One may thus see similar links between ethnographic analysis and many kinds of social disenfranchisement or marginality. Examples include Driessen's Kabyle migrants, Kideckel's Romanian village ethnographer, and Svensson's prisoners (all in this volume). In counterpoint to those and many other groups' displays of improvisatory skill – of "making do" in the face of formal restraint (Reed-Danahay 1996) – bureaucrats, exercising the self-ascribed right of the powerful to remain personally undisclosed, provide a *basso continuo* of formality and regulation, which does not mean that they do not have similar tales of their own, were they only free to recount them.

In a sense, in exploring such personal reworkings of state symbolism, I am revisiting intellectual terrain already partially traveled, as the mention of Greenwood and Kapferer might indicate (see Herzfeld 1992: 22–23, 62–65). This retracing is deliberate and serves the goal of placing a part of my own intellectual history in a context of comparison with the vicissitudes of the people about whom I write. For in the present exploration I turn back to my own ethnographic interests and visit three different "populations." Here I thus become doubly autoethnographic: I revisit "my" ethnographic sites, here conjoined by the thread of my personal trajectory (a syntagmatic link) while also placing that trajectory in direct comparison with those of the people among whom I have worked (a paradigmatic link).[2]

Three Ethnographies and an Ethnographer

The first of these three contexts is a community of shepherds and farmers in the foothills of Mount Ida (Psiloritis) on Crete, where to own and maintain a flock is to be able to participate in the sometimes violent give-and-take of reciprocal animal-theft. Among these people, responsibility for one's actions is a matter of categorical ascription deftly managed in the agnatic clan politics of a small, intensely social village community – I so describe it because at one point, for a total population of 1,450, it boasted 29 cafés for the exclusive use of its adult males. I mention the logic of feuding principally because the issue of responsibility, or *account-ability*, is central to the kind of comparative analysis that I wish to focus on styles of narrating selfhood and is also an important starting-point in the history of anthropological writings on the self (e.g., Evans-Pritchard 1936; Lienhardt 1961). Indeed, one of the most significant early forays into this terrain was conducted in Greece by my own mentor, John Campbell (1964).

The second population consists of the large, nationally dispersed, and professionally as well as personally diverse community – if I may call it that – of bureaucrats: the very people whom the sheep-thieves most despise, but who, while cordially reciprocating that dislike, have domesticated – not the savage mind – but a revolu-tionary idiom, now represented as nationalistic historiography, based on a highly similar population. This group of people figures prominently, if schematically, in the stories that ordinary people tell about "the system" in order to displace blame for their own failures, a device in which the bureaucrats themselves share (see Herzfeld 1992). Here the self is not (usually) that of the narrator but that of a stereotypical ot icial. Most of the tales told in this arena concern the *denial* of responsibility and the play of excuses, fertile grounds for exploring the official construction of selfhood and its vicissitudes in everyday social practice.

The third constellation is a population of the literary imagin-ation, created by a man whose own origins in the wild Cretan mountains may have been his greatest asset in his mordant decoctions of bureaucratic pretension and of the repressively anodyne representation of the national past in which they are engaged, and that their actions reproduce. The selves recounted here are multiple: men and women, artists and workers, thugs and academics. While the author often writes in the first person singular, these are detached selves that comment ironically on others' foibles but show less interest in promoting their own virtues in some competitive arena.[3]

The novelist himself bridges the worlds of the sheep-thieves, the small townsfolk, and the modernist project of Athens. Andreas Nenedakis was born in 1918 in Rethemnos, the Cretan town where I have conducted research on the politics of historic conservation and on artisans and apprentices. His parents' marriage was arranged as a result of animal-theft between their respective families, an activity that had been at the core of my earlier fieldwork in Crete (see Herzfeld 1985, 1991); his later experiences in Athens as an art gallery entrepreneur placed him in some of the spaces that I was to inhabit many years later. I am currently engaged in writing his biography, a project that allows me to explore, through his public representation of his own and his characters' innermost thoughts, something of the complex and usually inaccessible relationship between collective representation and personal volition. While it has been far from rare for anthropologists to explore novels as a source of insight, the chance to do so with an author first encountered in the course of conventional fieldwork, and with one who is so closely tied to its physical and social contexts, makes for exceptionally direct correlations.

Thus, the three topics I have grouped together here – a community of shepherds, the imagined world of bureaucrats produced by its clients' experiences, and the autobiographical and fictional selves of the novelist – are not as disparate as they may seem at first. Moreover, they represent major way stations on my own route through the Greek nationscape. To juxtapose them in this way is thus to explore some of the ways in which one anthropologist's own interests articulates their common ground.

That common ground is not only the accidents of that anthropologist's life; nor is it a besetting fascination with the relationship between classification and human experience. Not that the latter aspect is unimportant. On the contrary, it defines a fundamental source of my training and curiosity. It led me from deep dissatisfaction as an undergraduate student of prehistoric archaeology, irritated by the reduction of human experience to classifications of safety pins and pottery types, to my later susceptibility to the analysis of taxonomic anomalies in various structuralist modes, and on to highly disconcerting encounters with the culturally self-fulfilling disjuncture between bureaucratic order and social practice in Greece.

But there is something even more fundamental at stake in this trajectory: many of the real and fictional people I am going to describe hold views radically antithetical to my own. The sheep-thieves sometimes seem to have difficulty deciding whether they are talking about their animals or their wives; their use of feminizing narrative strategies when talking about stolen animals suggests an ideology hopelessly at odds with my own. Their views on vengeance were scarcely more attractive, especially in retrospect now that I have come to see much of what they believe as part of an ideology of blood that underlies much of the killing and rape elsewhere in the Balkans. Then again, the bureaucrats, however well-meaning, seemed too easily to stoop to the kinds of racist exclusion, petty power play, and venal unfairness that I found particularly distasteful and that sometimes seem to lend official force to the kinds of racism that I had occasionally encountered while growing up as a schoolboy in England.[4] Even Nenedakis, not to speak of his characters, would often say things that I found acutely discomfiting, especially in his acceptance of ideas about blond Europeans and the ancient roots of the mountain Cretan stock – although, not surprisingly, his remarkable ability to approach everything we talked about with a fresh eye, and especially his thoughtful reassessment of his own national pride, always commanded my respect and did not occasion me the kind of dyspepsia that so much else I am going to describe could sometimes do, perhaps because much of his talk shimmered with subtle hints of irony and self-deprecation.

The point of all this is not that I disliked everybody with whom I worked. The opposite is patently true, and *that* is the point. Why, if these people could all make me feel so deeply uncomfortable with views they obviously cherished, did I entertain such warmth for them? I came to realize that the very aspects of their styles that caused me the most discomfort were grounded in larger histories of inconsistency and reversal, leading to nationalist rhetorics in which inventive subversions like their own had acquired, through a process of routinization, all the deadliness of bureaucratic sclerosis. This gave me pause: for an ideology that is grounded in the ironic self-awareness for which it has since lost the capacity can surely, or so I thought, return to that gloriously unstable condition.

Conventional History and its Discontents

Let me explore these historically grounded contrasts in respect of one defining sequence in particular. In Nenedakis's (and most other left-wing Greek intellectuals') vision of national history, the country's independence was due to the activities of guerrillas, appropriately known as "thieves," whose insubordination against Ottoman rule became transmuted into disobedience to the equally intrusive – because foreign-imposed – control of the bureaucratic Greek state (see also Kondoyoryis 1979; Kordatos 1924). For Nenedakis especially, with his recent origins in the pastoral communities of western Crete and their endemic institutions of reciprocal animal-theft, as well as his protracted sufferings in the prison camps of Cold-War Greece, the analogy between foreign tyrant and domestic bureaucrat is compelling, while his irreverent sense of humor suggests a direct kinship with the mischievous delight of shepherds who dismiss the conservatives as virtual Turks – on the eve of the socialists' 1981 election victory, one of their local supporters in Crete remarked to me that it was time to get rid of the political Right as "we've had them for 400 years," a stock phrase for the Turkish occupation – and who are not above tricking the police into eating the meat of stolen animals and so destroying the evidence against the thieves (see Herzfeld 1985: 141, 220–221).

Thus, shepherd and intellectual share a sense of the reversibility of convention, and they cast this conceptual mischief in immediately similar terms. Their subversion of the formalities of language is grounded in their common, and insubordinate, perception of a national history stolen from the people by the agents of foreign powers. Their perspective reverses, especially, that of the bureaucrats, for whom claims to an absolute and literal understanding are the key to their strategies of power. It does so, not only in terms of the law, but also in those of the normative semantics of a national language. In Greece, where until 1975 that language was an archaizing formal dialect that only figured in everyday speech as a source of irony or among a small coterie of elite conservatives, any challenge to the pervasive literalism of official utterances used to be deeply disturbing to the educational, legal, and military authorities, and still grates against the conventional tenor of much everyday speech.

In considering this inversion, I am drawing the central analogy from an insight I owe to Mary Douglas, who once remarked to me that in Britain punning appeared to be popular with the working class and with the aristocracy, but not with the bourgeoisie; those who are most closely identified with the formal structures of power are also likely to be the least happy with anything that threatens the assumption of a universal semantic stability. Although Greek class structure possesses none of the rigidity usually associated with the British, Greece's rapid post-1960 *embourgeoisement* found ready-made models of occidentalist respectability to feed a rhetoric of law and order, as well as a passionate anticommunism closely paralleled – even to the point of opposing communism to "national" identity – in the United States during the period of the McCarthy witch-hunt. In that context, it is perhaps hardly surprising that language-play and irreverence toward the idea of authority should be associated with rebellious shepherds and urban intellectual leftists, especially when the latter are deeply conscious of a genealogy linking them literally and metaphorically with the former.[5]

Thus, the sequence shepherds-bureaucrats-novelists is not in any sense an evolutionary one, but it does have the advantage of allowing us to see clearly both the reversibility of routinization through generational time (Nenedakis, the literary grandson of shepherds, recovers the sense of playful subversion that the bourgeois state has suppressed) and the deep interpenetration of apparently contradictory values. The paradoxes of Greek identity, which often take the form of an internalized battle between orientalizing and occidentalizing self-stereotypes,[6] are also usefully seen as an almost unbearable tension between extreme political insubordination – the revolutionary slogan "Freedom or Death," emblematically celebrated by Kazantzakis (1956), comes to mind – with equally extreme cultural conformism.

This tension has major political consequences. In contrast to what happens in neighboring Italy, for example, Greek localism does not produce strong separatist movements, least of all in Crete, where against a background of powerful claims to *cultural* distinctiveness we encounter strong *political* conformism. Even when Cretans protest what they see as government submission to foreign pressure, as when they demonstrated against the display of ancient Cretan artifacts in foreign museums, their challenge to the national government's stewardship of the national patrimony (Hamilakis and Yalouri 1995) is an expression of loyalty to national causes. Such tensions become especially interesting when they appear as the defining parameters of personal experience and of the social realization of selfhood – of autoethnography, in other words.

The intense paradoxes of Greek identity relate the personal to the national in another way. Richard Handler (1988) has argued that Québecois nationalism, and most other forms by extension, displays an expansion of the characteristically European ideology of "possessive individualism" to the nation-state: just as individuals "own" personal property, character, and values, so too nations are supposed to possess territory, "national character" (see Caro Baroja 1970), and "a culture" (Handler 1985). This argument works especially well for Greece, where the transmission of *property* supposedly follows that of genetically transmitted character *properties*, symbolized and indexed by the parallel transmission of baptismal names (Herzfeld 1982; Kenna 1976; Vernier 1991). Moreover, although Handler does not himself discuss this, the Québecois *patrimoine* is implicitly a patrilineally inherited possession, which brings it into line with the powerfully agnatic idiom of much European and Middle Eastern, and especially Greek and Turkish, nationalist ideology (see Delaney 1995; Herzfeld 1992). Indeed, David Sutton (1995) has recently suggested a direct link between personal naming in Greece and the continuing Greek demands for exclusive rights to the name "Macedonia."

This is also the context for the construction of Greek *eghoïsmós* as both individualism (in which case it represents the heroic and European heritage of Classical Hellas in official discourse) *and* atomism (when, for the bourgeoisie and the state, it becomes the antisocial and Oriental taint of the Turkish era). Thus, the stakes involved in self-presentation and in its interpretation by others link personal performance to national ideology in ways that enable both the policing of sentiment (or at least of its public expression) and the subversion of official and bourgeois pretensions. Self-representation thus writes an ethnography of the nation at the same time.

A Night at the Opera: Epiphanies of an Ethnographer

Let me add a personal note of my own here. All of us, I suspect, recognize the inconsistencies to which any critique of essentialism commits us; since inevitably such critiques carve a privileged space out of the essentializing in which social life largely consists, we become aware of the necessary partiality of what we are doing. Feminist scholars have recognized this as the ground on which they inscribe what some have called, almost tautologically in this context, "strategic essentialism" (see Schor and Weed 1994). Thus, we may become aware of the inconsistencies of nationalism and its easy slippage between self-liberation and the repression of others, yet still be deeply moved by its rhetoric, its music, and its visual art.

In my own adolescence, as I grew increasingly skeptical of the absolutist claims of Jewish identity politics (including Zionism), I was nevertheless overwhelmed at the age of 14 by a rousing performance of Verdi's Old Testament masterpiece *Nabucco*, an opera about the redemption of the Israelites from their exile under the Babylonian king Nebuchadnezzar. That opera became on its very first night an allegory of the Italians' own struggle for national independence (the *Risorgimento*) as well, subsequently, as a recurrent index of climactic moments in Verdi's own life. How could I not be moved by the story of how the libretto had inspired the recently bereaved young Verdi to return to writing operas – "note by note, line by line; and so the opera composed itself," as Verdi later recalled (Weaver n.d.)? Or of how the first production introduced him to the lead soprano, who became his second wife and who, decades later, played the music of *Nabucco* to him on the piano as he lay on his deathbed? Or of how it made of him an instant national hero? Ettore Bastiniani, who died young only six short years after that night in Florence, sang in the title role, his rich, many-hued baritone soaring beyond the constraints of time. For me that shock of pleasure in the Teatro Comunale in Florence in 1961 was an epiphany, brought back to me with explosive force 23 years later when I found a live recording of the very same production and again in 1994 when, trembling with hesitation on the brink of my first attempt at fieldwork in Rome (and nervous about doing fieldwork in a language other than Greek, which had become naturalized for me as *the* field language), I found my courage after hearing, quite by chance, a band concert that began with the great *Nabucco* chorus of the Israelite slaves. But the true epiphany was indeed that first night in 1961. It was then that I discovered the appeal that romanticism and patriotism could have even at the very moment at which I seemed to be parting company with such sentiments forever, as I set out on the path of skeptical inconvenience that led me to become a social anthropologist.

This story gives an experiential twist to Greenwood's insight into the extraordinary lability of one of the most natural – and therefore, one might have supposed, one of the semantically most fixed – symbols of national but also of kinship identity, that of blood. I "know" that nationalism is not "natural," but cultural, constructed, and contrived; and yet I am still moved by the memory of that Florentine night. I recall, too, that I had not wanted the first act to end, for that would presage the end of the performance and the end of life itself: a first, glorious discovery of the exquisite tragedy that we call mortality, not merely intimated but wonderingly embraced. And there was the central paradox in all its stark immediacy: for, as Anderson (1983) reminds us, nationalism promises a collective immortality that should subsume the destinies of individuals. Why, then, should my skepticism be unable, even today, to stem the joyous tears that the strains of *Nabucco* evoke in me with undiminished force? Certainly there is the force of association with a formative moment in my late childhood. But at some level to explain the paradox away is to betray the emotions that have guided me to my present, intense interest in such questions.

These experiences may have given me some empathy with the sometimes strident patriotism of those I have met in Greece and many other places. (For some reason I find it much harder to accept the enjoyment of Wagner by stoutly antifascist friends!) For I know that I cannot claim innocence of such sentiments. Because they derive order from the chaos of social experience and personal feelings, identity choices are, of necessity, contradictory, and the symbolism that expresses them is correspondingly unstable in its meanings. It is intellectually easy to dismiss the easily aroused patriotic, masculinist, or statist emotions of others with a superior smile. But one may soon discover, in a perhaps unwelcome flash of introspection, that we are part of what we oppose: we are historically, socially, and emotionally entailed in it, and we can only come to terms with that entailment if we first recognize it. This is a hard reflexivity. But, to the extent that accounts of the self must address issues of *accountability*, we can hardly deny these connections.

Thus, inasmuch as I have argued for the recognition of a direct (and no less discomfiting) parallel between anthropology and nationalism, I should also acknowledge both the strain and the convergence between my enjoyment of the discourse of honor and destiny in Verdi's operas and my impatience with the anthropological emphasis on precisely those values in the analysis of circum-Mediterranean societies. Moreover, I most fully express this impatience in the same context as I explore the paradoxical links between nationalism and a discipline now inimical to all manner of cultural essentialisms (Herzfeld 1987). This is not simply perverse: like Richard Handler, also a critic of the relationship between anthropology and nationalism (Handler 1985, 1988), I believe that the "destructive analysis" of such linkages is the most productive approach. Taxonomies are at their most useful when their flaws are exposed and their contingency becomes apparent, for it is then that they reflect the intense paradoxes, as I call them here, of social life.

Paradoxes of Patriotism

So it is that I have no difficulty in understanding how the outlaw shepherds of the Cretan mountains remain loyal to the nation even as they despise the state which they regard as its enemy and betrayer. They dispute the legitimacy of officeholders and even of institutions, but not to the point of betrayal: a segmentary worldview assures their loyalty in times of crisis. Their rebellion in times of peace is the price of that loyalty, and fits the logic of "obligation" (*ipokhréosi*).

This even applies to the international relations, as in the Cretans' conventional denunciation of Great Power ingratitude (*akharistía*) for Greek – and, revealingly, *especially* Cretan – support for the Allied cause, revealed in West European responses to Greek concerns over Cyprus and Macedonia. Even while they rail at their European Union partners over these matters, they continue to take full advantage of EU support for the weaker economies and to proclaim their European identity. This is the play of resentment and obligation that also motivates the shepherds' dealings with politicians who, schooled in these entailments at the local level, presumably also often view their international activities through the same prism.

The Cretan shepherds' rebelliousness does not, therefore, make them unpatriotic. On the contrary, lack of patriotism is the stick with which they, like the guerrillas who fought the Turks in the dawn of Greek independence (see St. Clair 1972), beat the "pen-pushers" (*kalamarádhes*) in Athens. While I may be out of sympathy with the bloodthirstiness of their attitude to local and international enemies alike, I also recognize their capacity for appreciating the paradoxes of their own situation. Not only do they ruefully concede the strain between patriotism and lawlessness, but they appreciate that the absolute rhetoric of their moral code may conceal ample negotiating space. Thus, for example, in the context of revenge for homicide they exhibit an explicit and entirely pragmatic understanding that less directly affected parties to a feud will find it possible and even desirable to interact discreetly among themselves. Similarly, Cretan guest-workers newly returned from Germany recognize the common cultural ground they found with their Turkish colleagues even as they declare their willingness to be the first to shed Turkish blood in times of war. But the models for recognizing such paradoxes existed long before the first guest-worker left Crete for Germany; they have long maintained that the goal of animal theft is making alliances with proven former foes, just as marriages often serve to unite previously feuding kin groups (see also Campbell 1964: 146, 206–209). For these people the metaphor of agnatic blood, which "boils" more intensely with *both* anger and love in direct proportion to the parties' degree of patrilineal proximity, makes perfect sense of these tense modes of relationship, grounded as they are in contradiction and the inevitable inconsistencies of social experience.

Crete is one of those southern European spaces where the language of blood infuses ideas about the self and where a well-established strain of literary traditionalism, notably in the writings of Nikos Kazantzakis, reinforces the image of haughty insubordination. It is a place where the language of blood – "taking the blood back" (revenge), "blood doesn't become water, and, when it does, it can't be drunk" – gives a literal "feel" to what are in practice manipulable ascriptions of categorical blame and solidarity.

The very fixity of these symbols provides a secret space for negotiating their contents. After a tractor accident, the victim's patrilateral first cousin called for revenge against the same victim's mother's brother because the latter had asked for the tow that led to the accident (Herzfeld 1985: 84–91). Those who were not involved disagreed: "he [the matrilateral uncle] hadn't wanted it [the accident to happen]." But those who belonged to the victim's patriline saw in the rhetoric of agnatic solidarity a legitimate basis for venting their grief, transmuted to anger in ways that Rosaldo (1989) and Behar (1991) have movingly explored. Conventional anthropological concerns also remain relevant, because the *channeling* of anger, its legitimation, places the social self in the framework of a socially specific calculus of risk. The maternal uncle's sons faced their cousins down and restored peace through a demonstration of fearless manhood. Their risk was considerable, but their action set a limit to the legitimate expression of anger. The predictability of risk in feuding societies increases with the bellicosity of the situation, reaching a horrific climax in the rigidly agnatic logic of rape, infanticide, and selective breeding of the rapists' offspring (and murder of their mothers) in the Bosnian war. At such moments it requires international intervention to break the cycle of retributive justice and of the *categorical* ascriptions of blame that legitimize the most destructive expressions of anger. Note that the inflammation of war makes exceptions to the classification correspondingly difficult to sustain.

In peace, of course, such rigidity is relatively fragile, but bureaucrats – at least in the popular imagination – have much at stake in trying to maintain it. They and their more disgruntled clients are most likely to agree on attributing the ultimate blame to a nameless, faceless "system." The violence of war is a perversion of bureaucratic intentions and not their necessary consequence, but the pettier infractions of state functionaries who discriminate against ethnic and religious minorities or settle old personal scores from the privileged side of their desks follow the same logic, if not on the same scale: it is a redeployment for selfish or sectarian purposes of the symbolic capital of statehood, including immunity from blame. In a country where patronage remains rife, such exploitations of the democratic ideal are well-protected and relatively common. For our present purposes, their great advantage is that they showcase the social management of responsibility in ways that make bureaucratic interactions and blood feuds mutually comparable within a single framework.

Nenedakis writes of bureaucratic classification with great contempt. For him there is a radical disjuncture between unthinking chauvinism and the patriotism that he admires, the legitimate defense of the native land against tyranny that sent him off to the Foreign Legion and then the Allied forces at El Alamein to fight against the Nazis, but that also led him to a death sentence for participating in a left-wing insurrection against the royalist and Allied commanders of the Middle East forces. Similarly, shepherds dislike the bureaucrats because of their policing functions. For both Nenedakis and the shepherds, bureaucratic rigidity affords a backdrop for displays of selfhood that depend on weakening the identification of nation with state – a distinction that Campbell (1964: 258) was the first to note from an anthropological perspective. The shepherds also recognize the human failings of bureaucrats, which is why the shepherds are able to mock the authority of even the most senior functionaries.

Two complementary and mutually opposed conceptual operations are thus involved: *detaching* the nation from the state at the level of ideology, and *attaching* bureaucrats to the realm of ordinary people at that of social engagement. Because the shepherds often engage the police in friendly acts of hospitality and because Nenedakis can identify the decency of those among his fascist tormentors who have been forced by others to their degrading task, both the shepherds and Nenedakis recognize the representatives of the state primarily as human beings rather than as automata. This places a burden of responsibility on shoulders perhaps more accustomed to shrugging it off. But it also reveals the relationship between agency and taxonomy in the conduct of relations between citizen and state. The state is comprised of real people with whom one can do business precisely because they are as liable to temptation as oneself.

Scrutinizing the System: Two Views

Both the communist and the rebel place those relations under a particular scrutiny. Much of this is achieved by irony, like punning a means of disturbing semantic complacency. Often, too, narrative accounts of animal-theft situate the action in the context of a pragmatic cynicism about official motives: while the state ("the system") is blamed in a generic sense, the shepherds know perfectly well that this is a convenient device for disguising the mutual involvement of patrons and clients.

Thus, for example, a notorious animal-thief reflected on the relationship among theft, blame, and patronage in local politics:

Here we now at any moment are in need, so to speak, for [such things as] building constructions, because all of these things involve illegalities (*paranomíes*). Most things happen [that way]. That is to say, we move in the direction of illegality. Do you get it? Like, when you go to be with the sheep, too, you must carry your pistol. Isn't that the case? And at any moment the police may get you, and you can't [do anything about it]. In other words, you are continually a violator [i.e., lawbreaker], how else should I put it to you? Well, as for me, in any case, I like this government, in which there exists this business of influence-peddling (*méso*). (How should I put it to you, now?) Of course, I'm talking about myself, I don't know how others feel.

Here the shepherd describes an encompassing system of blame and exoneration. Much as popular historiography borrows from official ideology to treat the persistence of endemic animal-theft as the product of centuries of Turkish oppression, so this shepherd articulates a system of inequality that effectively forces him to break the law, and he does so in a way that makes government officials look distinctly like the stereotypical image of Turkish tax collectors.

But note: he "likes this government." Is this simply an ironic jest? Perhaps it is; but his disclaimer – "I'm talking about myself, I don't know how others feel" – suggests otherwise: as an expression of individuality it is actually very conventional, an acceptance of responsibility for apparently amoral views that, by its very form, proclaims that everyone else feels the same way. In this fashion the narrative form reproduces the paradox of an *eghoïsmós* – here, pride in personally shouldering the responsibility for outlaw attitudes – that is in practice socially determined. In that sense we may read his admission that he "likes this government" as subscribing to a larger pattern of complicity between state officials and outlaws. It also allows the animal-thief to admit that he has worked matters out to his own advantage, a key element in *eghoïsmós*, but in a way that fits the popular local representation of the government in Athens as successors to the Turks – as rapacious but corruptible intruders into the edenic pastorale of village life. As the same animal-thief remarked:

Animal-theft comes from the people who are in government, that is, parliamentary deputies, things like that. That's where it comes from. The deputy gives you wings and you go off on a raid (*klepsá*). That is, you go with a certain "air" about you. I, too, at this very moment, if captured, will call on a deputy of my own [to look] into the matter, in these things you always get the government involved.

It is clear that "the government" is perceived as a set of more or less independent agents, while the thief's own agency in the construction of these mutually beneficial arrangements is also strongly asserted. The thief also gave a revealing picture of the personal psychology involved:

There are many whom he [a high-ranking party official and deputy] has helped. That's where the whole business begins, because when I, for example, think that I have a deputy who at any moment can [help me], you [*sic*] go with more of an "air" about you. In other words, you go from one point of view with the intention of not being caught, but you still say to yourself that if you *are* caught you have a person who can help you. And you always depend on this one person, do you get me? That's why I say that animal-theft [will never disappear] under any government, unless there's a[nother] dictatorship.

Here the animal-thief gives a revealing glimpse of the ways in which social actors' self-awareness – in the sense of Cohen's (1994) "self consciousness" – articulates with the nexus of moral values and political and social obligations so stunningly described for the Sarakatsani of northern Greece by Campbell (1964). This is true theoretical knowledge – discursive rather than practical consciousness, to use Giddens's (1984) terminology. I have argued elsewhere for the full recognition of this capacity on their part: were they not able to construct general accounts of social action, they would hardly be able to adapt so rapidly to the conditions of emigration and return or of cultural and social change at home. Moreover, as the shepherds themselves point out, quick wits are at a premium in their unforgiving social and natural environment: the ability to infer social rules from the comparison of experiences makes them acute ethnographers of their own society and pragmatic theorists of cultural comparison in their dealings with the outside world from Athenian politicians to German factory bosses and the international power brokers whose activities they follow so avidly in the news.

Our thief-*raconteur* thus imbues powerful social values ("obligations") with psychological ("you go with the intention of not being caught") and affective ("I like this government") implications. This is autoethnography: a coherent vision of the paradox-plagued self, described by people who, no less than anthropologists, are theorists – practical theorists, to be sure, but articulate exegetes of the politics of selfhood for all that. Their descriptions situate the self in a nexus of kin relations that define notions of *obligation* to both kin and to politicians in the larger sphere (see also Campbell 1964: 95–96 *et passim*). But they are also couched in terms of categories understood to be semantically labile; and in this the shepherds, who (like the working-class English) have nothing to gain from maintaining the sober face of semantic stability, differ radically from the bureaucrats (whose interests depend on it).

Such explicit self-construction is not unlike what we also find, as Cohen (1994: 180–191) argues, in novels. This has been a major motivation for my exploration of Nenedakis's writings. His representation of an enormous range of characters, from tough rural Cretan youths to sophisticated Athenian women, must satisfy the demands of plausibility, especially as he writes in a realist mode and grounds virtually all his fictional work in autobiography and in historically documented events. When he describes how encounters with Turks feed the young Cretan peasant's progressive disenchantment with his own braggadocio and with the strident chauvinism on which it feeds, for example, Nenedakis (in his novel *Bir Hakeim* [1975a]) gives us a portrait that is significantly different from that of the stereotypical Greek military hero we encounter in school textbooks. The young man discovers that he is unable to avenge the sexual insults of a Turkish official against some Greek prostitutes. Clearly the idea that Greek women are pure becomes absurd in that situation; but, as a result, so do his well-learned pretensions of all-avenging Cretan masculinity. He encounters fear. It is not the fear to which sheep-thieves sometimes admit in order all the more to glorify their eventual daring, but a more visceral terror of being pointlessly killed in an unworthy cause. The sexual politics, in which Greeks as much as Turks engage, undermines for him the very idiom of chauvinism that is allegorically constructed upon it in the language of rape and sexual exposure, and so causes him to rethink his values.

The animal-thief is interested in preserving the *status quo*. It serves his interests and provides him with a familiar context, besides putting him in direct contact with the official representatives of the bureaucracy that is supposed to punish him. Thus, his narratives contain little self-doubt, much self-justification. In this regard they strikingly resemble the stereotypical talk of, and about, bureaucrats. In both cases the idiom of self-justification is instantly recognizable and so satisfies the necessary "felicity conditions" (Austin 1971 [1956–57]) for plausibility in what is indeed a national rather than a local space.

The novelist's interests are rather different here. He, too, is interested in the idiom of introspection, but in the sense that it will challenge the *practices* of those in power rather than just mischievously recast their *ideological idiom* for self-interested purposes. Nenedakis writes of the forces that create a sense of ideological conversion, of the paradoxes within the logic of state power that can be used to pry open its assumptions and pretensions. Thus, for example, he writes of the psychological effect of being subjected by the military régime (1967–74) to incessant demands for a declaration of loyalty even from someone who had hitherto considered himself to be largely apolitical and certainly not fiercely left-wing:

> All the irregularities, everything he heard or they told him, might not have made him think he should do anything against it [the junta]. But when they behaved this way toward him and even openly tried to bully him into signing, that he could not swallow. And, what was most important, all the pressure the police brought to bear on him showed that he had to resist.

And, as a result, the next time he was called to the police station, he declared, "I am against the dictatorship, sir!" (Nenedakis 1975b: 178–179).

Nenedakis, in other words, views the self, including his own, as responsive to the inconsistencies in the ideologies of power. Unlike the animal-thief, who enjoys the perquisites of client status (and supports a right-wing party), the left-wing author despises the allure of patronage and the traps that it lays for its supposed beneficiaries.

But both narrators are concerned with the preservation of human dignity. This is the common element, justified for both in self-consciously traditionalizing terms. For both operate in that idiom. The animal-thief is an aficionado of the social institution of blood-brotherhood as described in Kazantzakis's novels about nineteenth-century Crete; the novelist writes with deep nostalgia about the lost intimacies of small-town Cretan life and values. But whereas the animal-thief uses the conventional rhetoric of self-exoneration and preserves his *eghoïsmós* in that way, the novelist describes an active rejection of these conventions, which in other writings he ties explicitly to the taxonomic obsessions of a repressively bureaucratic state – thus ultimately appealing, after all, to the same "system" as the source of social evil.

The novelist (also an admirer of Kazantzakis, although a more nuanced one) has a longer conceptual reach. He sees, for example, that the logic of the blood feud would not suit his vision, although he did remark once, in connection with a literary dispute that entailed family squabbles in his native Rethemnos, "Had I not been an author, I would have killed [someone by now]!" – an ironic recognition of common grounds that inversely mirrors a Cretan villager's acute observation to me: you don't have children because you write books and we have children in order to resurrect ourselves through the baptismal naming system and through the promise of an unending bloodline.

Nenedakis also writes extraordinarily stoic tales of human dignity in the face of police brutality. His fictional diaries of the prison camps (Nenedakis 1974a, 1974b), for example, measure out the endless days of humiliation with dull thuds of phrasing that echo in the reader's bruised consciousness like the jackboots of the camp guards – a presence that has numbed its own capacity to terrorize by sheer repetition but also by the endurance that this realization makes possible. Indeed, the ability to reproduce its dull repetitiveness as prose snatches its victories away from it.

Remarkably, Nenedakis's vision also incorporates the recognition of humanity in some of those charged with brutalizing the prisoners. His contempt for most of them depended, it seems, on his ability never to reduce them all to a single stereotype, even as he mocked their attempts to reduce him to the cipher of just such a taxonomic device. Equally remarkably, he is explicit about condemning the atrocities committed by his own side in the Civil War as well as the errors of Soviet communism. Ever rueful, he recognizes the paradoxes that eventually limit the purity of all revolutions and that always mock the claims of any classification to a transcendent truth.

The Taming of Revolution: Classification and the Self

For social life has its constraints, and so the revolution gets tamed in multiple ways. (Bureaucratic classification, viewed in these terms, is simply the dead end of that process.) For the sheep-thief, it is his entailment in the state system of patronage that provides him with the "air" to commit acts of lawlessness even while it also reduces his capacity for drastic action. Even though the shepherd whose narratives we have heard here once boasted to me that he had hand grenades at the ready in his vehicle in case the police ever attacked him, when they *did* attack him he did nothing and was arrested and drew a long jail term, itself a mark of distinction among his peers. He had too much to lose by resisting violently, everything to gain by meekly accepting his sentence and the glory it brought him. And he had hopes, perhaps, of returning to fight another day. His accommodations served the maintenance of the *status quo*, and he knew it. As he remarked: "I like this government!"

The novelist, on the other hand, found that his profound acquaintance with the paradoxes of political actuality and, more particularly, his disappointment at the corruption of his ideals by those in power – he resigned from the Communist Party of Greece in protest against the Daniel and Sinyavsky show trials in Moscow in 1966 – undermined his most cherished assumptions and revealed the fragility of any political system that requires unthinking loyalty. It was the revolution's own failures – not just the failure to seize power in Greece, but the failure to use it wisely in the Soviet Union – that tamed its appeal for him and opened it up for his critical inspection.

The novelist achieves self-realization by refusing to bow to an authority that punishes him for this insubordination. Whether disgusted by the sanctimonious chauvinism of the military and religious anticommunism of the Cold War Greek régimes or disenchanted by the fallibility of the political left in turn, Nenedakis finds his own voice through opposition to the received values he was expected to adopt. The more violently he was pressed to conform, the more determinedly he defined his own moral space in opposition. Disenchantment thus offered him an independence that contrasted most tellingly with the apparently voluntary self-enmeshing of the animal-thief in the nexus of patronage – but that similarly, if with less of a sense of dependence, placed him at the margins and so gave him moral authority in his own eyes at the expense of real power in those of others.

Like the shepherds, he derives dignity from self-regard, from the *eghoïsmós* that allows the powerful to treat them, and him, as marginal and even as antisocial. The self that he dissociates from the official stereotype of national character is a more deliberately distinctive one, in part because he and the heroes of his books refuse the game of patronage – in his case, that of signing declarations of loyalty to right-wing régimes – through which, by contrast, the shepherds define their moral superiority over corrupt politicians and other power brokers. Nenedakis will not accord his tormentors the satisfaction they would derive from his betrayal of principle; the shepherds, in true Hegelian fashion, mock the politicians of the democratic right-wing parties for depending on the shepherds' subjection as clients to sustain the politicians' role as patrons.

The perspectives of the villagers (especially those of the animal-thieves) are thus not identical to those of the novelist, despite his affectionate traditionalism and their awareness of the encompassing cultural and political world of the nation-state. But these perspectives do draw on a common idiom of self-regard, one that we also, and more surprisingly, find in the utterances of bureaucrats. (Is autoethnography the transmutation of a static and categorical self-regard into process and prose?) If the differences among these populations are important, so too are the resemblances. In a universe in which people differentiate themselves by blaming others or by contrasting their respective understandings of personal accountability, they must share a common idiom in which to do it.

Such commonalities go against the grain of our cherished assumptions. Bureaucrat and outlaw define themselves in opposition to one another, yet they share the symbolic capital that makes it possible to do so. As I discovered so many years ago in the opera house and afterward, it is the common symbolic ground of our own ideologies and of those we profess to oppose that has the power both to disconcert and, by that fact, to instruct us. It disturbs our categorical certainties, producing what Fernandez calls "edification by puzzlement" (1974: 172–187) – in this case puzzlement about the a self that does not conform to its own ostensible imperatives. For such are the ineluctably intense paradoxes of the social being we call the self.

Notes

1. A version of this paper was presented on April 12, 1996, at the Department of Anthropology, Cornell University, as part of a celebration of Davydd Greenwood's election as a corresponding member of the Spanish Royal Academy of Moral and Political Sciences. Some elements are also incorporated from my inaugural lecture at Harvard in 1992 ("From the Coffee-House to the Opera House: Reflections on Ethnography in the Nation-State").

2. The value of the syntagmatic/paradigmatic contrast here is that it reminds us that the lineal ordering of our own lives, with all its attendant serendipity, imposes some practical constraints on our empirical and comparative vision (along the syntagmatic axis) but that this should not deter us from *also* including that trajectory as a *comparandum* – especially when the subject is autoethnography, with its double meaning (on which, see Reed-Danahay, this volume).

3. In this essay I shall necessarily confine my description of these events and characters to a minimalist and selective outline, but the goal of the "ethnographic biography" I am writing is to explore their complexity as it relates to issues of ethnographic representation.

4. For example, when applying for a residence permit I was told that I did not have the option of leaving the "religion" space blank but that both this and my "nationality" (*ethnikótita*), as opposed to my "citizenship" (*ipikoötita*), should depend on what my father was. In Britain at that time, I would never be asked for such information for legal purposes, but the argument that I was "not English" pervaded informal relations and is closely related to the legal status of "patrials" in current UK immigration laws.

5. There are parallels here in African-American literature in the United States. See Labov 1972, and compare Gates 1987. For an especially useful comparison with Greece, see Hart 1989: 21.

6. This has been a defining theme in my work; see especially Herzfeld 1995. For an early formation of occidentalism, see Carrier 1992; for a global view that offers some further insight for the present discussion, cf. Coronil 1996.

Chapter 8

Writing Birthright: On Native Anthropologists and the Politics of Representation

Pnina Motzafi-Haller

> Not just because they position themselves with reference to two communities [the academic and the one they describe] but because when they present the Other they are presenting themselves . . . both halfie and feminist anthropologists are forced to confront squarely the politics and ethics of their representations. There is no easy solution to their dilemmas.
>
> Lila Abu-Lughod (1991: 142)

> When exactly. . . does the "post-colonial" begin? . . . When Third World intellectuals have arrived in First World academe.
>
> Arif Dirlik (1994: 328)

> I participated, I "observed," I read my notes, recollect, and write, but is it not yet another emerging "stereotype," this time in the hands of a "native" anthropologist?
>
> José Limon (1994: 113)

> Not unlike other ethnographers, so-called natives can be insightful, sociologically correct, axe-grinding, self-interested, or mistaken.
>
> Renato Rosaldo (1989: 50)

In his recent critical review of intellectual debates within American cultural anthropology, Adam Kuper (1994) observes that "the view that only natives should study natives is a logical step from the orthodoxies of the previous decades" (1994: 545). This "American gospel" (that, to his relief, had not yet penetrated European social anthropology), Kuper notes, is based on the "curious" combination of elements of "the post-modernist programme with radical political engagements" (1994: 537). Although Kuper sees only the "potentially dangerous implications" of such a "nativist" turn, he is also clear that the question of the "ethnic identity of the investigator" raises "fundamental questions about the nature of anthropology and its uses" (547). The practice of "natives studying natives" is not an entirely new idea in anthropology. Earlier discussions written by anthropologists self-identified as "native" or "ethno" scholars, have been concerned largely with the methodological aspects of such autoethnographic work – whether one's native familiarity with the language, the unspoken cultural codes of the community, or one's social ties within the research site facilitated or hindered one's research project (Aguilar 1981; Fahim 1982; Jones 1970; Kim 1990). Later reflexive discussions centered on the personal ambivalences of those few ethno/writers struggling with the cross-cutting lines of their personal and professional identities (Kondo 1990; Nayaran 1993). But until quite recently these discussions were marginal; they had to do with the dilemmas of a small group of anthropologists.

After all, *most* anthropologists came from the "here" and left "home" to study "them" in remote, far-away locations "out there." So why has the question of "natives studying natives" burst into the very heart of anthropological discourse today, threatening, according to some, the very existence of the discipline? And why, at the very moment that anthropological theory has moved away from the essentializing depiction of "communities" and of unified collective identities into an exploration of the imaginative and contested construction of boundaries and multiple identities, has the distinctive identity of the scholar as "native," "halfi," "marginal," or "hybrid" become central?

In what follows I would like to explore these questions through my own experience as both "native" and "outsider" anthropologist. In reflecting here on my double experiences as a "native" writer on Israel and as the "outsider/foreign" ethnographer in Africa, I wish to problematize these two categories and explore some of the personal and epistemological questions of writing within, and moving between, these two positions. My explorations of such a double experience, with its inversion of hierarchy and power relations in one frame, intend to complicate the question of authorship and representation, a question that underlies much contemporary critical discussion within both anthropology and postcolonial studies.

"You are an authentic voice"

In the fall of 1995, I returned to Israel where I was born and raised, after seventeen years of "academic exile" in the US. I had finally landed a tenure-track position that permitted the luxuries of a limited load of teaching and extended time for research and writing. I was excited. I had not only returned to my native land and language, I was finally going to be able to devote serious time to complete the manuscript that had been sitting on my desk for almost three years. What I was finally finding time to return to was not merely another publication that would advance my career. It is an historical ethnography that explores the narrative of immigrants from North African and Middle Eastern countries, known as the Eastern (Mizrahim) or Oriental Jews. And I am a Mizrahi woman, born in Israel to immigrants from Iraq.

In 1991, I joined Dan Rothstein, a fellow research associate at Harvard's Center for Middle Eastern Studies, in writing the manuscript we entitled *Birthright: The Struggle for Equality in Israel's Early Years*. Upon my return to Israel, I wrote a book proposal that I submitted to an Israeli research and publication center. Dan shared my enthusiasm and emailed his encouragement. "We have an important contribution to make with publishing this book," wrote Dan upon hearing the news. "I urge you to think every day about how to just feel comfortable (without all those academic/ critical voices in your head) and just write it." He added: "Remember, you are an authentic voice, and the voices in the manuscript are authentic." What are these "academic/critical voices" and why do they prevent me from "feeling comfortable" in writing the book I deeply believe is the reason I became an anthropologist in the first place? And why did Dan's encouragement and his simple assertion that I am "an authentic voice" make me feel anything but comfortable?

I have tried this several times before – articulating, giving voice to, my painful struggles of writing *Birthright*, a coauthored historical ethnography on Israel, my native land.[1] My earlier essays felt incomplete and, for me, less than satisfactory. What am I trying to achieve with such reflexive, fragmented explorations of the

process that led me, almost despite myself, to the writing of
Birthright? Will such writing about my inner conflicts, the personal
and epistemological questions that underlie the project of doing
an autoethnography, help me resolve and work through the long
and agonizing process of writing the book? Can I indulge myself,
or even feel comfortable, in such fashionable postmodern "navel
gazing"?[2] Or is there a more valuable, theoretically relevant interest
in these reflections? The more direct and particularly critical
questions that I would like to explore here include: Are such
"critical academic voices" effectively silencing me? How? How
can I break through such silencing power? What kind of "voice"
can I claim?

These questions are not unique to my career nor novel in the
literature. I have been reading everything I can find about "native
anthropologists" and about what Abu-Lughod (cited above) calls
"their dilemmas." I have also tuned in to postmodern discussions
of the "positionality of the investigator" and, more recently, to
various attempts to write empowering historiographies of subaltern populations. During the summer of 1995, in a wonderfully
stimulating National Endowment for the Humanities Seminar on
"The Politics of Identity," I had the opportunity not only to read
but to meet academics (native and outsiders), community activists,
and others who were, from their various perspectives, struggling
with these very questions of representation and writing in the
Pacific region and in Hawaii in particular. "What do we foreigners
have to learn from Pacific Islanders by way of a methodology of
history? . . . What can we do to ensure that they do not become
simply a generalized faceless mass?" asks one Haoli (white)
historian. He also writes the more provocative statement: "Authentic Pacific history means far more than a pen in a brown hand
rather than a white hand" (Hezel 1992: 66). "We, who are more
fortunate," writes Epeli Hau'ofa, the celebrated writer and
historian, must "construct our pasts and present in our own way.
We cannot continue to rely heavily on others to do it for us because
autonomy cannot be attained through dependence" (1994: 2). As
I listened to the assertive voice of people like Hunani Trask,
who heads the Hawaiian Studies Center, and to the foreign
anthropologists who felt under attack by her powerful indigen-
ization agenda, I realized that I needed to examine my own dual
experience as "native" and "foreign" anthropologist/scholar
within the same frame. I also realized that my earlier explorations

of my dilemmas, framed only as those of a "native scholar," were partial, incomplete, and ultimately distorting.

"This is not how you write an academic paper"

> Among the reasons for choosing to be an anthropologist – to step in and out of society and to study it – are those connected with family background and personality. Class, religion, and other social (as well as personal) factors define certain experiences, and the reactions to them create new ones.
>
> Hortense Powdermaker, *Stranger and Friend* (1966: 15)

> Israel is a very young state, with a unique history – the return from exile of the Jewish nation which after two thousand years of exile had not lost its identity and attempts to build its spiritual and cultural life in its country. This country is a western enclave in eastern/oriental (*mizrahi*) Asia . . . . The Israeli rejects the *mizrahi* culture . . . he sees it as barbaric, and sees himself as superior to it . . . .. The victories in the battlefield . . . and the realization of such power brings with it contempt for everything that the Arabs symbolize . . . the contempt of that culture is expressed through the negation of values that are indeed beautiful and positive. Thus the Arab's generous hospitality is perceived by the Israeli as uncivilized eating while sitting on the ground and the adherence to family unity [of the Arabs] as the irrational blood feuds . . . the Israeli does not see the beauty in Arab poetry and folkloristic dances, only poverty and stagnation. The Arab represents the Oriental (*mizrahi*).
>
> Pnina Motzafi May 3, 1972 [An essay in Hebrew Lit class on the assigned topic "The Ugly Israeli – outline his character which to our regret is very common in our private and public life."]

I was seventeen when I wrote this essay. I was studying in a special boarding school that took gifted Mizrahi/oriental children out of their disadvantaged community schools in the periphery and placed them in the heart of "First Israel." We, the children of the boarding school, were the few Mizrahim who made it through this special program into the heart of the established, mostly Ashkenazi elite school system. In writing about "*the* Israeli" – ugly or not – I was adopting "their" understanding of *mizrahi* culture. Every third weekend, I returned home from my boarding school to a community of mostly Mizrahi poor immigrants in a peripheral town. My parents, who emigrated from an Arab country, Iraq, a few years before I was born, spoke Arabic at home, listened to Arabic music and were clearly not part of the hegemonic "western" model of "The Israeli" I was asked to characterize in my essay. Seven months after writing the above essay, I joined the Israeli army and served during the Yom Kippur war. I began studying "science" – "pure science" – in my first year in Jerusalem Hebrew University because it "proved," I was convinced then, that I could really "make it"; only people with less impressive academic achievements went into the soft, less prestigious social sciences. How I made it to a "Sociology of Israel" class that first year in Jerusalem is still unclear; but what I read there made me switch, in my second year, to a major in anthropology and sociology.

From the very beginning, my interest in the subject and the discipline was intense and very personal. I sat in huge, impersonal lecture halls and listened in absolute, visceral engagement to what my professors said. I searched for answers, for ways of grasping the confusing social reality I experienced in the logic of academic discourse, in the conceptual tools it provided. Most of what I heard in those years legitimized, explained away the very disturbing reality of inequality that corresponded to ethnic divisions in the grand narrative of "the mixing of exiles." I had to try very hard to find the very few critical voices that simply documented such reality. "Is this known and made public?" I asked one young lecturer who spoke about his new research on what he said were the paternalistic educational policies that created, rather than closed, the gaps between Ashkenazi and Mizrahi Jews in Israel.

In my first essay that year, on June 23, 1976, I wrote about the "Participation of immigrants from Asia and Africa in the Israeli political system." Without any model of academic writing,[3] I set out to document in my very first short essay not only the scope and nature of the under-representation of the Mizrahim in Israel's political life but also to examine the causes for such a state of affairs. I also wanted to explore the difficult questions of "Why has this situation continued unchanged over the last three decades of Israeli statehood?" and "What are the best ways of changing such a situation?" While struggling to adopt and make use of the style and logic of academic writing, it is clear that I wanted this investigation to provide me with "answers" to very burning existential questions. I wrote: "The struggle for greater representation of the non-Ashkenzi communities in the national and local political institutions in Israel is one of the most explicit expressions of the ethnic problem [in Israel]." I asked: "Does a person of Mizrahi origin represent, or are they able to represent, the interests of Mizrahi communities?" I went to see two Mizrahi members of parliament in search of answers. I concluded my first essay with a gloomy prospect: "It seems that in the existing power balance, Mizrahim in Israel do not have the political might to change Israel's political structure." But then I added: "I do not believe in a slow, integrative change initiated by those in power. The only avenue for change will occur when there is a wide social realization[4] of the extent and meaning of the existing political gap." "Such realization, when it comes," I closed the essay using a biblical idiom "will shake the foundation of the country." The grader of my paper jotted in the margins of my concluding paragraphs "This is not how you write an academic paper."

In retrospect, I see that I internalized, at that very early point in my career, my grader's notion of what "academic" writing should be: detached, objectified, "rational." I learned that my closing statements that had expressed anger and visceral feeling of rage should be censored out of any calm "academic" conclusion. Indeed, in the years and decades that followed, I became the best, the most merciless censor of such engaged writing in my academic work. Yet, what was my rage all about? And how did it shape, as I argue below, my eventual decision to leave, to put aside at least for a few years, my attempts to understand Israeli society and history? I think the answers to these two questions are closely linked. My anger stemmed not merely from my analysis of the impossible, dead-end situation of powerlessness among the Mizrahim, my people, in Israel, but from the frustration I felt at the success of the dominant discourse to silence any idea that challenged and exposed the simple logic of such injustice. An encounter with my two upwardly mobile sisters and their Mizrahi husbands illustrates this basic contradiction.

A few months before writing this student essay, I read an article by two Israeli sociologists[5] who documented, using statistical data, the social, economic, educational and political "gaps" between the two Jewish populations of Israel, the Ashkenazim and Mizrahim. I took the article home and read a direct quotation of it to my two older sisters and brothers-in-law. I forced it down their throats with joyous masochistic anger. "There is no discrimination" said these young, educated relatives of mine, all elementary school teachers in peripheral towns. "We can all make it." "It is a matter of one generation." "Look at us." "But listen to this," I triumphed, quoting the cold-blooded "scientific-sounding" sociological depiction of a reality we all were part of, "the gaps are expanding, not narrowing. How can you keep your heads in the sand?"

Like my own Mizrahi family, we all wish that what we have come to call the "ethnic problem" – the persistent correspondence between ethnic origin and socioeconomic position – would melt into thin air; that "intermarriage" (marriage between Mizrahi and Ashkenazi Jews), education, or mere time will bring about the promised "mixing of the exiles." Virginia Dominguez, one of the few non-Jewish, non-Israeli anthropologists to carry out intensive work in Israel, articulates what I am trying to say here best as she describes her original research question: "I had gone to Israel to explore the way in which social, political, and economic domination of one half of Israeli Jews by the other half took place *ideologically – without most people knowing or noticing*" (Dominguez 1992: 33, emphasis mine). I think Dominguez overstates her case here. I do not agree with her observation that most people in Israel do not know or even notice the very situation of their lives. We do.

The question is rather how and why has Israeli dominant discourse been so effective in explaining away, in delegitimizing, the systematic and persisting evidence that shows so powerfully that the Mizrahim as a category constitutes the lower classes. The Mizrahim are excluded and marginalized not only from social and political centers but – as my high school essay suggests – from the very definition of what it is to be "Israeli." The questions I dealt with were not abstract issues of social justice but pertinent to my daily existence. The discourse on *"adatiyut"* (ethnicity) with its strong humiliating tones that justified and legitimized "the gaps" – the continuing inequalities between Ashkenazim and Mizrahim – was all around me. When the Mizrahim learn to get rid of their debilitating oriental, cultural habits and become westernized, modern, civilized Israelis, the argument goes, then they will become equal. The ridicule dished out against anything that smacked of *"mizrahiyut"* (orientalist flavor) – of Mizrahi accent, music, way of life – in public discourse had its more "noble," paternalistic face in academic discourse.[6] The more I read such literature and the longer I thought about the research projects my teachers designed (I assisted in different roles in several such projects – it paid my bills), the more angry and confused I became. One example of the frustration I experienced will suffice here. In my second year of studies, I worked on a part-time basis in the Unit for Gifted Children in the Ministry of Education.[7] My duties included the administration of screening tests in various schools in the country and the organization of the lists of those who were identified as "gifted" before they were directed to special enriching schools. The whole project was – I am not sure what has happened with it in the last two decades – an elitist idea. The three special schools for gifted children were located in the most established neighborhoods of the three largest cities, and screening tests were administered only in these cities. Although I participated in all the planning meetings of the project and was invited into sessions with the educators and other professionals who helped design it, I did not criticize the very obvious elitist and discriminatory idea that the project was built on. All I noted was that a large number of letters sent to the homes of the few Mizrahi students who lived in the peripheries of the three established cities, had been returned to the office unopened. I pointed out this fact to my superiors, suggesting that many of the Mizrahim who were included in the target population were being effectively excluded from taking the screening tests. "Why do you think this is happening?" I was asked aggressively. I suggested that in my experience many of these Mizrahi children lived in large apartment buildings that had unmarked and disfunctional mailboxes, and that an official letter like the one we mailed out had very little chance of ever reaching its target. My idea was no more than a nuisance. I was told that if this was really important to me, I should follow up with a second letter or try to find the correct address myself.

At some point I decided that the emotional pain and direct involvement I had with the subject blinded my understanding and led me in circles I could not break out of. I felt that I needed to have a better grasp of conceptual and analytical tools and that the best way to achieve this would be to stay away from the Israeli material until I had acquired those tools. Underlying my decision was also the desire to return, to reenter the dominant academic and hegemonic discourse from a position of the relative power of an accredited academic and not that of an "angry Mizrahi woman." In September 1978, I left for graduate studies in the US with a stated interest in African ethnographies.

Africa . . ..

> How could I explain that I was not a gringa, not totally a gringa,
> anyway?
>
>   Ruth Behar, *Translated Woman* (1993: 32)

> The new mestiza copes by developing a tolerance for contradictions,
> a tolerance for ambiguity. She learns to be Indian in Mexican culture,
> to be Mexican from an Anglo point of view. She learns to juggle
> cultures. She has a plural personality, she operates in a pluralistic
> mode . . ..
>
>   Gloria Anzaldua, *Borderlands/La Frontera* (1987: 79)

In this section, I was going to oppose the experience of being "a
foreign anthropologist" in Africa with my struggle as a scholar
writing about her own ethnic group. I was going to talk about
how different my more remote academic interest and research
experience in Africa had been from my anguished, consuming
engagement with Israel. But then the ambiguous, less "picture
perfect" experiences of the "foreign ethnographer" pressed
themselves and demanded to be heard. What do I make of these
experiences that blurred the lines of difference between the two
types of anthropologists: the "native" and the "outsider?" How
do I understand that blurring of the lines of "self" and "other,"
subject and object in Africa, not only in my native Israel?[8]

Yes, it was easier to put together the research proposal that
brought me to Botswana in 1982 after four years as a graduate
student at Brandeis. I did not struggle and agonize over the very
categories and conception of the research project the way I did,
and continue to do, with my Israeli material. I wrote about
examining the links between macro- and micro-level politics, about
development programs, about the way people dealt with national
programs of directed change and land reform. My identity meant
nothing for such realist examinations, or so I thought. When my
proposal was accepted by more then one granting agency, I was
elated. It was not only that I was granted more money then I had
ever had access to in my life but that my academic research project
was legitimized, authorized by such grants. So here I was, with
all the privileges – material, institutional and ideological – that
this new position of a researcher/anthropologist bestowed. I had
prepared myself for the role before I arrived in Botswana: I read

and wrote about "fieldwork," learned Setswana, read anthropological monographs. I even picked "my people" and "my assistant/translator" in a short trip that preceded my great "professional fieldwork." But it proved hard – this simple, easy stepping into power and privilege, to "other" them as my "informants" and "assistants," to claim the crispness of my position there as a "researcher" and a much richer "*lekgoa*" (white). The tensions were there from the very start. A few days after arriving in Botswana, I left Gaborone, the capital, on my way to the small village where I had made contacts a year earlier. I knew I was terrified. I drove fast and had loud, very loud music on. My terror was so complete that I found myself (less than two hours after I had left town) with my newly purchased pickup in a ditch, at the side of the road, unharmed but with a bent front axle and a broken windshield. I had failed to hear the tire explode. I had my earphones on. I was listening to the music of the Mizrahi-pride group HaBrera Hativit. After getting the car towed into a garage, I hitched a passing truck loaded with sugar bags and arrived in the village with only a few personal belongings. Why did I feel so much better in my temporary poverty? And why did I struggle for all the months that followed to rid myself of the privileges of my position? "How could you eat in the privacy of your hut when children outside your door were fed bland white-corn porridge and had bloated bellies?" I asked one of my former teachers at Brandeis who had herself carried out fieldwork in Africa two decades earlier. Why don't I ever hear about these very prosaic struggles of "doing fieldwork?"

The few accounts that describe the field experience that I read before going to Botswana (Malinowski 1961, Mead 1928, Powdermaker 1966, and even the 1970 collection *Women in the Field*, edited by Peggy Golde) were all very clear about the definition of the anthropologist's position as Westerner and as researcher. I had ambivalent feeling about both. I did fill my notebooks with interviews, I took two comp ete village censuses, I carried out extensive oral history research – I had done this obsessively; I needed to justify for myself my being there. But I also lapsed into long days and weeks when my conviction of the inner logic of such practice escaped me. I sat long hours with Moses Basebi, my friend and guide, and tried to convince myself of the value of such academic logic by "teaching him anthropology." "How will you help us? We see only hunger," they told me the first day I arrived.

"I will write what I see and the people in America will read about you and know how to help," I answered lamely. Moses held the thick copy of my dissertation, which I brought him on my second visit, and promised with shining eyes: "I will read it all, Pnina." In Israel, my mother teased me: "This is very heavy."

Dealing with the identity of a "lekgoa," a "white woman," was even harder. When I drove with Moses in the village paths, the little kids shouting "lekgoa, lekgoa" reminded me of the songs we, the Israeli "blacks" use to sing to each other: "Kushi bambo Africa, Shokolada masriha" – "You are a black bambo from Africa, you are a stinking chocolate." I tried to tell Moses that I was the "black" in my native country, and I remembered the uneasy reaction a few years later when an African-American professor at Harvard reacted in the same way to my "confession." I told Serefete, my adoptive village mother, that my mother in Israel was not the privileged white woman with an elaborate "kitchen" she had imagined and that, in fact, she, Serefete, was more educated than my own mother who could neither read nor write in any language. I listened to the village girls speak about their relative beauty and the beauty of the photographed black models in the cheap clothing catalogues that were created in South Africa especially for these poor blacks ("she is so beautiful . . . she is so fair . . . she almost looks white . . . ."), and I remembered similar adolescent discussions in my own youth in Israel.

Ten years later, when I returned to Botswana for a second follow-up research, I took Serefete with me to Francistown to visit her brother and my friend Moses in the hospital. I had no car and we were to hitch a ride. As I stood there on the road holding a written sign indicating my destination, I knew very clearly that I was cashing in on my "whiteness." I was right. A beautiful new car stopped minutes later, avoiding the large group of Africans who stood steps away. I could feel Serefete's fear of entering the "rich white man's" car. I asked the driver politely if "she" could come in as well. "She is with me," I said, thinking that I would not have to ask this if she was not black and that he was sure to think she is my maid. Throughout that ride, I made a point of talking to Serefete, who sat in the back, in Setswana. Her answers were short and frozen. And all the time, while trying to make Serefete feel I had not deserted her, that I had not turned into the alienated "lekgoa," I was also telling the young English South African man (he said, I think, that he managed real-estate property for a

European company) that I was not only his equal but his class superior. I dropped references to my college teaching in America, to my friendship with publicly known whites in Botswana, to my credentials as a jet-flying researcher. I felt, to paraphrase Ruth Behar, another woman of "borderland identity," that the fault lines of race and class were "quaking within me."

"The pool is not open to all races," I heard the poor, unkempt Afrikaner woman announce when, in one of my rare visits to Johannesburg under apartheid, I tried to enter a public swimming pool. I could feel the burning hostility of the history students in the University of Botswana when I presented my very first synthesis of my oral-history interviews. How could I tell the young angry man in Moletemane that I am "not quite a lekgoa" when I returned ten years after my original long stay in that village. How else could he read my presence, sitting there with my dark sunglasses, a straw hat and a camera. Could I tell him that I understood his rage, that we were caught in a textbook-perfect scene of the "white exploiting outsider woman" and the "angry local black man?"

I had a hard time making the transition away from the "field" and into academic authorship. It was not merely the wrenching experience of rendering the real, complex reality I came to know and grasp so well in bloodless academic abstractions, or the fact that I was writing in a language that was not my own (it is my third after the Iraqi Arabic we spoke at home and the Hebrew of my schooling and national identity). Underlying the long and agonizing process of producing my dissertation was the dual painful sense of alienation from the practice of writing about "them," and my right to be "here," in a spacious Harvard office.[9] I forced myself to write about land tenure and changing definitions of rights to land in a language and style that was meaningless, that violated my own feeling of what I really learned in those hard fifteen months "in the field." I had very little satisfaction with the academic exercise I produced and, in the months and years that followed, I refused to even look at my dissertation, let alone publish it. I felt that there were enough works like it about this or that African tribe or group and that my proper "addition to the literature" was a violation of the very reason that brought me into anthropology in the first place. And during all those hard years of writing, as I waited on tables and supported myself through temp jobs (I had no salable skills, not even as a typist), I felt a terrible guilt for deserting them there, back in Botswana. I sent cheap digital watches, used clothing, and small amounts of money through Tswana students who were going home. I wrote and sent prints of their photographs, as I promised. And when I did not hear any reply from Moses for more then two years (it turned out he took a job in a South African mine and did not receive my mail) I "understood." I justified his anger at being left there, jobless and with few prospects in the poverty that surrounded him, while I was here, in affluent America.

All the time I knew that I would need to get back to my work on Israeli ethnography, but I was not quite sure how. When Barbara Swirski, a Israeli radical feminist, invited me to write a chapter for her edited book on *Women in Israel*, I was completely at a loss. "What kind of chapter? academic, personal?" I asked. "Any kind you want," she replied. I started writing a few "personal" lines. I talked about being thirty, feeling my first child stir in my growing belly, about writing in snow-covered Massachusetts – and I stalled. I did not see the "value" of such exposition. What was interesting about this? Was I invited to write as *the* Mizrahi woman? What do these reflections have to do with such an essentialized identity? I could hear the ridicule of my teachers, of those critical and cruel voices. I would not let anyone see my vulnerability as a woman, as a Mizrahi, as a fledgling academic. I would write when I felt secure in my credentials, in my academic tool-kit, in my crisp professionalism.

How do I understand my complex experience in Africa within this larger project of constructing my professional and personal "life story?" Reflecting on her own biography Ruth Behar writes, "In my years of graduate school and dissertation writing, I had been forced to put aside all the burning questions of my own identity . . . [questions] that propelled me into anthropology in the first place" (1993: 331). Did I put my own "burning questions of identity" on the back burner during those years? I think not. Even if I naively believed, before leaving Israel for graduate studies in the US, that "Africa" would be the absolute "other" for me, the professional "safe heavens" where my emotional involvement would not "stand in the way" of my analytical understanding, I was very conscious, from the outset, of the larger purpose of what I believed was this necessary "detour." The professional skills and recognition I planned to acquire in the relative emotional calm of "doing" an African ethnography were to empower me to return to those "burning questions." Looking at that "African experience" today, it is clear that it was not only the necessary "phase" towards the "great return" to dealing with those burning questions of identity, it was a very powerful experience that enabled me to rethink, from new and critical angles, the very basis of such identity. I am, like Anzaldua and others, a *"mestiza"* who learned to "operate in a pluralistic mode."

The political and historical circumstances within which I made these explorations – at the edge of apartheid South Africa – were indeed unique and powerful. Was I the exploitative *"lekgoa"* researcher who sat in dark sunglasses and a straw hat in a car driven by an African man? Or was I the "colored woman" not allowed into "whites only" public places in apartheid South Africa. ("What race am I?" I asked in my momentary shock as the Afrikaner woman told me "the pool is not open for all races".) And, what does it mean to be a *"Schwartse"* (black) Mizrahi woman in my native Israel? The dilemmas of my ambivalent racial and class identity were accentuated in these extreme, objectifying circumstances and made the process of self-understanding, my struggles for a greater self-knowledge more acute, perhaps easier. Should I fight the practice of apartheid's complete objectification of who I am? Should I try to make the enraged Tswana man who grabbed my straw hat understand that I was not who he thought I am? My feeble and contradictory attempts to do just that in both situations – entering the pool after showing my Israeli passport, and spending long hours of negotiation and discussion in Setswana with the enraged man – had taught me an important, if far from new, lesson: my ability to shape my own identity, and that of others, is closely linked and must work within the powerful objectification of such identity in a particular social and historical moment. To allow "them" to define me in essentialized, one-dimensional ways would be to submit to their power, to give up my "voice." Yet how do I write as a "Mestiza"?

Although none of these personal, reflexive thoughts made their way into my early academic writing, they did, I believe, shape the content and style of my more recent published work on Botswana. I have written about the struggle of these subaltern populations, at the margins of the colonial and precolonial Tswana centralized polities, to define their collective identity, and written about moments of resistance to state hegemony. I have analyzed the contemporary reproduction of marginality and intergener-

ational poverty among those defined as Basarwa/Bushmen in the
rural periphery of Botswana. I have tried to write in ways that
will be informed by my sensitivity to my position as an outsider
investigator. I "allowed the people to speak for themselves"
providing long quotes in Setswana of situations that unfolded in
the research situation; I recorded the independent investigations
of Moses, my research assistant, and explored his encounters and
thought processes; and I examined transcribed texts of interviews
carried out by Tswana students along with my own notes and
interviews. I have also made several efforts (all failed) to work
with Tswana "native scholars." In one such attempt, I invited a
resident of the Tswapong region, an American-educated young
man who worked in the capital, to write a collaborative essay with
me and gave him copies of all my taped interviews and unpublished notes. In our initial meetings, he talked about the need to
adhere to "our own values" and other such statements that
sounded so remote, so unrelated to the way Moses and the others
in the village had expressed themselves. Despite several attempts
to revive the collaborative project, I have not heard from him since.
Was he caught within the same contradictory feelings that have
doomed my own attempts to write as a "native daughter" at
Barbara's request?

Writing *Birthright*

> For critical to our writing of culture are the often socially dominated
> conditions of those we write about, our own ideological stances as
> ethno/writers, and a general failing to bring together political
> economy and cultural criticism.
>
> Jose Limon, *Dancing with the Devil* (1994: 14)

> You don't choose to write the books you write, any more than you
> choose your mother, your father, your brother, your children . . ..
>
> Ruth Behar, *Translated Woman* (1993: xi)

In 1989, about a year after I received my Ph.D. in anthropology
from Brandeis University, I went to visit my former teachers in
Israel and explore my options of getting a job in my native land.
"Oh, Pnina," said one (male, Ashkenazi) anthropologist who was
rushing to catch his bus, "have you completed your education?

Great!, Just come back! I can tell you there is going to be a lot of work for anthropologists now that the Falasha [Ethiopian-Jews] are here. It is a big problem, a big problem!" he muttered as he disappeared into his bus.

In my original description of this scene I wrote: "I could not explain why his friendly invitation made me feel extremely uncomfortable, almost noxious but it was enough to keep me away from the Israeli academy for several long years." A Israeli friend who read this phrase expressed her surprise at my strong reaction: "But isn't it what you wanted? To be considered an equal professional? What's wrong with using your skills and your particular sensibilities to lessen the pains of cultural transformations the Ethiopians have to undergo in Israel today?" I think she missed the point. What made me so angry was the blunt objectifying position I was invited to take. For in this brief encounter I was invited, because of my newly earned credentials, into the privileged hegemonic club of those who only thirty years ago described my own parents and their immigrant group as "a big problem, a big problem." I resented the moment that was going to transform me from the subject of those professional researchers into a member of the group who made their careers by writing about those "problematic" Others. I felt the same rage that I thought I would be able to harness by "becoming professional."[10] "They" continue to define "the problem" in the same objectifying, patronizing way; I felt noxious, not powerful, at that realization. That encounter, and what it communicated, did keep me away from the Israeli academy for a few years. But I must add that it did not stop my intense interest in the subject.

All those years, while working on my African ethnography in Boston, I could not stop myself from following the academic and popular discourse about "ethnicity" in Israel. Along with my regular teaching on Africa at Harvard College and then at Holy Cross College, I taught evening and adult education classes on Israeli group relations. I had a hard time reading the patronizing, exoticizing studies that Israeli anthropologists continued to produce – micro studies that documented this or that "*edda*" (ethnic community, always of Sephardi/non-European origin). But I also did not find intellectually and personally satisfying the few critical studies that pointed out that all is not so well in the "Zionist miracle" and that, to quote one angry writer, "The Sephardim, as a Jewish Third World people, form a semi-colonized nation-within-a-nation" (Ella Shohat 1988: 2). At one point I researched and proposed[11] a study of the political aspirations and life histories of politicians of Mizrahi origin. Then I met Dan Rothstein at the Harvard Center for Middle Eastern Studies. Dan was working on analyzing a large body of archival material he collected in Israel. When I read his draft, I was elated. Here, finally, was an approach to Israeli group relations that went beyond the essentializing preoccupation with "Sephardim" or "Mizrahim" as the exotic Others for the modern Israeli hegemonic voice. It also escaped the materialist reductionist arguments that saw the "Jews of the East" as the hapless victims of the relentless forces of capitalist expansion in Israel controlled by the similarly essentialized "Ashkenazim," the European Jews. Dan's central concern was to explore what he calls "the vision of equality" articulated by immigrants to Israel from Arab and North African countries in the early 1950s, a demand based on their sense of their birthright as Jews in a newly forming Jewish state. I read into Dan's humanist thesis a larger agenda. I heard for the first time the missing voice of the immigrants themselves. When Dan told me of his plans to go back to Israel for a short research trip that would add a few oral interviews with immigrant families to his archival material, I suggested that he see my parents who immigrated to Israel from Iraq in 1950. He did. When I called my mother to ask about the interview she said it went fine, and that Dan is a wonderful young man. But then she added knowingly: "He did not have a tape recorder. But I think it was hidden in his briefcase." When I saw the text Dan produced I asked half-jokingly if he was going to use the name "Motzafi" in the final version or opt, as we anthropologists often do, to use a different name for our "informants."

At one point, after we had jointly led a workshop on "Sephardim and Ashkenazim in Israel" for the New Israel Fund, an American progressive organization that supports innovative democratic NGO (Non-Government Organization) projects in Israel, Dan proposed to me that I join him as coauthor in revising and reorganizing the manuscript. I accepted the offer, knowing that I was endangering my fledgling academic career. I had not published enough of my dissertation material and the book that was to emerge based on my dissertation work was far from being completed. Dan had his own sacrifices to make. But we both felt that the work was important and that it should be made public.

My immediate concern at these early stages of my involvement in writing *Birthright* was to make the central argument of the book explicit: Immigrants from Arab lands, like my parents, had a clear understanding of the reality of those first turbulent years of statehood; they resisted in many ways the dominant hegemonic discourse that systematically marginalized them and excluded them despite its rhetoric of equality among Jews; they had articulated in pieces and patches an alternative vision of how such equality can be achieved but their voices were silenced, and in the collective memory of those years, they are portrayed as the bewildered primitive Others who could not understand the modern concept of democracy. Using my newly found skills at analytical/academic/anthropological writing, I sought to shape this book in the positivist discourse of those who dominated Israeli academic life. After all, the earlier version of the book was shot down by Israeli readers who did not find enough "data" to support the "unclear argument." As I chopped the flowing narrative of the manuscript and rearranged the presentation of the historical data to support our newly "coherent" argument, I gave sections new titles like "Defining 'Them,'" "Who is 'Us,'" "The Encounter." I suggested that we make explicit the discrepancy presented in the documents between the public and the private discourse of the Zionist elite. And I constantly worried that we might not have enough "data" to support our more specific argument suggesting that, while the immigrants' resistant voice was heard during those critical years, it was systematically excluded from public debates.

Dan and I both felt deeply committed to the project and to the important social message it delivers. We both believed strongly that writing such an historical narrative of the Mizrahim would be not only empowering for the Mizrahim but would make for a better historiography of Israel. Our collaborative work produced its own difficulties and dilemmas, however, many of which still remain unresolved. We never defined clearly who was the audience for this text: The Israeli academy? Popular readership in Israel that includes Mizrahi activists and scholars? Or is it a book in the language and stylistic requirements of standard academic scholarship in the "center?" (We did, after all, submit the book to the most prestigious academic presses.) And what was the nature of our complex collaborative work? The agenda Dan brought to the work was his sincere commitment to social change and grass-roots activism. My own interest and growing involvement in this project has been at once academic and deeply personal. For a long time I believed that I could suspend the personal and remain within my role as the analytical partner who would bring to this collaboration her "anthropological eye" to complement the activist perspective that Dan provided.[12]

My contribution to the collaborative work, we both agree, has been my ability to sharpen the argument and point to the links between the kind of argument we develop for the Israeli case and the critical theoretical interdisciplinary discourse in anthropology, cultural studies, and history. Yet the more involved I became in reshaping and in sharpening the analytical focus of the text – the more I became a coauthor rather than an editor and a critical reader – the more central my identity as "the native" became. Was I, by the sheer fact of my heritage and name – by being "the native" – claiming and lending the book a "moral legitimacy"? Should I speak explicitly as a "native scholar"? Should I make explicit my deep personal links to the historical realities we were documenting and analyzing?

I am keenly aware of the powerful force such a claim to authenticity brings with it in the contemporary mood of post-modern writing in the US. Upon returning to Israel in October 1996, however, I discovered that the battle for alternative historio-graphies, for "letting the powerless people speak" and for reflexive writing – ideas and phrases that had become cliches in the US – is only now beginning to be introduced and fought about in the Israeli academy.[13] But I found that I could not comfortably claim that position and speak from such a place. I have read bell hooks (1990), Smadar Lavie (1995), and Hunani Trask (1993), to mention just a few particularly vocal examples, who seem to have adopted the explicit "I *am* the native-woman-scholar" voice and wave it over the heads of the "bad white guys," the "members of the exclusive club." I could not share their triumph, much less their paradoxically elitist/obscure vocabulary.

bell hooks, who writes from her position as an African-American woman in the heart of the white American Academy, is one example of this self-assured moralist voice: "I write from the 'margin,'" "I am IT," I hear her say. You must come to me if you are an enlightened liberal white, but you can never reach my "space." In a more shrill version of such moralist stand, Hunani Trask warns off any non-native scholars and rejects their academic "mamo-jumbo" for "things native" (1993). I find little use in this kind of argument, not only because it opens itself to charges of the purity of the essentialized identity of the writer. (How "native are you, Smadar?" And what about class and other defining criteria that make the writer a "representative" of the "oppressed"?) My objection to the "I am a native scholar and you are not" position is directed at precisely the reductive essentializing of identities that it promotes. The direct and unproblematic self-definition of these scholars as the champions of the powerless and their cause[14] produces, in my view, an "overdetermination of both concepts ("Here"-"There"; Eurocenter-peripheries; oppression-resistance) and subjectivities" (the good-native-writer vs. the bad-powerful-Western writer; dominant vs. oppressed populations). It is too easy, and I would argue historically reductionist, to describe the Mizrahim in Israel as an oppressed Third-World population; to apply preconceived analytical categories and concepts that have little resonance among the people whose life, world, and struggle we try to understand. The historical record we examine in *Birthright* does not lend itself to such reading. The Mizrahi voices we record, *and my own life experiences*, point to great ambivalences and contradictions, and speak of the most powerful urge to belong to the collectivity along with rage and resistance against objectifying, othering dominant discourses. The challenge in writing *Birthright* (for me) has been the portrayal of such struggles and contradictions where the categories of dominant-and-oppressed and good-and-evil were never clear cut and visible; of depicting social difference and struggle in ways that are historically specific to the Israeli context. How do I write about the internal contradictions and conflicts within the dominated sector? How do I weave together diverse discourses that speak not only about resistance and pride but also of anxiety and about internal divisions along class, ethnic origin, and gender? How do I, as a "native scholar," avoid the danger of essentializing my people?

Ethnography and Autoethnography: Fields of Power and Identities

My exploration of a way of writing about "my people" has been directed at two closely related sets of questions. The first has to do with my own position as a native/indigenous writer/author:

How has my particular life experience and feelings shaped my scholarship? Should I claim a "native daughter" voice? What kind of voice is that? Has the prevailing academic discourse I sought to engage with facilitated, created a space for, or effectively silenced, my voice? The second set of questions has to do with my search for sensitive analytical tools and concepts that will enable me to grasp and describe with accuracy and subtlety a complex historical reality from the perspective of the powerless. If there is any lesson (or conclusion) to be drawn from this essay, it is that the two sets of questions are not and can not be separate. My identity as a Mizrahi woman has propelled me, in torturous and far from direct ways, as the life story presented above shows, to return again and again to the study of power and the workings of hegemony. It pushed me to examine these questions from a deeply committed position and forced me to face such questions both on the level of the actual fieldwork experience and from the intimately connected analytical and theoretical implications of such work. Rosaldo (1989) has movingly explored the way his own experience of grief had opened new, more meaningful ways for understanding such feeling among the Ilongot. I suggest here that one's positioning within marginalized communities – of ethnic, race, religion, or gender – shapes not only one's research interest and the epistemologies one chooses in developing such research, it also sensitizes one in conscious and/or unconscious ways to look at practices of exclusion and perhaps to write in ways that do not accept the status quo. I say "perhaps" because it is clearly a more entangled subject. Writers of "Third-World origin" and other scholars who are/were members of excluded communities, face serious "dilemmas" in their presentations and might be "axe-grinding," "self-interested," or "mistaken" as Abu-Lughod, Rosaldo, Dirlik, and Limon note in the opening quotes above. Indeed, the life story I construct here is in no way a tale of my "heroic" resistance to dominant rules. In many ways it depicts, on the individual level, the more common compliance to, despite some efforts to maneuver within, dominant structures and forces.

The issue, I argue, is not that all "native writers" are conditioned by virtue of their birth to write about oppression and exclusion in insightful ways and clearly not that we have some "moral right" or a monopoly over such work. The point here is not one's indigenous qualifications but rather the connection that is always there between the researcher's positioning in society and history and the kind of research agenda and understanding such personal background shapes. And here I return to Adam Kuper's opening questions. I agree with Kuper that the view that "only natives should study natives" must be rejected. In fact, as I have argued throughout this essay, the binary categories of "native" and "non-native" are themselves superfluous and misleading. A researcher who had experienced in her own life oppression and had become conscious of it in ways that significantly inform her scholarship *is more likely*, I suggest, to write critically – to write from a position of social and political engagement. Because we are all, researchers and subjects, the products of our history and culture, an experience of social and political exclusion is likely to shape more critical thinking and writing about such experiences in the collective, structural domain. The alarm about "the nativist turn," I suspect, does not center on the "ethnic origin of the researcher" (although the last two decades have seen a rapidly growing number and greater visibility of formerly excluded subjects in academe) but exists because of the associated trend of a more radical, politically engaged scholarship advocated by many of these scholars.

But what kind of radical scholarship should we write? I have rejected what I call "the easy way out" of vulgar radicalism both for its reductive claims to represent "the oppressed" ("I am a native woman, you are the bad-white-male") and its limited analytical power. Instead, I have called for the exploration and development of more sensitive tools and terms that narrate histories of oppression, and hope to enact change. I wish to propose here that the personal narrative I have presented (and the larger autoethnographical project it signals) is one step towards that kind of writing and constitutes an act of resistance. It is an act of what bell hooks calls "talking back" to power in two ways: in the kind of genre it adopts and in its opening up a space for alternative understandings of the work of power in Israel and elsewhere.

Let me begin with the second point and make explicit the wider social meaning of the individual story presented here. I offer this narrative of self-understanding, this limited and temporal effort of making sense of the flow of my professional life, not for the dubious joy of making myself the center of attention, but because I hope that through the telling of my lived, direct experience I can tell best about existing power dynamics and the complex process of domination in my native land. My story is neither unique nor exemplary. It tells about an anxious mixture of challenge to, and the acceptance of, dominant rules and values of Israeli society and Israeli academe. When I was offered the option of escaping the limited options I had in my marginal, mostly Mizrahi hometown by attending a prestigious school in the heart of "First Israel," I did not hesitate. But as the short high-school essay quoted above attests, I continued to question the hegemonic definition of Mizrahi and Arab subjectivities. Like many other members of marginalized groups, I sought to enter the public domain of professional academic life only to find out that its claim to neutrality and scientific objectivity effectively silenced my fledgling attempts to develop my voice and scholarship with a meaning from my position as a Mizrahi woman. On a deeper level, I offer this story as a social and historically specific document that asks the reader to consider the complex ways in which marginalized people, in Israel and elsewhere, reproduce the structures and forces that exclude them despite their best efforts to resist their provided subjectivities. Using what bell hooks calls my own "experientially based history," I have sought in this chapter to develop a more nuanced understanding of the way hegemonic practices in Israel shape the compliance of Mizrahi subjects in subtle ways; ways that do not require – as in the case of Arabs and other excluded minorities in Israel – the use of force; ways that are effective because of their invisible, less explicit nature.

Judith Okely (1992: 3) has argued that "autobiography dismantles the positivist machine" and that "positivism destroys the notion of experience." Contemplating these statements through my own experience, I would like to propose here an idea that will need to be more fully explored in future work. By presenting my lived experience as a Mizrahi woman and anthropologist, I deflect the positivist critique (those "critical voices" that Dan wrote about) that may argue "you don't have your 'facts' straight;" "you need to read more;" "support your argument with better 'data.'" The power – and the "truth" – of this and other autobiographical accounts, is that they can not be undermined on such positivist terms; their "reality," their poignancy is given, built into the very definition of a lived experience.

I have struggled for all these years, and perhaps continue to do so, to fit into the dominant male-Ashkenazi-positivist discourse of Israeli scholarship.[15] When my identity and my personal experiences as a member of the marginalized and powerless did not fit with dominant academic discourses and public descriptions of the center – a dominant discourse that undermined the very existence of such alternative collective identity and the need for its narration – I sought to secure my professional armor outside the Israeli arena. I continued to split off my personal experiences and learning from my distant analytical self in my work in Africa, producing a disembodied text that adhered to all the prevailing conventions of a classic realist ethnography. Looking inward and claiming my voice in a more personal way – I was convinced, perhaps *because* of my vulnerability as a woman and a Mizrahi – undermined my professional standing and threatened my hard-won position of relative power and recognition. The flood of reflexive writing and the arguments made for the significance of such writing for the anthropological project were irrelevant for me from that position.[16] I needed to discover for myself, to construct from my own experiences, the links between such reflexivity and the analytical insights it produces, between the personal and the theoretical.[17]

"By giving them voice, she was giving herself voice," writes Caroline Brettell (this volume), with reference to her journalist mother. Exploring my contradictory experiences forced me to search harder for the unwritten, silenced, and internally contradictory experience of Mizrahim in Israel. By weaving together the experiential and the structural, the political and the theoretical, I wish to challenge the canonized genre of "objective" depictions of social reality. By collapsing the categories of native and non-native, subject and object, researcher and subject of study, I hope to go beyond the strict laws of the genre identified with traditional social-science practices. This is making me a better, not less able, anthropologist and analyst.

Notes

1. My first attempt, "Equality in a Jewish State: Material and Symbolic processes of Inclusion and Exclusion in Israel," was presented in an invited panel on "Redefining the Membership in the Collectivity: The Quest for Legitimation in the National Arena" at the 1993 AAA meeting in Washington D.C. The

second attempt was a paper that was read in my absence at 1995 AAA meetings, in the session on "Auto/Ethnography and Ethno/Biography: Anthropology, Life Stories, and Questions of Voice." I would like to thank Debbie Reed-Danahay, who organized this session, for her support throughout the writing process. I also thank John Comaroff, Nitza Yanai, Fran Markowitz, Vicki Shiran, Itzik Saporta, Andre Levi, Haim Hazan, and Daniel de Malach for their insightful comments and suggestions.

2. Commenting on my presentation of such questions in the 1993 AAA panel, Stanley Tambiah described my paper as a "moving" account and suggested that it belonged to "postmodern" writings.

3. We were trained to write exams that demonstrated we read the assigned bibliography for the course. Essay writing was a separate requirement towards the degree. No writing courses or direct interaction with the teacher framed this essay writing.

4. I used the Hebrew "*mudaut hevratit.*"

5. The article was written by Smooha Sammy and Yochanan Peres. I read the Hebrew version. The Engish version was eventually published in 1975 in *Social Dynamics* under the title, "The Dynamics of Ethnic Inequalities: The Case of Israel."

6. I simplify here, but not a lot. At some point in the future, I hope to engage in such a dialogue with my precursors in ways that are less confrontational and more constructive. Jose Limon (1994 chapter 1–4) presents me with an inspiring example of such exploration.

7. Unlike the boarding school for Mizrahi children I mentioned above, these were elementary-level schools and programs that enriched the children in their own elite schools and neighborhoods. A bitter-sweet note of such difference are the discussions we (the Mizrahi boarding-school children) used to have questioning our designation as "gifted."

8. There is, of course, a large body of work that theorizes and directly discusses the questions I am raising here. I could have put my "professional postmarks" here citing Fabian, Dumont, Geertz, Tyler, Crapanzano, Dwyer, Rabinow, Tedlock, and others who speak about the various aspects of fieldwork, objectification, writing the other, positioned researchers, etc. I choose to stay close to my own experiences and the inner process of my own coming to terms with these issues. This is

my voice and these are my struggles. I had to resist my urge to engage in this academic discursive convention of citing the authoritative voice of others in order to lend my voice greater credibility. I refer the interested reader to Kirsten Hastrup's article "Writing Ethnography" (1992) as one source, an overview of the "state of the art" for discussions and references.

9. The office was given to me, I still believe, because of some administrative mistake. I was after all only a "graduate student associate"; my home institution was Brandeis.

10. Bannister (1991) describes at greater length a parallel struggle of a Jewish woman to escape her gender and ethnicity via what seemed to her to be a universal/neutral domain of professional academic life. I return to some of these questions in the concluding section of this chapter.

11. I submitted the proposal only to the Harvard Academy of Scholars. When I did not secure financing, I left the project for some future point in time.

12. The particular nature of our collaborative work – between an academic and a grass-roots activist, a "native" Sephardi/ Mizrahi woman and an American/Ashkenazi Jewish man, an anthropologist and a historian – as I noted elsewhere (Motzafi-Haller 1994) can, and has been, a source of strength and creativity in this work and for any project that goes beyond and tries to expand on narrow academic and disciplinary limits. But it also give rise to more banal dilemmas from the ones outlined by Abu-Lughod: social and political activism has demands and structures that do not allow for the extended time or energy necessary for academic writing. (Dan has founded and now directs a nonprofit grass-roots organization, "The Right Question Project," that works to empower poor minority people.) And the requirements of the academic job market also work against such creative projects: as an Africanist with expanding interest in Israel, I was asked more than once (especially when the job description asked explicitly for an "Africanist") if my interest in Israel will undermine my African work. For several long years of job searching, I was defined and had to "sell myself" as "an area specialist."

13. See for example Uri Ram 1993, 1995. Yet the critical "new historiography" that was written until now in Israel has been largely concerned with articulating the alternative counter-

history of the non-Jewish Palestinian minority. The Mizrahi narrative has not yet been developed.

14. I borrow the phrase "overdetermination of concepts and subjectivities" from Arif Dirlik (1994: 342). Arif Dirlik observes, in a cynical eye, that in some cases such radical scholarship expresses not the "voice" of the powerless but the voice of the "the newlyfound power of 'First World intellectuals of Third World origin'" (1994: 342). The recent debate between Sahlins (1995) and Obeyesekere (1992) is a case in point.

15. Alexandra Jaffe portrays a similar tension in her portrayal (in this volume) of Corsican authors and intellectuals. I felt like one of the Corsican poets she writes about. Like him, I was "dominated by a discourse" that I "do not master."

16. I have been asked several times by colleagues who have heard presentations of my dilemma and read fragments of this paper: "but why did you write in such bloodless abstractions despite what you felt?" I think the answer goes back to my point about the ways oppression and effective silencing worked in my case The difficult and long journey I had made in search of points of resistance, of breaking away from the discursive pressure to comply, is an illustration of the links between the personal and the political.

17. Since writing these lines I have explored in greater depth the feminist literature that strongly advocates the value and the power of personal narratives.

Chapter 9

Blurred Genres and Blended Voices: Life History, Biography, Autobiography, and the Auto/Ethnography of Women's Lives

Caroline B. Brettell

> Biography – the optic that fuses individual and event into both a
> worldview and a narrative genre – lies at the methodological core of
> much ethnography and history.
>
> Comaroff and Comaroff (1992: 25)

Introduction: Blurred Genres

In 1980 Clifford Geertz published an essay titled "Blurred Genres: The Refiguration of Social Thought" in *The American Scholar*. In this essay Geertz drew attention to the significant amount of genre mixing in postmodern intellectual life – "philosophical inquiries looking like literary criticism, scientific discussions looking like belles lettres *morceaux*, baroque fantasies presented as deadpan empirical observations, histories that consist of equations and tables . . . documentaries that read like true confessions, parables posing as ethnographies, theoretical treatises set out as travelogues, ideological arguments cast as historiographical inquiries" (Geertz 1983: 20). The result, he suggests, is that it is difficult both to situate authors within particular disciplines and to classify their works.

In some sense this chapter offers further consideration of the blurring of genres, particularly as it pertains to the task of writing about women's lives.[1] My interest in this subject stems from the questions I have confronted in trying to describe how and why I, as an anthropologist, have written a book about the life and career of a Canadian woman journalist who also happens to have been my mother. My considerations can be situated within the broader context of reflexivity that has characterized both postmodern and feminist anthropology[2] and that has resulted in what Barbara Tedlock (1991: 81) has labeled a "growing meta-anthropological literature." Among other things, feminism and postmodernism have directed our attention to the autobiographical dimension of the anthropological encounter (Moore 1994; Okely and Callaway 1992), to a reconsideration of the contributions of life history to anthropological research (Abu-Lughod 1993; Behar 1990; Cole 1992), to the rising interest in the role of biography in women's history (Alpern et al. 1992), and to an exploration of auto-ethnography (Denzin 1989; Hayano 1979; Strathern 1987).

In this chapter, I explore some of these issues by comparing the current textual undertaking with work I engaged in many years ago that involved recording the life stories of three Portuguese migrant women. My discussion focuses specifically on issues of genre and voice and the implications that these have for the ethnographic enterprise.

Defining Terms and Situating Genres

Despite Geertz's recognition of the blurring of genres, where life-writing is concerned there is a very clear desire to delineate boundaries and define distinct approaches. Michael Angrosino (1989), for example, differentiates biography – a narrative account of one person's life, reconstructed mainly, though not exclusively, from records and archives and written or otherwise recorded by another – from autobiography – a narrative account of a person's life that he or she has personally written or otherwise recorded.

By contrast, the life history in Angrosino's view is an account of one person's life as told to another, the researcher.[3] Angrosino goes on to distinguish the life history from the life story, the former a narrative that records the entire span of a life and the latter a narrative that highlights a few key events or focuses on a few important relationships (1989: 3). A further elaboration of this distinction is provided by Peacock and Holland (1993). They begin with the premise that reservations about how representative or typical a life history is are no longer an issue because life histories are now accepted as subjective documents.[4] They then suggest that the concept of life story is preferable to life history precisely because it moves us away from any presumption that the narrative is true (Peacock and Holland 1993: 368). Finally, they differentiate a life-focused life story that treats a life as a window on the objective facts of historical and ethnographic events, from a story-focused life story that emphasizes the subjective experience of the narrator and the form of the narrative itself.

Nowhere is the diversity of genres of life-writing more apparent than in the literature by feminist ethnographers who write about women's lives.[5] The best examples of this genre focus on the life of a single women in a particular cultural context (Behar 1993; Blackman 1982; Brown 1991; Gmelch 1991; Kendall 1988; Shostak 1981). These works differ, however, in the manner in which they give voice to the narrator and in the extent to which the ethnographer inserts herself in the text and comments on the words of the woman whose story is being told.

For example, in the telling of her own life, Nisa is also telling the lives of !Kung women in general. The anthropologist Marjorie Shostak has organized Nisa's "life" into a written text and the ethnographic conclusions drawn from the life narrative are included in the introductions to each of the chapters/phases of Nisa's life. Gmelch, in her life history of the Irish traveling woman, Nan, alternates between the first person and the third person throughout her text. "I decided," she states, "to include myself explicitly as the narrator and the person to whom Nan tells her story in order to portray the collaborative and interactional nature of anthropological research and to reveal my own relationship with Nan" (Gmelch 1991: 21).[6]

Perhaps the most complex blending of voices is contained in Karen McCarthy Brown's "intimate spiritual biography" of the Vodou priestess Mama Lola (Brown 1991: ix). "I developed a style of narrative analysis," Brown claims, "in which the flow of the text is determined by story lines that from time to time evoke an analytic voice" (Brown 1991: 15). However, in addition to Mama Lola's voice, and to Brown's scholarly and self-revelatory voices, there is also the voice of the story-teller, Gede, who operates in the realm of fiction.

If early criticism of the use of life history in anthropology revolved around questions of representativeness and objectivity, today the most heated debates center on the authorial hand of the ethnographer. In the process of editing and rearranging an oral text in order to create a translation that is comprehensible to a reading audience far removed from the Kalahari Desert, the Irish countryside, or the ritual worlds of a voodoo priestess, the ethnographer may ignore indigenous methods of story-telling and constructing a life (Behar 1990: 226). They may also overlook the autoethnographic aspects of such accounts. For example, in an earlier essay in this volume, Kay Warren alludes to the authorial controversy surrounding the life testimony of the Guatemalan woman, Rigoberta Menchu.

Lila Abu-Lughod's response to the problem of "shaping the words of people living in societies other than our own" (1993: 17) is to call for a clear articulation of how we have worked. She bluntly admits that she reshaped the stories she was told by Bedouin women in order to juxtapose their interests with those most salient for specific audiences in the West. The stories she presents in *Writing Women's Worlds* follow what she calls an "anthropological logic" (Abu Lughod 1993: 18); they are organized around issues of patrilineality, polygyny, reproduction, patrilateral parallel-cousin marriage, and honor and shame.

It is in the context of such discussions about authorial voice, the nature of life history, the various ways in which women's lives have been written in the late twentieth century, and the ethnographic and autoethnographic character of such narratives that I consider my own texts.

Life His/Stories and Ethnography: Three Portuguese Migrant Women

We Have Already Cried Many Tears (1982/1995) is a book that brings together the migration stories of three Portuguese women – Ana, Ricardina, and Virginia – who left Portugal for France in the late 1960s. When I wrote it I had some specific goals in mind. I wanted to show the diversity of lived experiences of Portuguese migrant women in general, through the lives of three particular women. I chose these three women from the approximately forty women I had come to know quite well during a year of fieldwork in France in the mid 1970s.

Each of these women represented a different pattern of migration. Ricardina was a young single woman at the time of her departure for France. Ana followed a husband abroad, leaving her two children in Portugal in the care of their maternal grandmother. Virginia, mother to a teenage boy who had been born illegitimately in the mid 1950s, left for France with a married sister who was joining her husband. Prior to her departure, she had been working as a domestic servant in Lisbon. In addition, each of these women came from different social and economic backgrounds: Ricardina from a small village deep in the interior of Portugal; Ana from the city of Porto and hence a working-class background; Virginia from a village not far from the Atlantic coast that for centuries had been affected by emigration. Each of these women had a different reason for choosing to emigrate, but all were shaped by the gendered contexts of their lives within Portuguese culture and society.

In the general introduction to the book, I used the terms life history and life story interchangeably. However, two were collected through a series of ethnographic interviews or conversations that were spread out over several months. The third was recorded more formally in a shorter period of time and expressly as a life story. Today, and in light of the distinctions drawn by Angrosino on the one hand and Holland and Peacock on the other, I would probably refer to the narratives as life-focused life stories. These were women who shared the experience of migration. In attempting to understand that experience, it was necessary to situate it in personal and historical time. George Gmelch (1992) has observed that ethnographers are rarely on the scene to watch migration as it happens. They must rely on memory and recollection, and they inevitably shape the narratives in certain ways as they record and write. Such narratives are themselves quite appropriate to the goals I had in mind for it is individuals, or at most families, rather than groups or communities who migrate.

At the time that I published these life stories, I acknowledged my editorial hand in organizing them into chronological order, editing out redundancies, and creating a balance between the three accounts that would permit systematic analysis as a unit, as well as separately. However, I also tried to maintain the impression of the spoken language of these three women, using their phrases and adages, and the short expressive sentences that are so much a part of conversational autobiography. Like Shostak, I did not insert myself in the text of the narratives; my own comments were limited to the introductions to each of the narrative chapters where I noted matters of more general ethnographic significance that could be learned from each of their lives. I used the general introduction to address the history of Portuguese migration and the legal, religious, and structural aspects of women's status in Portuguese society.

While the exercise of such editorial authority would not please some contemporary proponents of the life history method, I feel comfortable with my decision in light of the purpose with which the narratives were collected and written. Susan Geiger (1986: 343) has argued that life histories help us to gain access to the particularities of women's experiences under the changing political, economic, and social conditions of the twentieth century. In addition, "they permit comparative cross-cultural studies of women's responses to such conditions in different settings" (Geiger 1986: 343). It was precisely with these aims in mind that I composed the text of *We Have Already Cried Many Tears*. I mediated the words of Ana, Ricardina, and Virginia for the broader purposes of illustrating how women experience migration. I recorded with the written word lives that would otherwise have remained unrecorded. These were, in short, distanced and transcriptive interpretations of the lives of others based on oral accounts that nevertheless gave voice to Ana, Virginia, and Ricardina. I had, or at least I thought I had, a clear sense of the genre I was using and of the ethnographic contributions that I was making through its use.

Writing a Mother's Life: Biography, Autobiography, and Auto/Ethnography?

If the genre, the voices, and the ethnographic intent of *We Have Already Cried Many Tears* were clear, the same cannot be said for my book about my mother, Zoe Browne-Clayton Bieler. Zoe was born in 1915 in a small farm community called the Okanagan Mission in the interior of the province of British Columbia, Canada. She went on to pursue a career in journalism, beginning with a position on the weekly news magazine, *The Montreal Standard*, from 1942 to 1949. Eventually, she became the women's editor (1957–1969) and later the medical reporter (1971–1979) for *The Montreal Star*, the evening English-language newspaper in Montreal, Quebec, until its demise in 1979.

As a book by a daughter about a mother who was a writer, this text involves a blending of voices and, by extension, a blurring of genres. It draws on a variety of sources and it describes a number of cultural contexts. It is both biography and autobiography, not only because it weaves my words with those of my mother but also because the lives of a mother and a daughter are inextricably intertwined. At certain points I discovered, as I made the journey through my mother's life, examples of the mirroring effect between a mother and a daughter that Ruth Behar (1993) addresses in her life history of the Mexican woman, Esperanza.

In *Of Woman Born*, Adrienne Rich (1976) drew attention to the unwritten story of mother-daughter relationships. Since that time mother/daughter writing has emerged as a particular genre, albeit a genre with several subgenres (Cahill 1988; Hirsch 1981; Wagner-Martin 1991). Some of this work, written within a psychological or psychoanalytic framework, makes the relationship itself central, emphasizing its intensity (Gornick 1987) or the daughter's search for identity and selfhood apart from a mother who is the source of all her problems (Friday 1977). Others record powerful emotional moments, such as the experience of a mother's death (Beauvoir 1965; Ernaux 1992; Schreiber 1990) or the exchange of roles that can occur when a mother is debilitated by physical or mental illness (Stanley 1993; Steinem 1983).

Many are biographies, but within the biographical format there are diverse approaches. Some focus on the interconnections of biography and autobiography in the telling of two, and sometimes three, lives (Chang 1991; Steedman 1987). Others, like Mary Catherine Bateson's (1984) biography of her mother Margaret Mead or Sissala Bok's (1991) of her mother Alva Myrdal, are highly personalized accounts of famous professional women who made some sacrifice in their motherly role in order to meet the public demands of their careers. Still others reveal a journey of discovery by daughters who elicited the life histories of famous and not so famous mothers because they felt it was important to save an unusual life from obscurity (Chernin 1985; Kikumura 1981). Finally, there are some, as Phyllis Rose (1990: 23) observes, who use the memoir of a mother "to make a point, blurring the traditional line between academic scholarship and personal narrative." She cites Carolyn Steedman's *Landscape for a Good Woman* as a good example of such an approach. My own account draws inspiration from each of these biographical subgenres.[7]

Adrienne Rich (1976) has cautioned that it is hard to write about one's own mother because ultimately it is one's own story (hence

autobiography?), one's own version of the past. The words in my
text are my words about my mother's words; but they are also
her words *chosen* by me because they help to compose her life.
They are, furthermore, her words about herself, as well as her
words about the world she lived in and particularly about the
world of women that she observed and commented upon throughout her life. She often used her own experiences as a prism through
which to view the lives of others (hence autoethnography?).
Periodically, I do situate myself in the text and some of what I
write is based on personal memory. I also include other people's
words about my mother, words that were largely gathered during
interviews with those who were her friends and colleagues, and
those whom she mentored during the years that she served as
women's editor of *The Montreal Star*.

Women have written about themselves by using a variety of
genres: letters, memoirs, journals, diaries, fiction, and poetry. My
mother used all of these, in addition to her professional *oeuvre*, to
tell her story (a life story?). But it is I who have taken these genres
– an adolescent diary she kept from 1930–1932, a college scrapbook, a travel journal and letters to her father dating to the period
between September 1938 and September 1939 when she traveled
to Europe, newspaper and magazine articles, poems and short
stories – and woven them into a narrative. In addition I draw on a
number of photographic images, many of which provide visual
support to the written word. Indeed, I have been struck by the
power that these images, themselves, have as both record and
representation of a life, and include a few of them in this chapter.

In a short chapter, I cannot do justice to the richness of the
material or to the subtle ways in which these materials come
together to tell a life. What I wish to do in the remaining pages is
to suggest how this life narrative, be it biography or autobiography,
can also be viewed as autoethnography in the sense that, as my
mother wrote about herself or others, she was also "writing
cultures" – engaging in the world through her own experience as
both a participant and an observer.

Like many adolescent girls, Zoe kept a personal diary. "I really
don't know why I am writing this," she began on November 22,
1930, "and I don't suppose I'll keep it up for long. But here goes:
This is a journal not a daily one to record impressions so as I can
laugh at myself in the future." Zoe used this diary not only as a
vehicle to express her individuality, but also as a mechanism for

developing her ambitions and skills as a writer. It was also a place where she recorded her observations of the community into which she was born, a community of well-born, well-educated but not necessarily well-off immigrants from England and Ireland who settled on farms in the west of Canada in the early twentieth century. By the time she was sixteen, Zoe had made up her mind to leave her past behind:

> It will be awful if I spend my life in this one small town. There is precious little chance of getting married here. Only the sons of United Church business men marry and they marry United Church girls, or girls they meet at their work. The poor stay home and the only men they really meet are the men of good family but poor who come here to earn money and rarely succeed. Altogether it's a pretty poor lookout for us. The only thing seems to be to get out and find out if its the same everywhere else.

Zoe's transnational family provided her the opportunity to "get out." Her father, as the third son of a gentrified Anglo-Irish family, was forced to leave his homeland; and yet, throughout his life, he maintained contact with his nine sisters who lived in various parts of the United Kingdom. Zoe wrote to these aunts and about these aunts; she also spent time with them when she visited England in 1938-39. Her journal of that year abroad contains graphic descriptions of a way of life that was soon to be disrupted and changed forever. For example, about a visit to the Lake District home of her Aunt Lucy and Uncle Claude, she wrote:

> They all just do what work they want – picnic when they like, dress for dinner, have elaborate meals, lovely gardens, etc. – all sort of a leftover from another age. Uncle Claude sketches, watches birds and finds their nests, fishes a bit, does business when he wants and putters around. Aunt Lucy gardens and has servant trouble like most other English houses of any size.

This life of leisure was foreign to Zoe's experience and to the life she had known as a child on the simple farm captured in image in Figure 1. In 1973, using the journalistic genre, she drew from memory to write about this way of life, one not all that distant from those that Virginia and Ricardina had described to me in their oral accounts of the daily routine in village Portugal.

Figure 9.1: Browne-Clayton Farm, Okanagan Mission, British Columbia, Canada, ca. 1915. Reprinted with kind permission of Caroline Bieler Brettell.

My father's working day started at 5 a.m. in summer and 6 a.m in winter with the milking, and ended at 7 p.m. when the cows were again milked and bedded down. He always bathed and dressed in clean clothes for dinner. We had no milking machines, so he milked by hand and the milk was separated by a hand-run separator. Each week the cream went to the local dairy while the skim milk was used to feed pigs and calves or for cooking. Some of the cream was used by my mother to churn her own butter. Because there was no electricity on our road until after I had finished high school, we had no refrigeration. Twice each day in summer the cream was lugged some distance to a cold running irrigation ditch to be kept cool. In winter it was kept in the cellar. One of the daily chores was pumping water for all domestic use. My brother and I had to do so many strokes of the pump each day, extra if the tank ran dry. This discouraged us from taking baths more than an inch deep and we were expected to flush the toilet only when necessary. In summer we were encouraged to use outdoor plumbing, used by my father year round, and to swim in the creek.

From the end of April to the end of September we went barefoot on the farm, a fact I'm reminded of every time I buy shoes and am told I have "a very wide foot." My chores included feeding the calves, pigs and chickens. My brother was assigned heavier jobs such as chopping wood for the cooking stove, a space heater and the Franklin stove in the living room, as well as hoeing and looking after irrigation ditches in the orchard. We both picked raspberries and strawberries in season and the whole family pitched in to pick cherries, peaches, greengages, and, of course, apples. The smaller fruits were mostly canned for family use or made into jam. In making jam the problem in our family was finding the money for sugar rather than finding the fruit.

On our farm all, or nearly all the animals were destined for the butcher. My father did all the killing. It was a job he hated, but one he never tried to pass on. Pigs had to be slaughtered at home. Usually the butcher sent out someone to help and my father made sure the job was done when we children were at school. If possible, he wanted my mother away too. Pigs always seem to know what is going to happen and the squealing could be heard on the neighboring farm. Although I was not unfond of pigs, they were not the same as the little calves. I remember once we had a promising heifer and my father decided we could keep her. I was thrilled. She became known as "Zoe's calf." By the time she was ready to be bred she had decided she was a pet, not a cow. She was, my father discovered, quite spoilt. Not only did she resent being milked but she was a poor producer and delighted in kicking the milk bucket on the barn floor whenever she could. She too, had vanished one day when I came home from school (*The Montreal Star*, July 11, 1973)

Zoe's years in college (at the University of British Columbia in Vancouver) are recorded in the newspaper articles that she wrote for *The Ubyssey* (the college newspaper) or for local Vancouver newspapers and in a scrapbook that she assembled from those days. A rather telling article published in February 1935 in the *Vancouver Sun* evokes a character in a novel by Theodore Dreiser. She described a country-bred coed trying to make her way at the university amid a student body that was largely composed of individuals from the Vancouver area. These less experienced students, she wrote,

> . . . wander around with a map of the campus in their hands; they flee to the library out of shyness and at night they sit in their boarding house rooms writing cheerful letters home to show they are not homesick. If classes are going okay, and friends are slowly found, there are still problems with nagging landladies who cannot cook . . . and money that always runs short. The shy little country freshette often finds she has brought down a trunk of hick country clothes unsuitable for campus wear and Vancouver weather.

Zoe began working for *The Ubyssey* soon after she arrived on campus and by her third year she had moved up the ranks to news manager. By then the campus newspaper had become an all-consuming world for her; it was where she made lifelong friends and it was where she decided on her future. Descriptions of her in this world come from photographs and from her cohorts. "Our brown-eyed blonde," wrote fellow *Ubyssey* staff member Allan Morley, "is as vivacious as ever. At one and the same time she appears to be eating a delayed breakfast of sinkers and Java, answering the telephone, and dispatching half-a-dozen bewildered reporters (amateurs) about their business."

After her graduation, Zoe returned to the Okanagan to nurse her dying mother. In the fall of 1938, and with her mother's blessing in the form of a note that she left for Zoe to read after her death, Zoe left for Europe. It is impossible to describe in any detail either the events of that year or the rich observations of a world living on borrowed time that were captured by Zoe in letters, a travel journal, and an account written from notes and memory once she was safely back in Canada. Here I share two short selections – one about the Parisians who went on with life as usual during the pre-war summer of 1939, a summer that *New Yorker* writer Janet Flanner (1972: 220) characterized as full of gaiety and hospitality; the other of English preparation for war as the summer of denial turned into a fall of doom.

> The French have the art of living down to a fine science, and most of them look so happy – quite different from the English. In the Latin Quarter nearly everyone seems to know everyone else, full of students. Lloyd knows masses of people and when he goes into a cafe he has to make a procession shaking hands; that is a French custom . . . . In the cafe everyone talks to everyone else, so different from the silent English meals . . . . Life here is very much like that at Varsity or that at home – friendly and easy – people talk instead of grunt like they do in England.

and:

> The general feeling of tension loosened English reserve; strangers spoke to each other in busses and theatres. And in our apartment block all the tenants became most friendly and talkative. There was an air of false gaiety about; the restaurants around Picadilly and Soho were crowded each evening and the theatres were packed. We all got fitted with gas masks and after reading the warnings in the papers decided that it would be a good idea to combine together war supplies. The expectation was that in the event of war a general food shortage would result. So with pooled resources we bought a giant box of rye-vita, seven shilling bars of chocolate, three pounds of tomatoes, a bottle of rum and one of sherry. In addition we had an immense Dutch cheese, which Jim had brought back from a weekend excursion in Holland, and we filled the decanters with water.

It took a while for Zoe to launch her career in journalism after returning from Europe, a function of the limited opportunities, especially for women, during the latter years of the Depression. After working for a few years in public relations and advertising in Vancouver, she moved to Toronto and later to Ottawa to work for the War Prices and Trade Bureau. There she met and married Jacques Bieler and in the spring of 1943 she and Jacques moved to Montreal.

Zoe soon found a job as a staff writer for a weekly magazine called *The Montreal Standard*. During the war years, the era of Rosie the Riveter, she was able to work on a range of stories, but once the war was over her options became narrower. Always one to turn disadvantage into advantage, Zoe began to develop her interests in writing about women's issues and women's lives, turning out a series of articles that are as timely today as they were in the 1940s.

For example, in the May 10, 1947, issue of the *Standard* (Figure 2) she wrote about how the shortage of males commits one out of every ten women to spinsterhood. "For the average woman there is no real substitute for a husband and children, but failing marriage there are alternatives around which a girl can build her life – all of them are second best . . .. Undoubtedly, feminist propaganda has made it possible for the modern spinster to be more independent than her old maid great aunt, but the life of a spinster is still no bed of roses" (p. 6). In other articles she addressed questions such as "Can Wives Afford to Work?" and "Politics' Weakling Sex" (about the low participation of women in politics) (Figure 3). "Today, Canadian women apparently still believe that politics is a man's game and a dirty game. They have made no move to unite to use their votes for their own benefit or for the benefit of the country" (*The Standard*, September 25, 1948, p. 3).

Zoe's perspective in all this writing was subjective as well as objective – often the ideas for stories came from personal experiences. Gloria Steinem (1983) has suggested that the lives of some women can be found between the lines of their professional writing. It is precisely in this sense that my biography is also my mother's autobiography, a story she is telling me about herself not only through the more obvious personal genres of female writing (diaries, journals, letters) but also through the medium of her professional pen.

In September of 1949, Zoe and Jacques adopted a baby boy they named Brian; within ten months, when Zoe was 35, they had a child of their own. Zoe used the written word to deal with her new motherhood, hoping, I think, to help others who might be confronted with a similar life experience of raising one natural child and one adopted child.

Figure 9.2; "Women Without Men", *The Montreal Standard*, May 10, 1947. Reprinted with kind permission of Thomson Newspapers, Toronto, Canada.

Figure 9.3: "Politics' Weakling Sex", *The Montreal Standard*, September 25, 1948.
Reprinted with kind permission of Thomson Newspapers, Toronto, Canada.

Brian is ours by adoption. He is our first child.
He is ours because we felt we needed him and because as soon as we saw him we knew he was just the boy we wanted . . . . I must admit that I very seldom think of Brian's real mother. On his birthday I am reminded that somewhere else there is probably another woman who is remembering what day it is too, but otherwise I can forget her for months on end. But I'm glad to know that she was not rushed into the decision of giving up her child permanently. During Brian's first six months she had plenty of time to make up or change her mind. I believe that she was entitled to those six months even if it meant I missed them. (*Weekend*, September 15,1951)

Zoe also used another form of writing to wrestle privately with what she was experiencing. She composed an unpublished short story titled "The Changeling" that I found among her papers after her death. In this story the main character, a young mother named Molly, is confronted with the fact that Tony, the child she has been raising, is not her natural son. When she is offered her natural child in exchange, she comes to a decision to keep both boys. "Once I told my husband that I didn't want to adopt a baby because I was afraid I could never love him as my own. Well I know now that I was wrong. All today I've been trying to face the fact that there is a possibility that Tony isn't really mine. I've found it makes no difference to my love."

Years later, she used two other written vehicles to deal with these experiences. In a letter to my college roommate, who had adopted a baby girl and then conceived a child of her own when she was in her late thirties, she offered advice on how to deal with two children who are very much your own despite differences in biological parentage. And, in an article published in *The Montreal Star*, she addressed the increasing frequency of motherhood after age thirty-five. These were cultural trends that she captured with a unique perspicacity.

The working mother (illustrated so dramatically in Figure 4 – an early 1950s image of "tak≥ not only your daughter but also your son to work") was a consistent theme in Zoe's writing. This was a category into which she fit but which she addressed by writing about others who had similar experiences. By giving them voice, she was giving herself voice. Her story about Lois Smith, a ballerina who was married to a dancer, did not fail to address how Ms. Smith juggled her career with the responsibilities of raising a daughter. She quoted Eartha Kitt, who hoped that her daughter, who often traveled with her, would "grow up to be an independent person who can think for herself. People today are not bred for thinking anymore; they are too concerned with belonging" (*The Montreal Star*, March 15, 1963). Similarly she quoted Ludmilla Chiriaeff, the founder of Les Grands Ballets Canadiens, as being "proud to have managed to develop in my children an understanding of my work, not merely as a profession but as a dedication" (*The Montreal Star*, April 3, 1962). Madame Chiriaeff told Zoe that she believed that all three of her children had learned to be self-sufficient as a result of her own career and eager to develop their own abilities. In her emphasis on these issues of independence and self-reliance, Zoe was in fact telling us about the core mothering values in her own life. In addition, in all these stories she was writing about women who did not fit the norm for the 1950s and early 1960s and thereby raised the question of how normative the stay-at-home mother really was.

Years later, in the fall of 1967, when both her children had left for college, Zoe would put into print her philosophy of the working mother. "I can't make any formal study of mothers who choose to work outside the home," she wrote, "but it is my firm conviction that as a group they rank among the most conscientious of mothers. They are, comparatively speaking, a very small group, hardly a threat to society" (*The Montreal Star*, November 23, 1967, p. 4). How resonant these words of more than a quarter-century ago are to us today!

From time to time, in her writing about women, Zoe adopted the ethnographer's life history method. The best example is found in an article published in the September 1953 issue of *The Canadian Home Journal*. The article is a sensitive portrait of an unwed mother that reflects the mores of the time. Kay, the fictional name of the thirty-year old mother featured in "I Kept My Illegitimate Child," recounts all the problems and prejudices that an unwed mother during the 1940s had to face. Kay's parents made up a story about a husband who was overseas and later they told their friends and neighbors that Kay was separated. Many of the men she dated walked away when they found out about her daughter. "I've learned that most men, though they don't object to a widow with a child, won't accept a girl who has a baby."

Zoe struggled herself with the prevailing prejudices against unwed mothers. In the late 1950s she hired an Italian housekeeper named Dina through the Salvation Army. Dina had an illegitimate

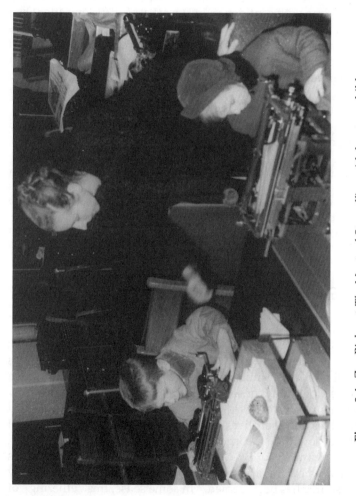

Figure 9.4: Zoe Bieler at *The Montreal Star* office with her two children. Reprinted with kind permission of Brian Bieler and Caroline Bieler Brettell.

baby girl named Paola who had been born in 1958. Zoe worried about what kind of impression bringing Dina and Paola into her home would have on her children. In the end she decided that Dina, who resisted every pressure from social workers to give up her child, was a loving women to whom she could entrust her two children with confidence. In February of 1970, long after Dina had left the household, Zoe returned to the topic of unwed mothers in an article that demonstrates the ideological changes that had occurred in less than two decades. This time, the young woman she interviewed declared quite forthrightly: "My son will be told as soon as he is old enough to understand. I don't plan to put Mrs. in front of my name nor wear a ring unless I do get married. Any boy I date will be told the truth." Zoe, mentioning the 1953 article, comments:

> The unmarried mother of today looks at herself in a very different light than did the girl in the same predicament 25 years ago. She is less self-punishing, her guilt is often minimal and she is far more hopeful about her ability to raise her children by herself. She is less concerned about the emotional damage her child may suffer when he learns he is illegitimate. (*The Montreal Star*, February 28,1970)

Conclusion: Blended Voices in the Writing of Women's Lives

Mary Catherine Bateson argues, in her book *Composing a Life* (1990: 5), that women read and write biographies to gain perspectives on their own lives. Similarly, Stuart (1992: 59) suggests that women read the biographies of other women "because they want to know about their private worlds, about how other women perceived themselves and their lives, about their sources of power, as well as about how they incorporated work into their domestic lives. Women want to know these things because other women's experiences can be a resource to them, and because previously this resource has been denied." In some sense, this "othering" of women in the genres of biography and autobiography is similar to the "othering" that characterizes ethnography.

In this chapter I have compared two texts about women's lives, one with a clear sense of genre and the other a good example of blurred genres.[8] Although Ruth Behar (1990: 224) has drawn attention to the awkwardness of blending the voices of the "native," the "I was there" ethnographer, and the authoritative and more distanced analytical anthropologist, there are a number of life histories that do this imaginatively and successfully; and, in the process, they take us into the private worlds of women in other cultures whose lives might otherwise have remained obscure and whose voices might otherwise have remained silent. This would certainly have been the case for Ana, Virginia, and Ricardina. Thus, I am not very comfortable using the term autoethnography to categorize the texts that describe their lives. For better or worse, I played a strong authorial role, and prevailing customs of anthropological writing kept me from interjecting personal experience into the work. And yet, if these women are not autoethnographers, their life stories nevertheless make an important contribution to ethnography. Just as the "Isle" of Corsica is narrated in the "I" life histories of the individuals discussed by Alexandra Jaffe earlier in this volume, the meaning of migration in Portugal is embedded in the biographical lives of its people.

If the issues of authorship, genre, and ethnography appear more straightforward, at least to me, in the text about three Portuguese women living a world of experience that is different from my own, these same issues are much more difficult and challenging to address in the text about my mother. Motzafi-Haller, in her contribution to this volume, discusses her double experiences as insider and outsider in relation to two cultural worlds – that of Africa and that of Israel. In the latter context she is "writing birthright" in a native land from which she was temporarily removed. In the text about my mother I am "writing birthright" in a more personal sense. But, each of us must struggle with the concept of authenticity. As a daughter, is my voice any more authentic than that of another biographer and can I create the kind of distance necessary to analyze the life of someone with whom my own life is so intimately connected? In short, I am confronted with some of the same dilemmas with regard to life-writing that "native" or autoethnographers must face when they study their own culture.

In the text about my mother, I am also dealing with multiple narratives drawn from a variety of genres of life-writing. I have suggested that even in some of her journalism my mother was writing about herself. And yet, there is also much that she did not place in the public domain, and thus I have given voice to her

THREE IS SUCH A FEMININE AGE

At this stage they act like grown-up ladies

A LITTLE GIRL of three often surprises her mother by turning, almost overnight, into a miniature woman. In a few years, or even months, she may revert to a complete tomboy, but right now she's intensely feminine. She takes pride in her appearance—pretty dresses and party shoes rate as high as toys in her estimation. She loves flowers (see cover).

Those who have a wide experience of children regard three as a delightful age. Three-year-olds are usually easy to handle; they can be quaintly serious; they want to conform; they like to please and they enjoy praise. These traits often encourage a three-year-old girl to model herself on mother. She takes pride in the fact that she's going to grow up into a "mummy" herself some day and often boasts about it. She loves to dress up in mother's clothes—a hat, bag, scarf and a pair of shoes—and pretends to be going downtown shopping or out with daddy. She likes to "mother" her dolls.

Everything that belongs to mother possesses great fascination for her. This can lead to disaster — a bottle of French perfume poured over a three-year-old elbow, a puddle of hand lotion on the bathroom floor, face powder on the carpet, smears of lipstick or cold cream in places where they're not wanted. But the little three-year-old woman can be a great help, too, if given a chance. If mother is patient and understanding she finds that small daughter is surprisingly competent at many light household tasks. She can lay a table, dust unbreakables, dry dishes, run a light vacuum cleaner or carpet sweeper, and do a multitude of small household errands such as fetching and carrying from upstairs to down. And she gets real satisfaction from doing the same work as mummy and working alongside her.

One of the things a three-year-old enjoys most is helping mother dress to go out. Although she's not completely efficient, she's an admiring and uncritical ladies' maid—in her eyes mother's taste in clothes and cosmetics is perfect and her looks flawless. Provided mother is not rushed, she's a lot of fun to have around. She'll patiently hold combs and pins, make suggestions as to perfume, nail polish and lipstick. She'll pick out earrings and necklaces from the jewelry box and bring the right shoes and bag from the cupboard.

When mother and daughter are both going out together the fun of getting ready is doubled, as each helps the other in a sort of mutual-aid, mutual-admiration society. A three-year-old girl is a mother's joy — mother and daughter may never again be so close and so free from friction until years later, when they get together over grandchildren. The harried mother of an adolescent daughter often looks back with nostalgia to that delightful period when "she was three — and seemed so grown-up and mature."

Zoe Bieler

"I must get into town before the stores close."

"There! I knew it was somewhere in my purse."

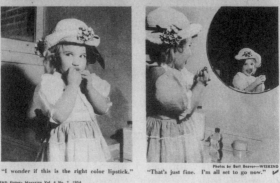

"I wonder if this is the right color lipstick."

"That's just fine. I'm all set to go now."

Photos by Bert Beaver—WEEKEND

WEEKEND Picture Magazine Vol. 4 No. 7, 1954

Figure 9.5: "Three is such a Feminine Age", *Weekend*, volume 4 (7), 1954. Reprinted with kind permission of *The Gazette*, Montreal, Canada and Caroline Brettell.

silences as both witness to, and reader of, her life much as I have given voice, as an ethnographer, to three women who never wrote down any aspect of their life in any genre prior to my engagement with them.

Finally, I have suggested that my mother was equally writing about the gendered and "cultured" worlds that shaped her life as she lived it; in this sense, she was an autoethnographer. She too straddled the boundary between insider and outsider, embedding elements of her own life experience in the stories that she wrote about others, many of which tell us much about what it was like to be a woman in Canadian society in the 1940s, 1950s, and 1960s.

But, the editor of this volume once asked me whether I too was an autoethnographer in relation to this text? If I answer yes to this question, it is because parts of my life story and my cultural world are also contained within it. "Three," my mother observed in an article published in *Weekend* in 1954 (Figure 5) "is such a feminine age." Here, an event in my personal experience, which in this moment of writing I choose to make salient, has become a powerful representation of the socializing force of gender ideology. If I leave the reader at the close of this volume with a sense of incertitude, it is precisely because the boundaries among the various genres of life-writing and writing about culture are indeed blurred. Paul Kendall (1965) once suggested that any biography uneasily shelters an autobiography within it; there are, perhaps, many ethnographies that shelter autoethnographies within them.

Notes

1. Behar and Gordon's book *Women Writing Culture* (1995) offers another example of the blurring of genres – not in a single text, but by bringing together in a single volume works of fiction and poetry, biographical, literary and historical essays, accounts of fieldwork, life stories, and travelogues. See also Freedman (1992).
2. Cole (1992: 122) has suggested that postmodernism is concerned with reflexivity in the text while feminism is concerned with

reflexivity of the context within which we carry out research and produce the texts based on that research. See also Gordon (1993).

3. Susan Geiger (1986: 336) sharpens this definition of life history by suggesting that it is an extensive record of a person's life told to and recorded by another who then edits and writes the life as if it were autobiography. For general discussions of the method and genre of life history see Langness and Frank (1985) and Watson and Watson-Franke (1985).

4. Cole (1992: 117) describes the negative responses she faced when she discussed her interest in life history with her professors in graduate school. As a method of research and a mode of writing, life history was viewed as "too individual, idiosyncratic, subjective, anecdotal."

5. Heilbrun (1989: 11) suggests that there are four ways to write a woman's life: "the woman herself may tell it, in autobiographical form; she can tell it in what she may label as fiction; someone else, woman or man, may write a biography; or the woman can write her own life in advance of living it." For more general discussions see Bell and Yalom (1990), Iles (1992), and Stanton (1987).

6. A similar attempt at interaction and collaboration is evident in Sally McBeth's work with Esther Horne, a Shoshone Indian woman (McBeth 1993).

7. I have omitted here any discussion of the fictional genre. Amy Tan, for example, used the stories her mother told her about her own life as the basis for her first two novels, *The Joy Luck Club* and *The Kitchen God's Wife* (see Lyall 1995: B14). In a somewhat different vein, Zora Neale Hurston writes in her autobiography *Dust Tracks on a Road* of her mother who, in her dying moments, "depended on me for a voice" (Hurston 1991: 63).

8. The blurring of genres is equally prevalent in literature and feminist literary criticism (Freedman 1992). "American feminist authors and critics," writes Barbara Tedlock (1995: 276), "have begun to weave autobiography into history and criticism, journals into analysis, and the spirit of poetry into interdisciplinary prose. This more personal writing at times even obfuscates the boundary between the author's self, the subject of the discourse, and the audience."

Bibliography

Abu-Lughod, Lila (1986), *Veiled Sentiments: Honor and Poetry in Bedouin Society*, Berkeley: University of California Press.
——, (1991), "Writing against culture," in Richard Fox (ed.), *Recapturing Anthropology*, Santa Fe, N.M.: School of American Research Press, pp. 37–62.
——, (1993), *Writing Women's Worlds: Bedouin Stories*, Berkeley: University of California Press.
Adams, Richard N. (1994), "A Report on the Political Status of the Guatemala Maya," in Donna Lee Van Cott (ed.), *Indigenous Peoples and Democracy in Latin America*, New York: St. Martin's Press, pp. 155–186.
Aguilar, J.L. (1981), "Inside Research: An Ethnography of a Debate," in D.A. Messerschmidt (ed.), *Anthropologists at Home in North America: Methods and Issues in the Study of One's Own Society*, Cambridge: Cambridge University Press.
Ak'abal, Humberto (1993), *Guardian de la Caída de Agua*, Guatemala: Serviprensa.
——, (1995a), *Ajyuq': El Animalero*, Third edition, Guatemala: Cholsamaj.
——, (1995b), *Hojas del Arbol Pajarero*, Mexico: Editorial Praxis.
Akerström, Malin (1993), *Crooks and Squares: Lifestyles of Thieves and Addicts in Comparison to Conventional People*, London: Transaction Publishers.
Alpern, Sara, Joyce Antler, Elisabeth Israels Perry and Igrid Winther Scobie (eds.), (1992), *The Challenge of Feminist Biography: Writing the Lives of Modern American Women*, Urbana: University of Illinois Press.
American Anthropological Association (1995), "Monkey Business in Chiapas," *Anthropology Newsletter*, vol. 36, no. 7, p. 41.
Americas Watch (1982), *Human Rights in Guatemala: No Neutrals Allowed*, New York: Americas Watch Committee.
——, (1984a), *Guatemalan Refugees in Mexico: 1980–1984*, New York: Americas Watch Committee.
——, (1984b), *Guatemala: A Nation of Prisoners*, New York: Americas Watch Committee.
——, (1985), *Little Hope: Human Rights in Guatemala; January 1984 to January 1985*, New York: Americas Watch Committee.

——, (1986), *Civil Patrols in Guatemala*, New York: Americas Watch Committee.

Amnesty International (1983), *Amnesty International Report 1983*, London: Amnesty International Publications.

Amrouche, F. (1988), *My Life Story. The Autobiography of a Berber Woman*, trans. D. S. Blair, London: The Women's Press.

Anderson, Benedict (1983), *Imagined Communities: Reflections on the Origin and Spread of Nationalism*, London: Verso.

Angrosino, Michael V. (1989), *Documents of Interaction: Biography, Autobiography, and Life History in Social Science Perspective*, Monographs in Social Sciences, no. 74, Gainesville: University of Florida Press.

Anzaldua, Gloria (1987), *Borderlands/La Frontera: The New Mestiza*, San Francisco: Spinsters/Aunt Lute.

Appiah, Kwame Anthony (1995), "African Identities," in Linda Nicholson and Steven Seidman (eds.), *Social Postmodernism: Beyond Identity Politics*, Cambridge: Cambridge University Press, pp. 103–115.

Archetti, Eduardo P. (ed.), (1994), *Exploring the Written: Anthropology and the Multiplicity of Writing*, Oslo: Scandinavian University Press.

Ashcroft, Bill, G. Griffith and H. Tiffin (1989), *The Empire Writes Back: Theory and Practice in Post-Colonial Literatures*, London and New York: Routledge.

Ashley, Kathleen, et al. (eds.), (1994), *Autobiography and Postmodernism*, Amherst: University of Massachusetts Press.

Atkinson, Paul (1992), *Understanding Ethnographic Texts*, Qualitative Research Methods Series 25, Newbury Park, London, and New Delhi: Sage Publications.

Austin, J.L. (1971 [1956–57]), "A Plea for Excuses," in Colin Lyas (ed.), *Philosophy and Linguistics*, London: Macmillan, pp. 79–101.

Bălan, Aurel (1979), *Contribuţii la Cunoaştera Înfinţării şi Activtăţii Cooperativei de Consum Hîrseni*. Paper delivered at the "Session of Scientific Communications," Hîrseni, Romania. Feb., 1979. Typescript.

Bammer, Angelika (ed.), (1994), *Displacements: Cultural Identities in Question*, Bloomington: Indiana University Press.

Barbat, Alexandru (1941), *Studiul Economic al Satului Drăguş-Făgăraş*, Bucharest: Imprimeria Naţională.

Bateson, Mary Catherine (1984), *With a Daughter's Eye: A Memoir of Margaret Mead*, New York: Morrow.

Bauman, Zygmunt (1989), *Modernity and the Holocaust*, Cambridge: Polity Press.

——, (1993), *Postmodern Ethics*, Oxford: Blackwell.

Beattie, Ann (1995), *Another You*, New York: Alfred A. Knopf.

Beauvoir, Simone de (1965), *A Very Easy Death*, London: G.P. Putnam's Sons.

Behar, Ruth (1990), "Rage and Redemption: Reading the Life Story of a

Mexican Marketing Woman," *Feminist Studies*, vol. 16, no. 2, pp. 223–258.

——, (1991), "Death and Memory: From Santa Maria del Monte to Miami Beach," *Cultural Anthropology*, vol. 6, pp. 346–384.

——, (1993), *Translated Woman: Crossing the Border with Esperanza's Story*, Boston: Beacon Press.

Behar, Ruth and Deborah A. Gordon (eds.), (1995) *Women Writing Culture*, Berkeley: University of California Press.

Beirne, Piers (1993), *Inventing Criminology: Essays on the Rise of Homo Criminalis*, New York: State University of New York Press.

Bell, Susan Groag and Marilyn Yalom (1990), *Revealing Lives: Autobiography, Biography, and Gender*, New York: State University of New York Press.

Benhabib, Seyla (1992), *Situating the Self: Gender, Community and Postmodernism in Contemporary Ethics*, Cambridge: Polity Press.

Bennoune, M. (1985), "What does it mean to be a Third World Anthropologist?," *Dialectical Anthropology*, vol. 9, pp. 357–364.

——, (1988), *The Making of Contemporary Algeria, 1830–1987. Colonial Upheavals and Post-Independence Development*, Cambridge: Cambridge University Press.

Benson, P. (ed.), (1993), *Anthropology and Literature*, Urbana: University of Illinois Press.

Bernard, H. Russell and Jesús Salinas Pedraza (1989), *Native Ethnography: A Mexican Indian Describes His Culture*, Thousand Oaks, Calif: Altamira Press.

Beronius, Mats (1994), *Bidrag till de sociala undersökningarnas historia: Eller till den vetenskapliggjorda moralens genealogi*, Stockholm: Symposion.

Berteaux, Daniel and Martin Kohli (1984), "The Life Story Approach: A Continental View," *Annual Review of Sociology*, vol. 10, pp. 215–237.

Blackman, Margaret (1982), *During My Time: Florence Edenshaw Davidson, A Haida Woman*, Seattle: University of Washington Press.

Bok, Sissela (1991), *Alva Myrdal: A Daughter's Memoir*, Reading, Mass: Addison-Wesley.

Bondeson, Ulla (1989), *Prisoners in Prison Societies*, New Brunswick: Transaction Publishers.

Bourdieu, Pierre (1984), *Homo Academicus*, Paris: Les Editions de Minuit.

——, (1986), "L'Illusion Biographique," *Actes de la Recherche en Sciences Sociales*, no. 62/63 (juin), pp. 69–72.

Brandes, Stanley (1982), "Ethnographic Autobiographies in American Anthropology," in E. Adamson Hoebel, Richard Currier and Susan Kaiser (eds.), *Crisis in Anthropology: View from Spring Hill*, New York and London: Garland Publishing Co., pp. 187–202.

Braudel, F. (1976), *The Mediterranean and the Mediterranean World in the Age of Philip II*, 2 vols, Glasgow: Fontana/Collins.

Brettell, Caroline B. (1982), *We Have Already Cried Many Tears: The Stories of Three Portuguese Migrant Women*, Cambridge: Schenkman Press (reissued by Waveland Press, 1995).

Brettell, Caroline B. (ed.), (1993), *When We Read What They Write: The Politics of Ethnography*, Wesport, Conn: Bergin and Garvey.

Brown, Karen McCarthy (1991), *Mama Lola: A Vodou Priestess in Brooklyn*, Berkeley: University of California Press.

Browne-Clayton, Zoe (1940), "Lights Out in Europe," *The Graduate Chronicle*, May 7, Alumni Association of the University of British Columbia.

Brunati, J. (1992), "O Zi Pà! Ou le père des récits," in Jacques Lovichi (ed.), *Corse: Défense d'une Ile*, Marseille: Editions Temps Forts, pp. 11–14.

Burns, Allan F. (1993), *Maya in Exile: Guatemalans in Florida*, Philadelphia: Temple University Press.

Cahill, Susan (ed.), (1988), *Mothers: Memories, Dreams and Reflections by Literary Daughters*, New York: Penguin.

Callaway, Helen (1992), "Ethnography and Experience: Gender Implications in Fieldwork and Texts," in Judith Okely and Helen Callaway (eds.), pp. 29–49.

Camilly, J. (1992), "Une mémoire indélible," *Etudes Corses*, vol. 38, pp. 111–116.

Campbell, J.K. (1964), *Honour, Family, and Patronage: Study of Institutions and Moral Values in a Greek Mountain Community*, Oxford: Clarendon Press.

Camus, Albert (1995), *The First Man*, trans. David Hapgood, New York: Alfred A. Knopf.

Carles, Emilie (1977), *Une Soupe aux Herbes Sauvages*, Propos recuellis par Robert Destanque. Paris: France Loisirs.

——, (1988), *Une Soupe aux Herbes Sauvages*, Propos recuellis par Robert Destanque. Paris: Editions Robert Laffont.

——, (1991), *A Life of Her Own. The Transformation of a Countrywoman in Twentieth-Century France*, trans. Avriel M. Goldberger, New York: Penguin Books.

Carmack, Robert (ed.), (1988), *Harvest of Violence: The Maya Indians and the Guatemalan Crisis*, Norman: University of Oklahoma Press.

Caro Baroja, Julio (1970), *El mito del caracter nacional: meditaciones a contrapelo*, Madrid: Seminarios y Ediciones.

Carrard, Philippe (1992), *Poetics of the New History: French Historical Discourse from Braudel to Chartier*, Baltimore: Johns Hopkins Press.

Cernea, Mihail (1981), "Trends and Methodological Developments in Village Monographs," in M. Cernea (ed.), *Rural Community Studies in Rumania*, Oxford: Pergamon Press, pp. 191–218.

Chernin, Kim (1985), *In My Mother's House: A Daughter's Story*, London: Virago.

Christie, Nils (1993), *Crime Control as Industry: Towards GULAGS, Western Style?* London: Routledge.

Clifford, James (ed.), (1988), *The Predicament of Culture; Twentieth-Century Ethnography, Literature, and Art*, Cambridge: Harvard University Press.

Clifford, James and George Marcus (eds.), (1986), *Writing Culture: The Poetics and Politics of Ethnography*, Berkeley: University of California Press.

Codaccione-Meistersheim, A. (1989), "Images d'iléité," *Cahiers de l'IDIM* vol. 1, pp. 30–36.

Cohen, Anthony P. (1994), *Self Consciousness: An Alternative Anthropology of Identity*, London: Routledge.

Cohen, Stanley (1985), *Visions of Social Control*, Cambridge: Polity Press.

——, (1992), "Social-Control Talk: Telling Stories about Correctional Change," in David Garland and Peter Young (eds.), *The Power to Punish: Contemporary Penality and Social Analysis*, Vermont: Ashgate.

Cohen, Stanley and Laurie Taylor (1993), *Escape Attempt: The Theory and Practice of Resistance to Everyday Life*, London: Routledge.

Cojtí Cuxil, Demetrio (1991), *Configuración del Pensamiento Político del Pueblo Maya*, Quetzaltenango, Guatemala: Asociación de Escritores Mayances de Guatemala.

——, (1994), *Políticas para la Reivindicación de los Mayas de Hoy*, Guatemala: Cholsamaj.

——, (1995), *Ub'aniik Ri Una'ooj Uchomab'aal Ri Maya' Tinamit; Confirguración del Pensamiento Político del Pueblo Maya*, 2da. Parte, Guatemala: SPEM/Cholsamaj.

Cole, Sally (1992), "Anthropological Lives: The Reflexive Tradition in a Social Science," in Marlene Kadar (ed.), *Essays on Life Writing: From Genre to Critical Practice*, Toronto: University of Toronto Press, pp. 113–127.

Comaroff, John and Jean Comaroff (1992), *Ethnography and the Historical Imagination*, Boulder: Westview Press.

Connor, Walker (1993), "Beyond Reason: The Nature of the Ethnonational Bond," *Ethnic and Racial Studies*, vol. 16, pp. 373–389.

Coronil, Fernando (1996), "Beyond Occidentalism: Toward Nonimperial Geohistorical Categories," *Cultural Anthropology*, vol. 11, pp. 51–87.

Cotaru, Romulus (1938), "Etica Drăguşenilor: criteriile morală şi filosofia practică în satul Drăguş," *Sociologie Românească*, vol. 3, no. 7–9, pp. 310–338.

Crick, Malcolm (1976), *Explorations in Language and Meaning: Towards a Semantic Anthropology*, New York: John Wiley/Halsted.

Culioli, Gabriel X. (1992), "La place pour un roman corse," *Etudes Corses*, vol. 38, pp. 43–36.

——, (1990), *Le Complexe Corse*, Paris: Gallimard.

Curruchiche Gómez, Miguel Angel (1994), *Discriminación del Pueblo Maya en el Ordenamiento Jurídico de Guatemala*, Guatemala: Cholsamaj.

Deck, Alice A. (1990), "Autoethnography: Zora Neale Hurston, Noni Jabavu, and Cross-Disciplinary Discourse," *Black American Literature Forum*, vol. 24, no. 2, pp. 237–256.

Delaney, Carol (1986), "The Meaning of Paternity and the Virgin Birth Debate," *Man* (n.s.), no. 21, pp. 494–513.

——, (1995), "Father State, Motherland, and the Birth of Modern Turkey," in Sylvia Yanagisako and Carol Delaney (eds.), *Naturalizing Power: Essays in Feminist Cultural Analysis*, New York: Routledge, pp. 177–199.

Delavalle, P. (1991), *La terre partagée*, Ajaccio: La Marge.

Denzin, Norman (1989), *Interpretive Biography*, Newbury Park, Calif: Sage Publications.

Desanti, J. (1990), Preface to *La Reconquête de la Dignité*, by Marie-Catherine Maroselli-Matteoli, Ajaccio: La Marge Edition.

——, (1984), "Effacer la mer," in Sébastien Giudicelli (ed.), *La Corse: une affaire de famille*, Marseille: Editions du Quai-Jeanne Laffitte, pp. 15–24.

Dirlik, Arif (1994), "The Postcolonial Aura: Third World Criticism in the Age of Global Capitalism," *Critical Inquiry*, pp. 328–357.

Dominguez, Virginia (1989), *People as Subject, People as Object: Selfhood and Peoplehood in Contemporary Israel*, Madison: The University of Wisconsin Press.

Dorst, John D. (1989), *The Written Suburb: An American Site, An Ethnographic Dilemma*, Philadelphia: University of Pennsylvania Press.

Douglas, Mary (1970), *Natural Symbols: Explorations in Cosmology*, London: Barrie and Rockliff.

Djura (1992), *The Veil of Silence*, trans. D. S. Blair, London: Quartet Books.

——, (1993), *La saison de narcisses*, Paris: Éditions Michel Lafon.

Driessen, Henk (ed.), (1993), *The Politics of Ethnographic Reading and Writing: Confrontations of Western and Indigenous Views*, Saarbrucken and Ft. Lauderdale: Verlag.

Dumont, Louis (1986), *Essays on Individualism: Modern Ideology in Anthropological Perspective*, Chicago: The University of Chicago Press.

England, Nora (1992), *Autonomía de los Idiomas Mayas: Historia e Identidad*, Guatemala: Cholsamaj.

Ernaux, Annie (1992), *A Woman's Story*, New York: Ballentine Books.

Esquit Choy, Edgar and Carlos Ochoa García (eds.), (1995), *Yiqalil q'anej, kunimaaj tziij, niman tzij; El respeto a la palabra*, Guatemala: CECMA.

Evans-Pritchard, E.E. (1937), *Witchcraft, Oracles and Magic among the Azande*, Oxford: Clarendon Press.

Fabian, Johannes (1983), *Time and the Other: How Anthropology Makes its Object*, New York: Columbia University Press.

Fahim, H. (ed.), (1982), *Indigenous Anthropologies in Non-Western Countries*,

Durham, NC: Carolina Academic Press

Favret, J. (1973), " Traditionalism Through Ultramodernism," in E. Gellner and C. Micaud (eds.), *Arabs and Berbers. From Tribe to Nation in North Africa*, London: Duckworth, pp. 307–324.

Favret-Saada, Jeanne (1980), *Deadly Words: Witchcraft in the Bocage*, Cambridge: Cambridge University Press.

Fernandez, James W. (1986), *Persuasions and Performances: The Play of Tropes in Culture*, Bloomington: Indiana University Press.

Fischer, Edward and McKenna Brown (eds.), (1996), *Mayan Cultural Activism in Guatemala*, Austin: University of Texas Press.

Fischer, Michael M. J. (1994), "Autobiographical voices (1,2,3) and Mosaic Memory: Experimental Sondages in the (Post)modern World," in Ashley et al. (eds.), pp. 79–129.

Foster, Stephen W. (1988), *The Past is Another Country: Representation, Historical Consciousness, and Resistance in the Blue Ridge*, Berkeley: University of California Press.

Foucault, Michel (1977), *Discipline and Punish: The Birth of the Prison*, London: Allen Lane.

——, (1980), "Prison Talk" and "Two Lectures," in Colin Gordon (ed.), *Power/Knowledge: Selected Interviews and other Writings 1972–77*, London: Harvester Press.

Fox, Richard G. (ed.), (1991), *Recapturing Anthropology: Working in the Present*, Santa Fe: School of American Research.

Filippi, P. (1992), "L'évocation de la Corse chez Angelo Rinaldi," *Etudes Corses*, vol. 38, pp. 79–90.

Franchi, J. (1992), "Bilinguisme, traduction et littérature," *Etudes Corses*, vol. 38, pp. 27–36.

Frankenberg, Ronald (1993), "Who Can Tell the Tale? Texts and the Problem of Generational and Social Identity in a Tuscan Rural Comune," in Sharon Mcdonald (ed.), *Inside European Identites*, Oxford: Berg Publishers, pp. 54–84.

Franzini, A. (1991), "Une île dans la tête," *Kyrn*, vol. 362, p. 35.

Fraser, Nancy (1989), *Unruly Practices: Power, Discourse and Gender in Contemporary Social Theory*, Minneapolis: University of Minnesota Press.

Freedman, Diane P. (1992), *An Alchemy of Genres: Cross-Genre Writing by American Feminist Poet-Critics*, Charlottesville: University Press of Virginia.

Freedman, Diane P. et al. (eds.), (1993), *The Intimate Critique: Auto-biographical Literary Criticism*, Durham and London: Duke University Press.

Friday, Nancy (1977), *My Mother, My Self: A Daughter's Search for Identity*, New York: Delacorte Press.

Furet, François and Jacques Ozouf (1982), *Reading and Writing: Literacy from Calvin to Jules Ferry*, trans. La Maison des Sciences de l'Homme and Cambridge University Press, Cambridge: Cambridge University Press, and Paris: Editions de la Maison des Sciences de l'Homme.

Fusina, J. (1992), "La question générique dans le prose d'aujourd'hui," *Etudes Corses*, vol. 38, pp. 15–24.

——, (1989), "Editorial: Lingua Corsa," *Kyrn*, vol. 203, p. 37.

Gadd, Pia (1991), *Att aldrig gå loss: Mekanismerna som gör fängelserna självförsörjande, intervju med Clark Olofsson*, Stockholm: Carlsson.

Gates, Louis Henry (1987), *Figures in Black: Words, Signs, and the "Racial" Self*, New York: Oxford University Press.

Geiger, Susan (1986), "Women's Life Histories: Method and Content," *Signs*, vol. 11, pp. 334–351.

Geertz, Clifford (1983), "Blurred Genres: The Refiguration of Social Thought," in *Local Knowledge: Further Essays in Interpretive Anthropology*, New York: Basic Books, pp. 19–35 (originally in *The American Scholar*, vol. 29, no. 2, Spring 1980).

——, (1983), *Local Knowledge: Further Essays in Interpretive Anthropology*, New York: Basic Books.

——, (1968), *Islam Observed. Religious Development in Morocco and Indonesia*, Chicago: The University of Chicago Press.

——, (1988), *Works and Lives: The Anthropologist as Author*, Stanford, Calif: Stanford University Press.

——, (1995), "Culture War," *New York Review of Books*, 11/30/95, pp. 4–6.

Genet, Jean (1967 [1949]), *The Thief's Journal*, New York: Harmondsworth.

Giddens, Anthony (1984), *The Constitution of Society: Outline of the Theory of Structuration*, Cambridge: Polity Press.

——, (1991), *Modernity and Self-Identity: Self and Society in the Late Modern Age*, Stanford: Stanford University Press.

——, (1992), *The Transformation of Intimacy: Sexuality, Love and Eroticism in Modern Society*, Cambridge: Polity Press.

——, (1994), "Brave New World: The New Context of Politics," in David Miliband (ed.), *Reinventing the Left*, Cambridge: Polity Press.

Gilroy, Paul (1993), *The Black Atlantic: Modernity and Double Consciousness*, Cambridge: Harvard University Press.

Ginsburg, Faye (1987), "Procreation Stories: Reproduction, Nurturance, and Procreation in the Life Narratives of Abortion Activists," *American Ethnologist*, vol. 14, no. 4, pp. 623–636.

Giudicelli, S. (1984), "Les Corses entre l'insularité et l'exil," in Sébastien Giudicelli (ed.), *La Corse: une affaire de famille*, Marseille: Editions du Quai-Jeanne Laffitte, pp. 179–216.

Gmelch, George (1992), *Double Passage: The Lives of Caribbean Migrants Abroad and Back Home*, Ann Arbor: University of Michigan Press.

Gmelch, Sharon (1991), *Nan: The Life of an Irish Travelling Woman*, Prospect Heights, Ill: Waveland Press.

Goffman, Erving (1991 [1961]), *Asylums: Essays on the Social Situation of Mental Patients and other Inmates*, London: Penguin.

González, Gaspar Pedro (1992), *La Otra Cara*, Guatemala: Ministerio de Cultura y Deportes, Serie Miguel Angel Asturias (Novela).

——, (1995), *A Mayan Life*, translated by Elaine Elliot, Rancho Palos Verdes: Yax Te' Press.

Gordon, Deborah (1993), "The Unhappy Relationship of Feminism and Postmodernism in Anthropology," *Anthropological Quarterly*, vol. 66, no. 3, pp. 109–117.

Gornick, Vivian (1987), *Fierce Attachments*, New York: Simon and Schuster.

Graziani, G. (1986), *Un ciel de fer*, Nucario: Cismonte e Pumonti.

Greenwood, Davydd J. (1984), *The Taming of Evolution: The Persistence of Nonevolutionary Views in the Study of Humans*, Ithaca: Cornell University Press.

Gubrium, Jaber F. et al. (1994), *Constructing the Life Course*, New York: General Hall.

Guillestad, Marianne (1996a), *Everyday Life Philosophers: Modernity, Morality, and Autobiography in Norway*, Oslo: Scandinavian University Press.

——, (ed.), (1996b), *Imagined Childhoods: Self and Society in Autobiographical Accounts*, Oslo: Scandinavian University Press.

Hacking, Ian (1995), *Rewriting the Soul: Multiple Personality and the Sciences of Memory*, Princeton: Princeton University Press.

Hagan, Jacqueline Maria (1994), *Deciding to be Legal: A Maya Community in Houston*, Philadelphia: Temple University Press.

Hale, Charles (1994), "Between Che Guevara and the Pachamama: Mestizos, Indians, and Identity Politics in the Anti-quincentenary Campaign," *Critique of Anthropology*, vol. 14, no. 2, pp. 9–39.

Hamilakis, Yannis and Eleana Yalouri (1996), "Antiquities as Symbolic Capital in Modern Greek Society," *Antiquity*, no. 70, pp. 117–129.

Hammel, E.A. et al. (eds.), (1982), *Among the People: Native Yugoslav Ethnography*, Ann Arbor: University of Michigan.

Handler, Richard (1985), "On Dialogue and Destructive Analysis: Problems in Narrating Nationalism and Ethnicity," *Journal of Anthropological Research*, vol. 41, pp. 171–182.

——, (1988), *Nationalism and the Politics of Culture in Quebec*, Madison: University of Wisconsin Press.

Hart, Janet C. (1989), "Redeeming the Voices of a 'Sacrificed Generation': Oral Histories of Women in the Greek Resistance," *International Journal of Oral History*, vol. 10, pp. 3–30.

Hastrup, Kirsten (1992), "Writing Ethnography: State of the Art," in Judith Okely and Helen Callaway (eds.), pp. 116–134.

Hau'ofa, Epeli (1994), "Pasts to Remember," a paper delivered at the University of the South Pacific, October 1994.

Hayano, David M. (1979), "Auto-Ethnography: Paradigms, Problems, and Prospects," *Human Organization*, vol. 38, no. 1, pp. 99–104.

Heider, Karl G. (1975), "What Do People Do?" Dani Auto-Ethnography," *Journal of Anthropological Research*, vol. 31, pp. 3–17.

Heilbrun, Carolyn G. (1989), *Writing a Woman's Life*, New York: Ballentine Books.

Hélias, Pierre-Jakez (1975), *Le Cheval d'Orgueil: Memoirs d'un Breton du Pays du Bigouden*, Paris: Plon.

——, (1978 [1975]), *The Horse of Pride: Life in a Breton Village*, trans. June Guicharnaud, New Haven and London: Yale University Press.

——, (1990), *Le Quêteur de Memoire: Quarante ans de recherche sur les myths et civilisation bretonne*, Paris: Plon.

Herseni, Traian (1944), *Drăguş : Un Sat din Ţara Oltului (Făgăraş)* – *Unităţi Sociale*, Bucharest: Institutul de Ştiinţe Sociale al României.

——, (1977), *Forme Străvechi de Cultura Poporană Românească: Studiu de Paleoetnografie a Cetelor de Feciori din Ţara Oltului*, Cluj-Napoca: Editura Dacia.

——, (1982), *Sociologie: Teoria Generală a Vieţii Sociale*, Bucureşti: Editura Stiinţifică.

——, et al. (eds.), (1972), *Combinatul Chimic Făgăraş: 50 de Ani de Existenţă*, Sibiu: Întreprindera Poligrafică.

Hertz, Rosanna (1996), "Introduction: Ethics, Reflexivity and Voice," *Qualitative Sociology*, vol. 19, no. 1, pp. 3–9.

Herzfeld, Michael (1982), "When Exceptions Define the Rules: Greek Baptismal Names and the Negotiation of Identity," *Journal of Anthropological Research*, vol. 38, pp. 288–302.

——, (1985), *The Poetics of Manhood: Contest and Identity in a Cretan Mountain Village*, Princeton: Princeton University Press.

——, (1987), *Anthropology through the Looking-Glass: Critical Ethnography in the Margins of Europe*, Cambridge: Cambridge University Press.

——, (1991), *A Place in History: Social and Monumental Time in a Cretan Town*, Princeton: Princeton University Press.

——, (1992), *The Social Production of Indifference: Exploring the Symbolic Roots of Western Bureaucracy*, Oxford: Berg.

——, (1995), "Hellenism and Occidentalism: The Permutations of Performance in Greek Bourgeois Identity," in James G. Carrier (ed.), *Occidentalism: Images of the West*, Oxford: Oxford University Press, pp. 218–233.

——, (1996), *Cultural Intimacy: Social Poetics in the Nation-State*, London and New York: Routledge.

——, (1997), *Portrait of a Greek Imagination: An Ethnographic Biography of Andreas Nenedakis*, Chicago: University of Chicago Press.

Hezel, Francis (1992), "Recolonizing Islands and Decolonizing History," in D. Rubenstein (ed.), *Pacific History*, Mangilao: University of Guam, pp. 63–67.

Heyck, Denis Lynn Daly (1990), *Life Stories of the Nicaraguan Revolution*, New York and London: Routledge.

Heywood, Colin (1988), *Childhood in Nineteenth-Century France*, Cambridge: Cambridge University Press.

Hirsch, Marianne (1981), "Mothers and Daughters," in Jean F. O'Barr et al. (eds.), "Ties that Bind: Essays on Mothering and Patriarchy," *Signs*, vol. 7, pp. 177–200.

Hobsbawm, Eric (1994), *Age of Extremes: The Short Twentieth Century 1914–1991*, London: Penguin.

Hofer, Tamás (1968), "Comparative Notes on the Professional Personality of Two Disciplines: Anthropologists and Native Ethnographers in Central European Villages," *Current Anthropology*, vol. 9, no. 4, pp. 311–315.

Hogan, Joseph and Rebecca Hogan (1991), "Telling Two Lives: Ethnographical Self-Fashioning in Jane Tapsubei Creider's My Spirit and I," unpublished manuscript.

hooks, bell (1990), "Marginality as Site of Resistance," in R. Ferguson et al. (eds.), *Out There: Marginalization and Contemporary Cultures*, New York: New York Museum of Contemporary Art, pp. 341–343.

——, (1993), "Keeping Close to Home: Class and Education," in Tokarcyzk (ed.), pp. 99–111.

Houston, J.M. (1964), *The Western Mediterranean World. An Introduction to its Regional Landscapes*, London: Longman.

Huntington, Samuel P. (1993), "The Clash of Civilizations?", *Foreign Affairs*, vol. 72, no. 3, pp. 22–49.

Hurston, Zora Neale (1991 [1942]), *Dust Tracks on a Road*, New York: HarperCollins.

Ignatieff, Michael (1994), *Blood and Belonging: Journeys into the New Nationalism*, London: Vintage.

Iles, Teresa (1992), *All Sides of the Subject: Women and Biography*, New York: Teachers College Press.

Irwin, John (1985), *Jail: Managing the Underclass in American Society*, Berkeley: University of California Press.

Jacobson, David (1991), *Reading Ethnography*, Albany: State University of New York Press.

Jackson, Anthony (ed.), (1987), *Anthropology at Home*, London: Tavistock ɣ Publications.

Jones, Delmos (1970), "Towards a Native Anthropology," *Human Organization*, vol. 29, no. 4, pp. 251–259.

Jönsson, Linda (1988), *On Being Heard: A Study of Discourse in Two Institutional Contexts*, University of Linköping.

Just, Roger (1989), "Triumph of the Ethnos," in Elizabeth Tonkin, Malcolm Chapman and Maryon McDonald (eds.), *History and Ethnicity* (A.S.A.

Monographs 27), London: Routledge, pp. 71–88.

Kapferer, Bruce (1988), *Legends of People, Myths of State: Violence, Intolerance, and Political Culture in Sri Lanka and Australia*, Washington: Smithsonian Institution Press.

Katz, Jack (1988), *Seductions of Crime: Moral and Sensual Attractions in Doing Evil*, New York: Basic Books.

Kazantzakis, Nikos (1956), *Freedom or Death: A Novel*, trans. Jonathan Griffin, New York: Simon and Schuster.

Kendall, Laurel (1988), *The Life and Hard Times of a Korean Shaman: Of Tales and the Telling of Tales*, Honolulu: University of Hawaii Press.

Kendall, Paul Murray (1965), *The Art of Biography*, London: George Allen and Unwin.

Kenna, Margaret E. (1976), "Houses, Fields, and Graves: Property and Ritual Obligation on a Greek Island," *Ethnology*, vol. 15, pp. 21–34.

Kenyatta, Jomo (1938), *Facing Mount Kenya: The Tribal Life of the Gikuyu*, New York: Vintage Books.

Khellil, M. (1979), *L'exil kabyle. Essai d'analyse du vécu des migrants*, Paris: L'Harmattan.

Kideckel, David A. (1982), "The Socialist Transformation of Agriculture in a Romanian Commune, 1945–1962," *American Ethnologist*, vol. 9, no. 2, pp. 320–340.

——, (1993), *The Solitude of Collectivism: Romanian Villagers to the Revolution and Beyond*, Ithaca: Cornell University Press.

Kikumura, Akemi (1981), *Through Harsh Winters: The Life of a Japanese Immigrant Woman*, Novato, Calif: Chandler & Sharp Publishers.

Kim, C.S. (1990), "The Role of the Non-western Anthropologist Reconsidered: Illusion Version Reality," *Current Anthropology*, vol. 1, pp. 191–201.

Kincaid, Jamaica (1995), "Homework," *The New Yorker*, 10/16/95, pp. 54–64.

Kligman, Gail (1988), *The Wedding of the Dead: Ritual, Poetics, and Popular Culture in Transylvania*, Berkeley: University of California Press.

Kondo, Dorinne (1990), *Crafting Selves: Power, Gender, and Discourses of Identity in a Japanese Workplace*, Chicago: The University of Chicago Press.

Kondoyoryis, Yorgos D. (1979), *Elladhiki laïkí idheoloyía*, Athens: Nea Sinora.

Kordatos, Yanis (1924), *I kinoniki simasia tis ellinikis epanastaseos tou 1821*, Athens: I. Vasiliou.

KOS, *Kriminalvårdens officiella statistik 1994/95*, Kriminalvården.

Krupat, Arnold (1992), *Ethnocriticism: Ethnography, History, Literature*, Berkeley: University of California Press.

Kuper, Adam (1973), *Anthropologists and Anthropology: The British School, 1922–1972*, New York: Pica Press.

——, (1994), "Culture, Identity and the Project of a Cosmopolitan Anthropology," *Man*, vol. 29, pp. 537–554.

Labov, William (1972), *Language in the Inner City: Studies in the Black English Vernacular*, Philadelphia: University of Pennsylvania Press.

Lacoste-Dujardin, C. (1992), *Yasmina et les autres de Nanterre et d'ailleurs. Filles de parents maghrébins en France*, Paris: La Découverte.

Langness, L.L and Gelya Frank (1985), *Lives: An Anthropological Approach to Biography*, Novato, Calif: Chandler and Sharp.

Lavi, Smadar, Kirin Narayan and Renato Rosaldo (eds.), (1993), *Creativity/ Anthropology*, Ithaca and London: Cornell University Press.

Lavie, Smadar and Ted Swedenburg (1995), "Between and within Boundaries of Culture," *Teorya VeBikoret*, no. 7, pp. 67–86. (Hebrew)

Lejeune, Philippe (1989), *On Autobiography*, Paul J. Eaken (ed.), trans. Katherine Leary, Minneapolis: University of Minnesota Press.

León Portilla, Miguel (1974), *El Reverso de la Conquista*, Mexico: Editorial Juaoquín Martiz.

——, (1984), *Visión de los Vencidos; Relaciones Indígenas de la Conquista*, Mexico: UNAM.

Lienhardt, R.G. (1961), *Divinity and Experience: The Religion of the Dinka*, Oxford: Clarendon Press.

Limon, José (1991), "Representation, Ethnicity, and the Precursory Ethnography: Notes of a Native Anthropologist," in Richard Fox (ed.), *Recapturing Anthropology*, Santa Fe: School of American Research Press, pp. 115–136.

——, (1994), *Dancing with the Devil: Society and Cultural Poetics in Mexican American South Texas*, Madison: The University of Wisconsin Press.

Linde, Charlotte (1993), *Life Stories: The Creation of Coherence*, Oxford: Oxford University Press.

Little, Michael (1990), *Young Men in Prison: The Criminal Identity Explored through the Rules of Behavior*, Vermont: Dartmouth.

Lionnet-MacCumber, Françoise (1993), "Autoethnography: The An-Archic Style of Dust Tracks on a Road," in Henry L. Gates, Jr. and K.A. Appiah (eds.), *Zora Heal Hurston: Critical Perspectives Past and Present*, New York: Amistad Press.

Lovell, W. George (1992), *Conquest and Survival in Colonial Guatemala; A Historical Geography of the Cuchumatán Highlands, 1500–1821*, Montreal and Kingston: McGill-Queen's University Press.

Lovichi, J. (1992), "Paese," in Jacques Lovichi (ed.), *Corse: Défense d'une Ile*, Marseille: Editions Temps Forts, pp. 177–196.

Lowenthal, David (1985), *The Past is a Foreign Country*, Cambridge: Cambridge University Press.

Lucchini, J. (1992), "Marie Susini: la réclusion solitaire," *Etudes Corses*, vol. 38, pp. 75–78.

Lyall, Sarah (1995), "A Writer Knows that Spirits Dwell Beyond Her

Pages," *The New York Times*, 12/29/95, pp. B1, B28.

Lloyd, G.E.R. (1990), *Demystifying Mentalities*, Cambridge: Cambridge University Press.

McArthur, Marilyn (1976), "The Saxon Germans: Political Fate of an Ethnic Identity," *Dialectical Anthropology*, vol. 1, no. 2, pp. 349–364.

——, (1981), "The Politics of Identity: Transylvanian Saxons in Socialist Romania," unpublished Ph.D. dissertation, Amherst: University of Massachusetts.

McBeth, Sally (1993), "Myth of Objectivity and the Collaborative Process in Life History Research," in Caroline B. Brettell (ed.), *When They Read What We Write: The Politics of Ethnography*, Westport, Conn: Bergin and Garvey, pp. 145–162.

Mahfoufi, M. (1994), "Le chanson kabyle en immigration: une rétrospective," *Hommes et Migrations*, no. 1179, pp. 32–40.

Malinowski, Bronislaw (1961 [1922]), *Argonauts of the Western Pacific*, New York: Dutton.

Manz, Beatriz (1988), *Refugees of a Hidden War: The Aftermath of Counterinsurgency in Guatemala*, Albany: State University of New York Press.

Marcus, George (1992), "Past, Present and Emergent Identities," in Scott Lash and Jonathan Friedman (eds.), *Modernity and Identity*, Cambridge: Blackwell.

Maroselli-Matteoli, M. (1990), *La Reconquête de la Dignité*, Ajaccio: La Marge Edition.

Mathiesen, Thomas (1965), *Defences of the Weak*, London: Tavistock Publications.

——,(1990), *Prison on Trial: A Critical Assessment*, London: Sage.

Matoub, L. (1995), *Rebelle*, avec la collaboration de Véronique Taveau, Paris: Éditions Stock.

Maynes, Mary Jo (1995), *Taking the Hard Road: Life Course in French and German Workers' Autobiographies in the Era of Industrialization*, Chapel Hill and London: University of North Carolina Press.

Mayle, Peter (1991), *A Year in Provence*, New York: Vintage Books.

——, (1993), *Hotel Pastis*, New York: Vintage Books.

McDonald, Maryon (1989), *We Are Not French! Language, Culture, and Identity in Brittany*, London and New York: Routledge.

Mead, Margaret (1928), *Coming of Age in Somoa*, New York: Morrow.

Menchú, Rigoberta with Elizabeth Burgos-Debray (ed.), (1984), *I Rigoberta Menchú: An Indian Woman in Guatemala*, trans. Ann Wright, London: Verso Editions.

——, (1985), *Me Llamo Rigoberta Menchú y Así Me Nació la Conciencia*, Mexico: Siglo Veintiuno Editores.

Merton, Robert (1988 [1972]), "Some Thoughts on the Concept of Sociological Autobiography," in Martha W. Riley (ed.), *Sociological Lives*, Newbury Park: Sage, pp. 17–21.

Messerschmidt, D.A. (ed.), (1981), *Anthropologists at Home in North America: Methods And Issues in the Study of One's Own Society*, Cambridge: Cambridge University Press.

Mezzadri, M. (1991), "Tous ne sont pas ministres," *Kyrn*, no. 375, p. 57.

Mitchell-Sambroni, Anne-Marie (1991), *Refuge*, Marseille: Editions Autres Temps.

——, (1992), "Donna," in Jacques Lovichi (ed.), *Corse: Défense d'une Ile*, Marseille: Editions Temps Forts, pp. 103–122.

Montejo, Victor (1984), *El Kanil; Man of Lightning*, Spanish-English edition translated by Wallace Kaufman, Carrbolo, N.C.: Signal Books.

——, (1987), *Testimony: Death of a Guatemalan Village*, translated by Victor Perera, Willimantic, Conn: Curbstone Press.

——, (1991), *The Bird Who Cleans the World and Other Mayan Fables*, translated by Wallace Kaufman, Willimantic, Conn: Curbstone Press.

——, (1992), *Testimonio: Muerte de una Comunidad Indígena en Guatemala*, Guatemala: Editorial Universitaria, Universidad de San Carlos de Guatemala.

——, (1993a), *The Dynamics of Cultural Resistance and Transformations: The Case of Guatemalan-Mayan Refugees in Mexico*, unpublished Ph.D. dissertation, Department of Anthropology, University of Connecticut.

——, (1993b), "In the Name of the Pot, the Sun, the Broken Spear; the Rock, the Stick, the Idol, Ad Infinitum & Ad Nauseam: An Expose of Anglo Anthropologists Obsessions with and Invention of Mayan Gods," *The Red Pencil Review, A Journal of Native American Studies*, Spring, vol. IX, no. 1, pp. 12–16.

——, (1995), *Sculpted Stones*, Spanish-English edition translated by Victor Perera, Willimantic, Conn: Curbstone Press.

Montejo, Victor and Q'anil Akab' (1993), *Brevísima Relación Testimonial de la Continua Destrucción del Mayab' (Guatemala)*, Providence, RI: Maya Scholars Network.

Moore, Henrietta L. (1994), *A Passion for Difference: Essays in Anthropology and Gender*, Bloomington: Indiana University Press.

Narayan, Kirin (1993), "How Native is a 'Native' Anthropologist?" *American Anthropologist*, vol. 95, pp. 671–686.

Nenedakis, Andreas (1974a), *Apaghorevete: To imeroloyio tis filakis*, Athens: n.p.

——, (1974b), *I margarites tou ayiou: Istories kratoumenon*, Athens: Orizondes.

——, (1975a), *Bir Hakeim: Sti Leyeona ton Ksenon*, Athens: n.p.

——, (1975b), *O mavros Aprilis*, Athens: n.p.

The New York Times Magazine (1996), "True Confessions: A Special Issue," 5/12/96.

Nichols, Bill (1994), *Blurred Boundaries: Questions of Meaning in Contemporary Culture*, Bloomington: Indiana University Press.

Obeyesekere, Gananath (1992), *The Apotheosis of Captain Cook: European Mythmaking in the Pacific*, Princeton: Princeton University Press.

O'Brien, O. (1993), "Good to Be French? Conflicts of Identity in North Catalonia," in Sharon Mcdonald (eds.), *Inside European Identites*, Oxford: Berg Publishers, pp. 98–118.

Ohnuki-Tierney E. (1984), "Native Anthropologists," *American Ethnologist*, vol. 11, pp. 584–586.

Okely, Judith (1992), "Anthropology and Autobiography: Participatory Experience and Embodied Knowledge," in Judith Okely and Helen Callaway (eds.), pp. 1–28.

——, (1996), *Own or Other Culture*, London and New York: Routledge.

Okely, Judith and Helen Callaway (eds.), (1992), *Anthropology and Autobiography*, London: Routledge.

Ottavi, A. (1992), "L'écrivain et son public en Corse," *Etudes Corses*, vol. 38, pp. 8–14.

Oxlajuuj Keej Mayab' Ajtz'iib' [Ajpub', Ixkem, Lolmay, Nik'te', Pakal, Saqijix, and Waykan] (1993), *Mayab' Chii'; Idiomas Mayas de Guatemala*, Guatemala: Cholsamaj.

Peacock, James L. and Dorothy C. Holland (1993), "The Narrated Self: Life Stories in Process," *Ethos*, vol. 21, no. 4, pp. 367–383.

Poli, M. (1991), *La Corse au Point*, Paris: L'Harmattan.

Powdermaker, Hortense (1966), *Stranger and Friend: The Way of an Anthropologist*, New York: Norton & Company.

Pratt, Mary Louise (1992), *Imperial Eyes: Travel Writing and Transculturation*, London and New York: Routledge.

——, (1994), "Transculturation and Autoethnography: Peru 1615/1980," in Frances Barker, Peter Holme and Margaret Iverson (eds.), *Colonial Discourse/Postcolonial Theory*, Manchester and New York: Manchester University Press, pp. 24–46.

Quandt, W.B. (1973), "The Berbers in the Algerian Political Elite," in E. Gellner and C. Micaud (eds.), *Arabs and Berbers. From Tribe to Nation in North Africa*, London: Duckworth, pp. 285–303.

Ram, Uri (1995), *The Changing Agenda of Israeli Sociology*, New York: State University of New York Press.

——, (n.d.), "Historians' Identity, A History of Identities: The Sociology of Historians Discourse in Israel," a paper delivered at the Behavioral Studies Department Seminar at Ben Gurion University, Beer Sheva (Hebrew).

Rancancoj A., Víctor (1994), *Socioeconomía Maya Precolonial*, Guatemala: Cholsamaj.

Rappaport, Joanne (1994), *Cumbe Reborn: An Andean Ethnography of History*, Chicago: University of Chicago Press.

Ravis-Giordani, G. (1983), *Bergers Corses*, Aix-en-Provence: EDISUD.

Redjala, R. (1994), "Le long chemin de la revendication culturelle berbère," *Hommes et Migrations*, no. 1179, pp. 25–31.

Reed-Danahay, Deborah (1995), "The Kabyle and the French: Occidentalism in Bourdieu's Theory of Practice," in James Carrier (ed.), *Occidentalism: Images of the West*, Oxford: Oxford University Press, pp. 61–84.

——, (1996), *Education and Identity in Rural France: The Politics of Schooling*, Cambridge: Cambridge University Press.

Reed-Danahay, Deborah and Kathryn M. Anderson-Levitt (1991), "Backward Countryside, Troubled City: Teachers' Images of Families in Rural and Urban France," *American Ethnologist*, vol. 18, no. 3, pp. 546–564.

Rich, Adrienne (1976), *Of Woman Born*, New York: W. W. Norton.

Rodriguez, Richard (1981), *Hunger of Memory. The Education of Richard Rodriguez: An Autobiography*, Boston: D. R. Godine.

Rodríguez Guaján, Demetrio [Raché] (1989), *Cultura Maya y Políticas de Desarrollo*, Guatemala: Coordinadora Cakchiquel de Desarrollo Integral, Departamento de Investigaciones Culturales.

Rogers, Susan Carol (1987), "Good to Think: The Peasant in Contemporary France," *Anthropological Quarterly*, vol. 60, no. 2, pp. 56–63.

Rosaldo, Renato (1986), "From the Door of His Tent: The Fieldworker and the Inquisitor," in James Clifford and George A. Marcus (eds.), *Writing Culture: The Poetics and Politics of Ethnography*, Berkeley: University of California Press, pp. 77–97.

——, (1989), *Culture and Truth: The Remaking of Social Analysis*, Boston: Beacon Press.

Rose, Phyllis (ed.), (1993), *The Norton Book of Women's Lives*, New York: W.W. Norton and Company.

RR. *Riksdagens revisorers förslag* 1994/95:RR13. *Den svenska kriminalvården*, Stockholm: Sveriges Riksdag.

Rutherford, Andrew (1986), *Prisons and the Process of Justice*, Oxford: Oxford University Press.

St. Clair, William (1972), *That Greece Might Still Be Free: The Philhellenes in the War of Independence*, London: Oxford University Press.

Sahlins, Marshall (1995), *How "Natives" Think: About Captain Cook, For Example*, Chicago: Chicago University Press.

Said, Edward W. (1996), *Representations of the Intellectual*, the 1993 Reith Lectures. New York: Vintage Books.

Salzmann, Zdenek (1981), "Nicknaming in Bigăr: A Contribution to the Anthroponymy of a Czech-Speaking Village in the Southern Romanian Banat," *Names*, vol. 29, pp. 121–137.

Sam Colop, Enrique (1990), "Foreign Scholars and Mayans: What are the issues?" in Marilyn Moors (coordinator), *Guatemala Scholars Network News*, February, Washington: GSN.

——, (1991), "Jub'aqtun Omay Kuchum K'aslemal: Cinco Siglos de Encubrimiento," Seminario Permanente de Estudios Mayas, Cuaderno No. 1, Guatemala: Editorial Cholsamaj.

Sarris, Greg (1994), *Mabel McKay: Weaving the Dream*, Berkeley: University of California Press.

Sawicki, Jana (1991), *Disciplining Foucault: Feminism, Power and the Body*, New York: Routledge.

Sayad, A. (1994), "Aux origines de l'émigration kabyle ou montagnarde," *Hommes et Migrations*, no. 1179, pp. 6–11.

Scarry, Elaine (1985), *The Body in Pain: The Making and the Unmaking of the World*, New York: Oxford University Press.

Schor, Naomi and Elizabeth Weed (eds.), (1994), *The Essential Difference*, Bloomington: Indiana University Press.

Schreiber, Le Anne (1990), *Midstream*, New York: Viking Press.

Scott, James C. (1990), *Domination and the Arts of Resistance*, New Haven: Yale University Press.

Shafir, Michael (1985), *Romania: Politics, Economics, Society*, Boulder, Colo: Lynne Riener Publishers.

Shohat, Ella (1988), "Sephardim in Israel: Zionism from the Standpoint of its Jewish Victims," *Social text*, vol. 7, pp. 1–37.

Shostak, Marjorie (1981), *Nisa: The Life and Words of a !Kung Woman*, Cambridge: Harvard University Press.

Sioui, Georges E. (1992 [1991]), *For an Amerindian Autohistory: An Essay on the Foundations of a Social Ethic*, trans. Sheila Fischman, Montreal and Kingston: McGill-Queen's University Press.

Smart, Barry (1992), "On Discipline and Social Regulation: A Review of Foucault's Genealogic Analysis," in David Garland and Peter Young (eds.), *The Power to Punish: Contemporary Penality and Social Analysis*, Vermont: Ashgate.

Smith, Carol (1990), "Conclusions: History and Revolution in Guatemala," in Carol Smith (ed.), *Guatemalan Indians and the State: 1540–1988*, Austin: University of Texas Press, pp. 258–285.

——, (1991), "Maya Nationalism," *NACLA*, vol. 25, no. 3, pp. 29–34.

Smith, Sidonie and Julia Watson (eds.), (1996), *Getting a Life: Everyday Uses of Autobiography*, Minneapolis: University of Minnesota Press.

Stahl, Henri H. (1936), "Vecinătăţile din Drăguş," *Sociologie Românească*, vol. 1, no. 1, pp. 18–31.

Stanley, Liz (1991), "The Knowing Because Experiencing Subject: Narratives, Lives, and Autobiography," *Women's Studies International Forum*, vol. 16, no. 3, pp. 205–215.

——, (1992), "Process in Feminist Biography and Feminist Epistemology," in Teresa Iles (ed.), pp. 109–125.

Stanton, Domna (ed.), (1987), *The Female Autograph: Theory and Practice of Autobiography from the Tenth to the Twentieth Century*, Chicago:

University of Chicago Press.

Steedman, Carolyn (1987), *Landscape for a Good Woman*, Brunswick, N.J.: Rutgers University Press.

Steinem, Gloria (1983), "Ruth's Song (Because She Could not Sing It)," in *Outrageous Acts and Everyday Rebellions*, New York: Holt, Rinehart, and Winston, pp. 129–146.

Stoll, David (1993), *Between Two Armies in the Ixil Towns of Guatemala*, New York: Columbia University Press.

Strathern, Marilyn (1987), "The Limits of Auto-Anthropology," in Anthony Jackson (ed.), pp. 16–37.

Stuart, Meryn (1992), "Making the Choices: Writing About Marguerite Carr-Harris," in Teresa Iles (ed.), pp. 59–67.

Sutton, David (1995), *Images of History: The Past in the Present of a Greek Island*, unpublished Ph.D. dissertation, Department of Anthropology, University of Chicago.

Svensson, Birgitta (1992), "On the Dark Side of Culture," *Ethnologia Europaea*, vol. 22, p. 1.

——, (1994), "When Offenders Became Delinquents: The Change in the Swedish Tinker Identity," *Journal of the Gypsy Lore Society*, series 5, vol. 4, no. 2.

——, (1995), "Lifetimes – Life History and Life Story: Biographies of Modern Swedish Intellectuals," *Ethnologia Scandinavica*, vol. 25.

Swirski, Shlomo (1981), "*Orientals and Ashkenazim in Israel*," Haifa: Mahbarot LeMehkar UleBikoret. (Hebrew)

——, (1984), "The Oriental Jews in Israel," *Dissent*, vol. 31, pp. 77–90.

Tambiah, Stanley J. (1989), "Ethnic Conflict in the World Today," *American Ethnologist*, vol. 16, pp. 335–349.

Taussig, Michael (1992), *The Nervous System*, New York: Routledge.

Tedlock, Barbara (1991), "From Participant Observation to the Observation of Participation: The Emergence of Narrative Ethnography," *Journal of Anthropological Research*, vol. 47, no. 1, pp. 69–94.

——, (1995), "Works and Wives: On the Sexual Division of Textual Labor," in Ruth Behar and Deborah A. Gordon (eds.), *Women Writing Culture*, Berkeley: University of California Press, pp. 267–286.

Thiers, J. (1992), "A propos de 'A funtana d'Altea," *Etudes Corses*, vol. 38, pp. 63–66.

——, (1990), *A Funtana d'Altea*, Levie: Editions Albiana.

——, (1992), *Les Glycines d'Altea*, Levie: Editions Albiana.

——, (1994), *Il Canto d'Altea*, trans. Noelle Tomasi, Basia: JPC Infograffia.

Tokarczyk, Michelle M. and Elizabeth A. Fay (eds.), (1993), *Working-Class Women in the Academy: Laborers in the Knowledge Factory*, Amherst: The University of Massachusetts Press.

Trask, Haunani-Kay (1993), *From A Native Daughter: Colonialism and Sovereignty in Hawai'i*, Monroe, Maine: Common Courage Press.

Van Maanen, John (1995), "An End to Innocence: The Ethnography of Ethnography," in J. Van Maanen (ed.), *Representation in Ethnography*, Thousand Oaks, London, and New Delhi: Sage Publications, pp. 1–35.

Verdery, Katherine (1991), *National Ideology Under Socialism: Identity and Cultural Politics in Ceauşescu's Romania*, Berkeley: University of California Press.

Vernier, Bernard (1991), *La genèse sociale des sentiments: aînés et cadets dans l'île grecque de Karpathos*, Paris: Éditions de l'École des Hautes Études en Sciences Sociales.

Vico, Giambattista (1744), *Principij di Scienza Nuova*, 3rd edition, Napoli: Stamperia Muziana.

Vincinguerra, M. (1992), "La Corse au miroir des îles," *Etudes Corses*, vol. 38, pp. 129–132.

Vulcănescu, Romulus (1966), *Etnografie – Ştiinţa Culturii Populare*, Bucharest: Editura Ştiinţifică.

——, (1970), *Coloana Cerului*, Bucharest: Editura Academiei.

Wagner-Martin, Linda (1994), *Telling Women's Lives: The New Biography*, New Brunswick, NJ: Rutgers University Press.

Walters, Glenn D. (1990), *The Criminal Lifestyle: Patterns of Serious Criminal Conduct*, Newbury Park: Sage.

Warren, Kay B. (1989), *The Symbolism of Subordination: Indian Identity in a Guatemalan Town*, second edition, Austin: University of Texas Press.

——, (1992), "Transforming Memories and Histories: The Meanings of Ethnic Resurgence for Mayan Indians," in Alfred Stepan (ed.), *Americas: New Interpretive Essays*, New York: Oxford University Press, pp. 189–219.

——, (1993), "Interpreting la Violencia in Guatemala: Shapes of Kaqchikel Silence and Resistance in the 1970s and 1980s," in Kay B. Warren (ed.), *The Violence Within: Cultural and Political Opposition in Divided Nations*, Boulder, Colo: Westview Press, pp. 25–56.

——, (1995), "Each Mind is a World: Dilemmas of Feeling and Intention in a Kaqchikel Maya Community," in Lawrence Rosen (ed.), *Other Intentions: Culture and the Attribution of States of Mind*, Seattle: University of Washington Press for the American School of Research, pp. 47–67.

——, (1996), "Reading History as Resistance: Mayan Public Intellectuals in Guatemala," in Edward Fischer and McKenna Brown (eds.), *Mayan Cultural Activism in Guatemala*, Austin: University of Texas Press.

——, (n.d.a), "Mayan Multiculturalism and the Violence of Memories," in Veena Das, Mamphela Ramphele and Arthur Kleinman (eds.), *Violence, Political Agency, and the Construction of the Self*, Delhi: Cambridge University Press.

——, (n.d.b), "Enduring Tensions and Changing Identities: Mayan

Family Struggles in Guatemala," in Dorothy Holland and Jean Lave (eds.), *History in Person: The Mutual Construction of Endemic Struggles and Enduring Identities*, Santa Fe: School of American Research Press.

———, (n.d.c), "Indigenous Movements as a Challenge to a Unified Social Movement Paradigm for Guatemala," in Sonia E. Alvarez, Evelina Dagnino and Arturo Escobar (eds.), *Cultures of Politics/Politics of Cultures: Revisioning Latin American Social Movements*, Boulder, Colo: Westview Press.

Watanabe, John (n.d.), "Neither As They Imagined Nor as Others Intended: Mayas and Anthropologists in the Highlands of Guatemala Since 1969," in John D. Monaghan (ed.), *Supplement to the Hand Book of Middle American Indians*, vol. 6, Austin: University of Texas Press.

Watson, Lawrence C. and Maria-Barbara Watson-Franke (1985), *Interpreting Life Histories: An Anthropological Inquiry*, New Brunswick, NJ: Rutgers University Press.

Weaver, William (n.d.), *Verdi: A Documentary Study*, London: Thames and Hudson.

Weber, Eugen (1976), *Peasants into Frenchmen: The Modernization of Rural France, 1870–1914*, Stanford: Stanford University Press.

Wilson, Richard (1995), *Mayan Resurgence in Guatemala*, Norman: University of Oklahoma Press.

Wolf. E. (1973), *Peasant Wars of the Twentieth Century*, New York: Harper Torchbooks.

Zimmerman, Marc (1995a), *Literature and Resistance in Guatemala: Textual Modes and Cultural Politics from El Señor Presidente to Rigoberta Menchú*, Vol. One: *Theory, History, Fiction, and Poetry*, Athens, Ohio: Ohio University Center for International Studies.

———, (1995b), *Literature and Resistance in Guatemala: Textual Modes and Cultural Politics from El Señor Presidente to Rigoberta Menchú*, Vol. Two: *Testimonio and Cultural Politics in the Years of Cerezo and Serrano Elias*, Athens, Ohio: Ohio University Center for International Studies.

Index